Copyright Infringement

Copyright Infringement

The Comparative Law Yearbook of International Business

Special Issue, 2018

PUBLISHED UNDER THE AUSPICES
OF THE CENTER FOR INTERNATIONAL LEGAL STUDIES

General Editor

Dennis Campbell

Director, Center for International Legal Studies
Salzburg, Austria

A C.I.P. Catalogue record for this book is available from the Library of Congress

ISBN 978-94-035-0083-6

e-Book: ISBN 978-94-035-0084-3

web-PDF: ISBN 978-94-035-0085-0

Published by:
Kluwer Law International B.V.
P.O. Box 316
2400 AH Alphen aan den Rijn
The Netherlands
Website: lrus.wolterskluwer.com

Sold and distributed in North, Central and South America by:
Wolters Kluwer Legal & Regulatory U.S. Inc.
7201 McKinney Circle
Frederick, MD 21704
United States of America
E-mail: customer.service@wolterskluwer.com

Printed on acid-free paper

© 2018 Kluwer Law International

All rights reserved. No part of this publication may be reproduced, stored in a retrieval system, or transmitted in any form or by any means, electronic, mechanical, photocopying, recording or otherwise, without prior written permission of the publishers.

Permission to use this content must be obtained from the copyright owner. Please apply to: Permissions Department, Wolters Kluwer Legal, 76 Ninth Avenue, Seventh Floor, New York, NY 10011-5201, United States of America. Email: permissions@kluwerlaw.com. Website: lrus.wolterskluwer.com

The Center for International Legal Studies

The Center for International Legal Studies is a non-profit research and publications institute established and operating under Austrian law, with its international headquarters in Salzburg, Austria.

The Center has operated since 1976 in Salzburg, and it has close cooperation with the faculties of law of the University of Salzburg, Boston University and Suffolk University in the United States, Lazarski University in Poland, Eötvös Loránd University in Hungary, and numerous other universities and educational institutions in Europe.

The Comparative Law Yearbook of International Business prints matter it deems worthy of publication. Views expressed in material appearing herein are those of the authors and do not necessarily reflect the policies or opinions of the Comparative Law Yearbook of International Business, its editors, or the Center for International Legal Studies.

Manuscripts proposed for publication may be sent by email to:

The Editor
Comparative Law Yearbook of International Business
office@cils.org

Acknowledgments

Argentina

Verónica Canese and Inés O'Farrell

Marval, O'Farrell & Mairal
Av. Leandro N. Alem 882
C1001AAQ Buenos Aires
Argentina
Tel: (54 11) 4310 0100
Fax: (54 11) 4310 0200
Email: VMC@marval.com

Austria

Carl Dominik Niedersüß

Fiebinger Polak & Partner
Am Getreidemarkt 1
1060 Vienna
Austria
Tel: (43 1) 58258
Fax: (43 1) 582582
Email: d.niedersuess@fplp.at

Brazil

Ricardo Barretto Ferreira da Silva, Camila Taliberti Ribeiro da Silva, and Vitor Rodolfo Koketu da Cunha

Azevedo Sette Advogados
Av. Pres. Juscelino Kubitschek, 2041
Torre E, 16º andar
04543-011 São Paulo SP
Brazil
Tel: (55 11) 4083 7600
Fax: (55 11) 4083 7601
Email: barretto@azevedosette.com.br

Germany

Ulrich Lohmann and Igor Barabash

Pinsent Masons
Ottostrasse 21
80333 Munich
Germany
Tel: (49 89) 20304 3500
Fax: (49 89) 20304 3501
Email: Ulrich.Lohmann@pinsentmasons.com

Italy

Riccardo G. Cajola

Cajola & Associati
Via G. Rossini, n. 5
20122 Milan
Italy
Tel: (39 02) 7600 3305
Fax: (39 02) 780177
Email: law@cajola.com

Mexico

Alfredo Pineda N. and Edgar Mata

Hogan Lovells
Paseo de los Tamarindos #150-PB
Bosques de las Lomas
México, D.F. 05120
México
Tel: (52 55) 5091 000
Fax: (52 55) 5091 0123
Email: alfredo.pineda@hoganlovells.com

Portugal

Vasco Stilwell d'Andrade

Morais Leitão, Galvão Teles, Soares da Silva & Associados
Rua Castilho, 165
1070-050 Lisbon
Portugal
Tel: (351) 213 817 400
Fax: (351) 213 817 499
Email: vsandrade@mlgts.pt

Russia

Taras Derkatsch

Beiten Burkhardt
Turchaninov per., 6/2
119034 Moscow
Russia
Tel: (7 495) 232 9635
Fax: (7 495) 232 9633
Email: Taras.Derkatsch@bblaw.com

Turkey

Yegân Liaje and Elçin Karatay

Pekin & Pekin
10 Lamartine Caddesi, Taksim
34437 Istanbul
Turkey
Tel: (90 212) 313 3500
Fax: (90 212) 313 3545
Email: YLiaje@pekin-pekin.com

United Kingdom

Gareth Dickson

Taylor Vinters LLP
Merlin Place, Milton Road
Cambridge CB4 0DP
United Kingdom
Tel: (44 1223) 423 444
Email: gareth.dickson@taylorvinters.com

United States

Jonathan I. Feil

Simburg, Ketter, Sheppard & Purdy, LLP
999 Third Avenue, Suite 2525
Seattle, WA 98104-4089
Tel: (1 206) 382 2600
Fax: (1 206) 223 3929
Email: jfeil@sksp.com

Table of Contents

Argentina

Introduction 1
Exceptions to Infringement of Copyright 3
Infringement Proceedings 4
Evidence in Copyright Infringement Proceedings 7
Provisional and Final Remedies in Infringement Proceedings 7
Arbitration in Copyright Infringement Disputes 9
Liability of Internet Service Providers 10
Conclusion 13

Austria

Introduction 15
Resale Right Regime of Berne Convention 16
European Harmonization of Resale Right
   through Directive 2001/84/EC 20
Infringement and Subject Matter of Resale Right 23
Conclusion 30

Brazil

Introduction 33
Rights Protected by Copyright 34
Copyright Enforcement in Brazil 41
Civil Enforcement Proceedings 45
Conclusion 48

Germany

Introduction 49
Infringement 52
Online Intermediary Liability 54
Limitations on Copyright 55
Remedies 56
Procedural Law 58

Italy

Introduction 69
Rights Covered by Copyright 70
Copyright Protection and Soundreef Judgment 72
Enforcement 84
Conclusion 95

Mexico

Introduction 97
Rights Covered by Copyright 98
Infringement 101
Infringement Proceedings 104
Non-Commercial File Sharing 106
Intermediary Liability 107
Piracy 107
Remedies 108
Economic Impact 109
Exemptions from Copyright Infringement 110
Conclusion 111

Portugal

Introduction 113
Works Protected by Copyright Law 115
Author's Rights 118
Copyright Infringement 119
Copyright Infringement Defense Strategies 124
Choice of Venue 126
Dispute Resolution Alternatives 128
Civil Copyright Infringement Proceedings in Judicial Courts 128
Interim Relief and Other Measures 135
MAPiNET — Movimento Cívico Anti Pirataria na Internet 139
Copyright Infringement Criminal Proceedings 140
Costs 142
Conclusion 142

Russia

Introduction 145
Russian Intellectual Property Law 145
Copyright 146
Liability for Violation of Intellectual Rights
    to Copyrighted Material 162
Conclusion 167

Turkey

Introduction 169
Works, Authorship, and Copyright under Turkish
    Intellectual Property Law 170
Conclusion 187

United Kingdom

Introduction 189
Subsistence 191
Authorship and Ownership 197
Infringement 200
Defenses 211
Criminal Liability 217
Remedies 218
Brexit 222
Conclusion 223

United States

Introduction 225
Legal Basis for Copyright Protection in the United States 226
Elements of Copyright Infringement 229
Rights Covered by Copyright in the United States 231
Works That Copyright Protects 234
Ownership of Copyright 239
Affirmative Defenses to Infringement 242
Remedies for Infringement 251

Index 255

Editor's Note

There is little doubt that, with the emergence of the Internet, social media, video streaming, and new technologies that facilitate the pirating of copyrighted content, the issue of copyright infringement is increasingly important in a global economy. Therefore, it is timely that copyright infringement be examined here from an international perspective.

In this edition of the *Comparative Law Yearbook of International Business*, lawyers from 11 jurisdictions examine recent developments in copyright infringement. Reports are provided by practitioners from Argentina, Austria, Brazil, Germany, Italy, Mexico, Portugal, Russia, Turkey, United Kingdom, and the United States.

Dennis Campbell, General Editor
Center for International Legal Studies
Salzburg, Austria, Europe

Argentina

Verónica Canese and Inés O'Farrell
Marval, O'Farrell & Mairal
Buenos Aires, Argentina

Introduction

In Argentina, copyright protection is based on the constitutional principle established in Section 17 of the Constitution, which specifically safeguards the rights of authors over their work. Argentina is a party to several international treaties on copyright protection, which have been approved by the Congress and are part of the legal system, namely:

(1) The Montevideo Treaty on Literary and Artistic Property of 1889;
(2) The Buenos Aires Convention on Literary and Artistic Copyright of 1910;
(3) The Washington Inter-American Convention on the Rights of the Author in Literary, Scientific and Artistic Works of 1946;
(4) The Geneva Universal Copyright Convention of 1952;
(5) The Berne Convention for the Protection of Literary and Artistic Works of 1886;
(6) The Rome Convention for the Protection of Performers, Producers of Phonograms and Broadcasting Organizations of 1961;
(7) The Geneva Convention for the Protection of Producers of Phonograms Against Unauthorized Duplication of Their Phonograms of 1971;
(8) The Geneva Treaty on the International Registration of Audio-visual Works of 1989;
(9) The Convention Establishing the World Intellectual Property Organization of 1971 (as amended in 1979);
(10) The World Trade Organization Agreement on Trade-Related Aspects of Intellectual Property Rights of 1994;
(11) The World Intellectual Property Organization Copyright Treaty of 1996; and
(12) The World Intellectual Property Organization Performances and Phonograms Treaty of 1996.

Copyright is specifically governed by the Copyright Law, Law Number 11,723 of 26 September 1933, which is regulated by Decree Number 41,223 of 1943. Other laws applicable to copyright are Law Number 17,648 on the Argentine Association of Authors and Composers of Music (SADAIC) and Law Number 20,115 on the General Association of Argentine Authors (ARGENTORES). The Copyright Law is the basic statute on copyright in Argentina. It protects the expression of ideas, not the ideas themselves, and confers protection to a broad variety of works. This protection extends to scientific, literary, artistic, or educational works, regardless of the process of reproduction.

Copyright protection has been granted to writings (dictionaries, books, almanacs, and articles); musical works and plays; cinematographic, choreographic, and pantomime works; drawings, paintings, and sculptural works; architectural, artistic, and scientific works; maps, plans, and other printed matter; plastic works, photographs, engravings, and phonograms; titles and characters as an integral part of a work; works of applied art; computer software and databases; and derivative works, new versions, compilations, and translations.

Argentine courts have found that works must be expressed in a tangible form and must contain a minimum degree of originality[1] in order to be protected. There is no requirement related to artistic merit. Regarding the term of copyright protection, the Copyright Law provides the following:

(1) Copyright protection is granted throughout the life of the author and for an additional seventy years, counted from 1 January of the year following the author's death. In cases of works involving cooperation, the seventy-year period will begin running as of the death of the last author. If the work was published after the author's death, the seventy-year term will begin running from 1 January of the year following the author's death.[2]

(2) Anonymous works belonging to institutions, corporations, or legal entities are protected for fifty years as from their date of publication.[3]

(3) Photographic works are protected for twenty years as from the date of their initial publication, while cinematographic works are protected for fifty years as from the date of the death of the last co-author.[4]

---

[1] Court of Appeals in Civil Matters, Division D, *AGISA* vs. *Kaiser*, Alberto, 1997.
[2] Copyright Law, Section 5.
[3] Copyright Law, Section 8.
[4] Copyright Law, Section 34.

In addition, the Argentine copyright protection framework recognizes authors' both economic and moral rights over their works. Economic rights refer to the rights an author has to the economic benefits that derive from a work, while moral rights refer to non-economic rights granted exclusively to the creator of a work in his capacity as author. Moral rights are an essential constituent element of copyright under Argentine law. They include the right to be named as the author, the right to preserve the work, and the right to decide whether to publish it.

Under the Copyright Law, works are granted protection from the moment of their creation. The Copyright Law does not include any registration or notice requirements. However, the *Dirección Nacional del Derecho de Autor* (Argentine Copyright Office), an administrative body within the Ministry of Justice and Human Rights, is responsible for the registration of works and the recordation of copyright-related agreements.

Registering copyrightable works before the Argentine Copyright Office is advisable for a number of reasons. Registering a work creates a legal presumption of the validity of the copyright, is beneficial for evidentiary purposes, and can lead to tax benefits. Furthermore, and from a practical standpoint, pursuing infringements on the basis of a registered copyright is easier. In particular, when referring to published works, Section 63 of the Copyright Law states that lack of copyright registration within three months from publication of a work results in the suspension of the editor's economic rights over such work.

In addition, copyright assignments must be recorded with the Argentine Copyright Office in order to be enforceable against third parties. Nevertheless, the courts have found that foreign works that meet the requirements of the Geneva Universal Copyright Convention are protected by Argentine law, regardless of whether they have been registered in Argentina.

Exceptions to Infringement of Copyright

There are a few exceptions to copyright protection and there is no "fair use" judicial doctrine. Exceptions are included in the Copyright Law and act as a limit to the authors' exclusive rights. Any actions falling within the scope of these specific exceptions will not constitute copyright infringement. The exceptions contained in the Copyright Law include:
(1) The right to quote up to one thousand words of literary or scientific works or eight bars of musical works, as long as they

are published for educational or scientific purposes or as part of a commentary or a review, and are necessary to that effect;
(2) The right to use and transmit news of general interest and publish the original version if the source is mentioned;
(3) The right to publish parliamentary speeches (as long as not done for profit);
(4) The right to perform literary or artistic works in public acts organized by teaching establishments, as long as the performance is not broadcasted and is free of charge;
(5) The right to publicly perform musical works in concerts, auditions, or shows by orchestras, bands, and other musical organizations belonging to government institutions, if admission for the general public is free of charge;
(6) The right to copy and distribute scientific and literary works in special systems designed for blind people or people with disabilities in their perception, as long as it is conducted by authorized entities;
(7) The right to make private copies for personal use is not considered, in principle, to violate copyright provided no multiple copies of the same work are made with a commercial use;
(8) The right to publish portraits if said publication is related with scientific, didactic, or cultural purposes or with events or facts of public interest or which may have taken place in public; and
(9) The right to use works that have fallen into the public domain provided the corresponding tax is paid to the *Fondo Nacional de las Artes* (National Arts Fund) as Argentina is one of the few countries where the *Domaine Public Payant* regime is still in force.

Infringement Proceedings

In General

The Argentine Copyright Office does not resolve copyright disputes. Copyright is enforced before either the criminal courts or the civil courts.

Criminal Proceedings

The Copyright Law contains several criminal sanctions. These would be pursued before the criminal courts. Section 71 of the Copyright Law provides that a fraud against intellectual property rights granted by the Copyright Law will be subject to the penalties established by Section 172 of the Criminal Code.

The penalty included in Section 172 of the Criminal Code is imprisonment for a period ranging from one month to six years. The specific penalty for each case is fixed by the court on the basis of the particulars of the offense. In principle, any type of willful infringement of copyright is subject to the penalties provided by Section 71 of the Copyright Law.

Furthermore, Section 72 of the Copyright Law refers to certain special types of fraud against intellectual property rights. They are sanctioned in the same manner as those included in Section 71 and may result, in addition, in the sequestration of infringing publications. The infringements listed by Section 72 are the following:

(1) Publishing, selling, or reproducing by any means or instrument an unpublished or a published work without the necessary authorization;
(2) Counterfeiting intellectual works;
(3) Suppressing or changing the name of the author or title of a work or willfully altering the text of a work, upon its publication, sale, or reproduction; and
(4) Publishing or reproducing a higher number of copies than those authorized.

Moreover, Section 72 *bis* of the Copyright Law applies to violations related to phonograms, which include:

(1) Reproducing for profit a phonogram, without the written authorization of the producer or of the producer's licensee;
(2) Facilitating for profit the illegal reproduction of phonograms by means of renting phonographic disks or other tangible elements;
(3) Reproducing unauthorized copies of a phonogram, upon request of third parties in exchange for a price;
(4) Storing or exhibiting illegal copies of phonograms, if the person thus acting is unable to show — by means of an invoice derived from a legitimate producer — the origin of such goods; and
(5) Importing illegal copies with the purpose of distributing them to the public.

Additionally, Section 73 of the Copyright Law provides a sanction of between one month to one year of imprisonment or a fine (the amount of which varies periodically) against one who performs or organizes the public performance of theatrical, literary, or musical works without the authorization of their authors or their assigns and one who performs or organizes the public performance of musical works without authorization from their authors or assigns.

Lastly, Section 74 of the Copyright Law establishes a sanction of between one month to one year of imprisonment or a fine (the amount of which varies periodically) for anyone who, claiming to be the author or right-holder of a work, suspends a licit representation or performance of such work. The statute of limitations on criminal actions for copyright infringement is six years as from the date of the infringement. Criminal procedures for copyright matter are governed by the federal procedural rules if the violation is subject to federal jurisdiction, or by the procedural rules enacted by each province if the violation is not subject to federal jurisdiction.

Civil Proceedings

In addition or alternatively to criminal proceedings, parties alleging copyright infringement can initiate civil proceedings, which are mainly regulated by the general provisions included in the Civil and Commercial Code. Under Argentine tort law, if anyone infringes copyrights and causes damages, whether due to negligence or with intent, the holder of such rights will be entitled to compensation. If a certain conduct infringes any copyright, it will also be possible to obtain an injunction from the civil courts to terminate such conduct.

Copyright infringement proceedings are ordinary court proceedings heard before the civil courts. In addition, Sections 80 and 81 of the Copyright Law establish a special summary civil procedure for cases involving copyright infringement. In particular, they provide that the parties may request that evidence be produced in a public hearing in which the parties, the court, and experts may be heard.

Depending on the complexity and nature of the case, the court may appoint a special jury of experts to issue an opinion as to whether there has been a violation of statutory rights. However, the jury of experts only provides an opinion. The final decision is still rendered by the court.

The statute of limitations for civil actions will vary, depending on the date of occurrence of the infringement. The Civil and Commercial Code came into effect on 1 August 2015 and replaced the prior Civil Code. Therefore, infringements occurring prior to 1 August 2015 will be held to the two-year statute of limitations established by the Civil Code for claims on non-contractual civil liability. Conversely, infringements occurring after 1 August 2015 will be held to the general statute of limitations of five years established by the Civil and Commercial Code.

The one exception to the above civil and commercial proceedings relates to works that have fallen into the public domain. Pursuant to Section 83 of the Copyright Law, anyone may file a complaint before the Argentine Copyright Office regarding a work that has become part of the public domain. In case of mutilation of any such literary, scientific, or artistic work, such as additions, transpositions, mistranslations, errors of concept, and deficiencies in the original language or version, a complaint may be filed by any Argentine inhabitant.

Alternatively, actions against such work may be initiated *ex officio*. A jury of experts will be formed to determine if a fault was committed. In case it finds that it was, the jury may order that the work be corrected and forbid the circulation of non-corrected versions. Anyone who disobeys this order will have to pay a fine.

Evidence in Copyright Infringement Proceedings

In Argentina, copyright infringement is assessed on a case-by-case basis. In principle, substantial similarity between a work protected by copyright and another work is enough to prove copyright infringement. In addition to a copy of the infringing work and the work protected by copyright, other evidence provided in infringement proceedings will depend on the particular circumstances of the case.

Moreover, as noted, under Section 81 of the Copyright Law, a court that considers that determining the existence of infringement in a particular case requires specialized knowledge can request the opinion of experts on the corresponding field. The Copyright Law provides that, while civil and criminal proceedings are independent and a final decision rendered in one will not affect the other, evidence obtained in one process may be used in the other.[5]

Provisional and Final Remedies in Infringement Proceedings

The Copyright Law specifically provides certain provisional remedies. Regarding criminal proceedings, Section 72 *bis* on copyright violations related to phonograms provides that courts may order the seizure of the

---

5 Copyright Law, Section 77.

illegal copies and the elements used for the illegal reproduction of phonograms *ex officio* or upon request of an interested party. Once seizure has taken place, the criminal action must be filed within fifteen business days or else the seizure order may lapse.

In addition, the Copyright Law provides that a party that alleges copyright infringement in civil proceedings may request the court to grant precautionary measures. In particular, Section 79 of the Copyright Law establishes that, upon compliance with a bond, courts may order as a precautionary measure the suspension of a theatrical, cinematographic, or other analogous exhibitions, the attachment of the works that have been indicated as in violation of copyright, the attachment of the proceeds derived from infringing exhibitions or works, and any other precautionary measure deemed necessary for the protection of the right involved.

In addition to the specific provisions of the Copyright Law, a party alleging copyright infringement can request the precautionary measures derived from the general rules of civil procedure. Precautionary measures that may be used in copyright cases include injunctions, deposit in court of property subject to litigation, attachments, and designation of court-appointed officers to receive the proceeds from exhibitions or other activities or to obtain information regarding such activities. However, courts may grant other types of precautionary measures if they consider that actions are required to prevent an imminent or irreparable damage to a legal right.

Additionally, Argentine courts have granted preliminary injunctions based upon Section 50 of the Trade-Related Aspects of Intellectual Property Rights Agreement. These would prevent the infringer from making any use of the infringing material until the court renders a final decision on the merits of the case. In order to obtain such a measure, the claimant has to prove the legal plausibility and the urgency or risk in the delay of the fulfillment of his material interest. In addition, the court may require the petitioner to deposit a cash bond to secure eventual damages before the measure is performed.

After the preliminary injunction is notified and any related measures performed, a lawsuit on the merits of the case must be filed within ten days in order to maintain the validity of the measures. Otherwise, the injunction and any other measured ordered would lapse.

In general, there are no specific final remedies in copyright infringement actions. The only specific provision is Section 72 *bis* of the Copyright Law regarding criminal proceedings in cases of violations related to phonograms, which states that the courts may order the seizure of the illegal copies and of the elements used for the illegal reproduction of phonograms. It also provides that illicit copies will be destroyed and the elements used to carry out the reproduction will be auctioned. In civil actions, the final remedies available will be determined by the measures the courts deem appropriate. A final judgment can order the discontinuance of the reproduction or performance of an infringing work, or eventually order a recall.

Moreover, copyright holders are entitled to claim compensation for any damages caused. Courts have consistently awarded damages on the basis of Section 165 of the Code of Civil and Commercial Procedure that allows judges to reasonably determine the amount of damages when they are legally established but not accurately quantified. The manner in which damages are assessed and the amount set by the final ruling will vary depending on the circumstances of the case. Ways of assessing damages include:

(1) Profits lost by the copyright holder;
(2) Profits obtained by the infringer;
(3) Loss of chance; and
(4) Expenses incurred in by the copyright holder as a consequence of the infringement.

Arbitration in Copyright Infringement Disputes

The Civil and Commercial Code introduced a provision that states that certain cases are exclusively subject to the jurisdiction of Argentine courts. Section 2609(c) of the Civil and Commercial Code provides that Argentine courts have exclusive jurisdiction to decide matters related to the registration and validity of patents, trade marks, designs or drawings, industrial models, and other analogous rights bound to deposit or registration in Argentina when such deposit or registration was requested or conducted or finalized in Argentina.

As noted, the Civil and Commercial Code came into effect on 1 August 2015. Despite the fact that there is no case law resulting from Section 2609(c) of the Civil and Commercial Code, a harmonic interpretation of this provision would be that, if a work is registered in Argentina (which requires its deposit with the Argentine Copyright Office), any dispute will be subject to the exclusive jurisdiction of Argentine courts. However, if the work is not deposited with the Argentine Copyright Office, the resulting dispute may be resolved by arbitration.

Liability of Internet Service Providers

The liability of Internet Service Providers (ISPs) under Argentine law is a matter that is still under discussion. Despite several attempts to regulate this issue, there is no legislation in Argentina that addresses ISP liability. There are three bills on the subject before Congress.[6]

When considering this matter, the courts have applied the principles of general civil law. The decisions issued by the courts are central to understanding ISP liability in Argentina. Originally, discussions focused on whether strict liability or a standard of fault should be applied. In 2014, the Supreme Court issued a landmark decision on search engine liability for third-party content.

In *Belén Rodríguez* vs. *Google Inc.*,[7] a model sued Google and Yahoo for linking her image and name to third-party websites displaying sexually explicit content. The court of first instance applied a standard of fault analysis and ruled in favor of the model. Conversely, the Court of Appeals also applied a standard of fault analysis but reversed the lower court's decision.

The Supreme Court found that the search engines were not liable for the third-party content. It stated that a search engine should not carry the burden of monitoring all the content it displays. Nevertheless, search engines could be found liable for third-party content if they had actual knowledge of the illicit contents and failed to take remedial action. It further held that actual knowledge could be established in two circumstances:

(1) If the infringing nature of the content was evident, an out-of-court notification would suffice; and
(2) If the infringing nature of the content was not evident, a judicial notification would be necessary.

There have been two rulings issued by courts of appeal in copyright infringement cases that follow *Belén Rodríguez* vs. *Google Inc.* The first ruling was issued in 2015 by the National Court of Appeals in Criminal Matters. The case, *Botbol, Hernan et al*,[8] involved the unauthorized posting by third parties of links that redirected users to files containing

---

[6] Congressional Files Number S-1865/15, S-942/16, and D-5771/16.
[7] Supreme Court, *Rodriguez, Maria Belen* vs. *Google, Inc.*, 2014.
[8] National Court of Appeals in Criminal Matters, Division I, *Botbol, Hernán et al*, 2015.

literary works by Jorge Luis Borges on the taringa.net, portalplanetasedna.com.ar, and zipete.com websites. The owner of the intellectual property initiated criminal proceedings against those responsible for the websites for copyright infringement.

Using a standard of fault analysis, the National Court of Appeals found that the websites were not liable for the postings of the third parties on their electronic platforms. It reasoned that the websites were mere intermediaries and not the owners' posted contents. Since, upon receiving actual knowledge of the illicit content, the websites took down the contents, the court did not find them liable.

The second case was decided in 2015 by the Federal Court of Cassation in Criminal Matters in *Page, Larry et al*.[9] Pampa Films SA, the holder of the copyrights to a film that was made available on YouTube, initiated a criminal complaint against the unknown users who uploaded the material and against executive officers of Google Inc. The claim was dismissed by the court of first instance and on appeal by the National Court of Appeals in Criminal Matters.

The Criminal Court of Cassation also dismissed the case. It held that those responsible for the platform had no monitoring obligation and that it was not possible to treat them as participants of any crime committed. It further stated that they could have been found liable in the absence of corrective measures after having actual knowledge.

In addition, some courts have found ISPs liable based on their having an active role, rather than being neutral intermediaries. Although these cases did not involve copyright, they illustrate under what circumstances courts may find ISP liable.

In 2013, the Argentine Supreme Court dismissed a request for appeal and left in place a ruling issued by the National Court of Appeals in Civil Matters in *Claps, Enrique Martin* vs. *MercadoLibre SA*,[10] in which e-commerce platform MercadoLibre was held liable for the sale to an unsuspecting buyer of two stolen concert tickets. MercadoLibre argued that it was a mere intermediary in the transactions carried out through its website. The ruling held that MercadoLibre was liable because it intervened in the transactions since it charged for the offers uploaded by users and for the sales made. It, therefore, profited not only from providing the space offered for users, but also from the transactions themselves.

---

9 Federal Court of Cassation in Criminal Matters, Division III, *Page, Larry et al*, 2015.
10 National Court of Appeal in Civil Matters, Division K, *Claps, Enrique Martin* vs. *MercadoLibre SA*, 2012.

Furthermore, the Federal Court of Appeals in Civil and Commercial Matters ruled in trade mark infringement cases *Nike International Ltd.* vs. *Deremate.com de Argentina SA*[11] and *Nike International Ltd.* vs. *Compañía de Medios Digitales CMD SA*[12] that an e-commerce platform could be liable for having an active role in connection with the postings of its users. In both cases, Nike sought to make an e-commerce platform liable for the online sale of counterfeit products by third parties. The Court of Appeals found both defendants liable based on their having an active role. In *Deremate*, the active role existed because Deremate:

(1) Provided a payment method; and
(2) Used a third party's trade mark as keyword on Google AdWords program to maximize use of its platform.

In *CMD*, the active role existed because CMD promoted the products of its users and collected five per cent of every transaction.

More recently, the Court of Appeals in Commercial Matters issued a decision on the liability of e-commerce platform Demotores for the sale of a stolen car in *Gómez* vs. *Dridco SA*.[13] In this case, a user who unknowingly purchased a stolen car from a third party sought to make the platform that published the advertisement liable. The court decision ruled that the platform was not liable because it merely provided a service (publishing the advertisement) and was in no way involved in the transaction itself.

In 2017, the Supreme Court generally reaffirmed the standard set in *Belén Rodríguez* vs. *Google Inc.* In *Gimbutas* vs. *Google Inc*,[14] a model sued Google for use of her image and sought compensation for damages. The court of first instance and the court of appeals rejected the claim. The Supreme Court confirmed the decision of the lower court, applying a standard of fault analysis and referring to *Belén Rodríguez* vs. *Google Inc.* It reaffirmed that ISPs are liable only for third-party contents once they have actual knowledge of illicit contents and fail to act diligently. In addition, it specifically stated that an ISP may also be liable if they act as more than mere intermediaries and take an active role in connection with the third-party contents. However, the concurring and dissenting opinions rendered by members of the Supreme Court in

---

11 Federal Court of Appeals in Civil and Commercial Matters, Division I, *Nike International Ltd.* vs. *Deremate.com de Argentina SA*, 2015.
12 Federal Court of Appeals in Civil and Commercial Matters, Division III, *Nike International Ltd.* vs. *Compañía de Medios Digitales CMD SA*, 2015.
13 Court of Appeals in Commercial Matters, Division B, *Gómez* vs. *Dridco SA*, 2017.
14 Supreme Court, *Gimbutas, Carolina* vs. *Google, Inc.*, 2017.

Gimbutas vs. *Google Inc.,* specifically regarding the scope of "actual knowledge" and liability for use of images as thumbnails, demonstrate that ISP liability is still a matter of legal debate in Argentina.

Conclusion

The Copyright Law was passed in 1933. Since then it has been amended several times. However, many consider that the Copyright Law is outdated. A possible reform of the Copyright Law is under study as part of the Ministry of Justice and Human Rights "Justice 2020 Program", which provides a forum for discussing legislative initiatives.

Some of the matters raised in the framework of this debate include the need to update regulations to respond to new technologies, to have clearer rules in connection with collective societies, to review the registration requirement as well as the public domain regime in force, to set more limitations or broader limitations, and to develop more-detailed procedural provisions.

Austria

Carl Dominik Niedersüß
Fiebinger Polak & Partner
Vienna, Austria

Introduction

It has been more than 15 years since the effort to harmonize European Union (EU) copyright doctrine with the enactment of Directive 2001/84/EC, creating a common standard of the resale right in the EU. The harmonized resale right (*droit de suite)* is constructed as an integral part of the authors' copyrights, and entitles them to royalties on the resale of original works of graphic and plastic arts, given the sale was effected with the involvement of a professional party or an intermediary.

The motivation behind the policy was an attempt to "redress the balance between the economic situation of authors of graphic and plastic works and that of other creators who benefit from successive exploitations of their works".[1] The European legislator thus argued the economic necessity of this harmonization by pointing towards a seeming peculiarity of the art market. Prices for works of arts may rise significantly once an artist has reached a certain level of notoriety.

At first sight, it seems unfair to bar artists' graphic and plastic works from this rise in value of their works. Painters and sculptors typically only benefit financially from the initial sale of the work. Subsequent sales, due to the harmonized principle of exhaustion, typically will not infringe the creator's right to distribution after a lawful first sale, and thus will not benefit the artist. Some artists will not be able to capitalize on an increase in value of his early work. These profits belong exclusively to members of the art market. This seems unfair when compared to other artists who benefit from successive exploitations of their works.

The Directive intends to uniformly strike a balance between members of the art market and the artist in the Common Market. Central to its application — and thus its infringement — is the definition of what is to be considered an "original" and thus susceptible to *droit de suite*. The European legislator chose to leave some aspects of the scope of the resale right opaque.

---

[1] Directive 2001/84/EC, Recital 3.

As practice has shown, this poses difficulties with regards to certain types of works. There has been an ongoing discussion whether it was the European legislator's intent to include works of applied arts, traditionally not subject to the resale right. Another aspect that appears to regularly emerge in legal practice is where to draw the line when it comes to works that have been serially reproduced in high quantities. Finally, the question of posthumously published works may challenge the definition of the term "original" as introduced by the European legislator.

As will be shown, most of the considerations set forth here will, due to the fact that the topic is in the harmonized *acquis*, be of relevance for the definition in all EU Member States.

In order to illustrate the concepts set forth, the focus here will be on analyzing infringement issues relating to infringements of the resale right with regards to a specific edition of furniture. This is defined as a set of furniture that has been conceived by a renowned modern artist and that is being reproduced and marketed in high quantities after the author's death. It combines both high artistic and applied value.

Regardless of its applied value, its reproductions are being traded as works of art, using artistic distribution channels (i.e., involvement of the art market). Although the works are finished posthumously, they are authenticated as originals by the artist's heirs. This example will allow us to address a wide variety of issues, concerning the scope of the European resale right, and its Austrian implementation.

Resale Right Regime of Berne Convention

Resale Right Enters International Stage

The resale right was introduced on an international level at the Berne Convention Revision Conference in Rome in 1928. It was added to the Berne Convention at the Brussels Revision Conference in 1948. Since then, despite being moved from Article 14 *bis* to Article 14 *ter*, the phrasing of the provision has remained unchanged (Article 14 *ter*, *Droit de Suite*):

> "(1) The author, or after his death the persons or institutions authorized by national legislation, shall, with respect to original works of art and original manuscripts of writers and composers, enjoy the inalienable right to an interest in any sale of the work subsequent to the first transfer by the author of the work.

"(2) The protection provided by the preceding paragraph may be claimed in a country of the Union only if legislation in the country to which the author belongs so permits, and to the extent permitted by the country where this protection is claimed.

"(3) The procedure for collection and the amounts shall be matters for determination by national legislation."[2]

The Berne Convention thus defines the subject matter as "original works of art and original manuscripts of writers and composers".

Subject Matter of Berne Convention

The Berne Convention itself does not provide further context as to how the crucial term "original" is to be interpreted. In addition to Article 14 *ter*, the Convention uses the term "original" in connection translations, which do not provide further clarification.[3]

While the Berne Convention does not define the term "original works of art", the World Intellectual Property Organization (WIPO) Guide to the Berne Convention provides a useful starting point, as it states that "it is generally agreed that these consist of drawings, paintings, statues, engravings, lithographs, always provided that they are the originals, made by the artist himself. The right does not apply to works of architecture or to applied art".[4] The WIPO Guide to the Berne Convention thus suggests a stringent interpretation by requiring the artist's direct involvement for the piece of art to constitute subject matter of the resale right.

This strict requirement may have been state of the art at the time of introduction into the Convention. The criterion, however, no longer holds up in light of a contemporary concept of art, where rules of authorship have been blurred ever since Warhol's Factory, and the dawn of assembly-line production of artworks. If one were to follow this strict requirement of the artist's personal involvement, one must conclude that

---

2 This wording is considered the World Intellectual Property Organization's official (non-binding) English version of the Berne Convention for the Protection of Literary and Artistic Works. See http://www.wipo.int/treaties/en/text.jsp?file_id=283698 #P188_36636. Slight variations found online (e.g., keionline.org suggests the wording "in respect of original works of art") are due to translation errors but, in the author's opinion, do not impact its legal meaning.
3 Berne Convention, Articles 8, 11, 11 *bis*, and 11 *ter*.
4 World Intellectual Property Organization, *Guide to the Berne Convention for the Protection of Literary and Artistic Works* (1978), 14 *ter* 4.

works of art finished or published posthumously are not subject to the *droit de suite*, even if the majority of the work was finished by the author before his death. One may deduct that series of works are not included, as implied by the phrase "provided they are the originals".[5] Finally, works of applied arts are explicitly excluded from the scope.

Applying this reasoning to the case study, the set of furniture created by a famous artist would not be subject to the Berne Convention's resale right, as it — regardless of the time and quantity of its production — will possess applied value in addition to its artistic value. Hence, it will qualify as work of applied arts. A further sale would not infringe the resale right according to the Berne Convention's definition. This reasoning does not seem very convincing. The mere fact that a work of art has applied value should not *per se* suffice to exclude applicability of the resale right. A purposive analysis of the norm's economic rationale might clarify its *telos*.

Mythical Economic Rationale for Resale Right

The WIPO Guide to the Berne Convention offers some insight on the underlying economic rationale that guided the members, stating that:

> "It is an attempt to look after the interests of artists and other makers of artistic works. The painter or sculptor often sells his work cheaply in order to make ends meet. The work may pass through a number of hands and, in going so, may considerably increase in value. It becomes a source of revenue for those engaged in sales (dealers, experts, art critics, etc.) and is often bought as a good investment. This provision therefore allows the artist to follow the fortunes of his work and to profit from the increase in its value each time it changes hands."[6]

This explanation introduces a repetitive theme[7] that has been used to provide for an economic foundation of the *droit de suite*, that of the romantic, yet naïve, image of a talented young artist, who is ahead of his time and who must sell his work underpriced, for it is only later generations who will be able to recognize the genius. It is difficult to blame

---

5 World Intellectual Property Organization, *Guide to the Berne Convention for the Protection of Literary and Artistic Works* (1978), 14 ter 4.
6 World Intellectual Property Organization, *Guide to the Berne Convention for the Protection of Literary and Artistic Works* (1978), 14 ter.
7 Commission Proposal 96/085 (COD), 13 March 1996, I-2 *et seq.*

the legislators, for this recurring theme in popular culture has been attributed to many of the greats, such as Mozart or Van Gogh, about whom it is said that he sold but one painting during his lifetime.[8] Both are said to have lived or died in relative poverty, only to gain tremendous fame *post mortem*.

A similar story is attributed to Rembrandt, Vermeer, and Gaugin, despite not always being factually justified. This image has become so often repeated that one might conclude that poverty and lack of recognition is every artist's lot. The myth is perpetuated by other artists — as was famously the case with artist and cultural icon Banksy — and the narrative probably resonates with everyone because it feels unfair; it seems that most great artists live a life of poverty while creating great values through their artworks. They enrich society, and yet are not rewarded.

O'Hagan introduced a capitalistic perspective by comparing this view of the art business to the image of a "collector who, having purchased a work of art for relatively little, resells it for a great deal more, pocketing the entire profit and leaving the artist whose effort created the work and whose subsequent accomplishments may have contributed to its increase in value, with no part of such increase. It is the image of Robert Rauschenberg and Robert Scull in tense confrontation after the 1973 action at which Scull resold for US $85,000 a work for which he had originally paid Rauschenberg less than US $1.000".[9]

However, this image does not universally apply, at least not generally. As commentators from the field of economics have explained, "there is a simple economic reason for the enormous differences in the prices at which dealers buy and sell art: from the dealer's point of view, the works of young and unknown artists are lotteries. He will frequently be unable to resell the pieces and, of those sold, only a few will be worth large sums".[10]

This popular narrative grossly undervalues the gallerists' role in making an artist successful, by promoting the artists' works at their own financial risk. The same can be said for the artist's management or estate, which both tend to play important roles in the creation of reputation. It would appear that the idea of the *droit de suite* is based on an inaccurate myth of how the art world and its economic mechanisms

---

8 Mareder, *The Lore: Van Gogh Sold Only One Painting during His Life*, see https://www.thoughtco.com/van-gogh-sold-only-one-painting-4050008.
9 O'Hagan, *The State and the Arts — An Analysis of Key Economic Policy Issues in Europe and the United States* (1998), at p. 100.
10 Kirstein and Schmidtchen, *Do Artists Benefit from Resale Royalties? An Economic Analysis of a New EU Directive* (24 April 2000), at p. 5.

work. This economic rationale offers only limited further clarification when attempting to analyze the intended subject matter of the resale right.

No Austrian Implementation of Droit de Suite

While the Berne Convention explicitly states that the resale right is subject to the rule of reciprocity, it does not create the necessity to transpose the resale right into national legislation. The resale right is optional in the sense that EU Member States are free to decide whether to introduce it.[11] Additionally, according to Article 2, Paragraph 1, of the Agreement on Trade-Related Aspects of Intellectual Property Rights (TRIPS),[12] Article 14 *ter* BC is not part of the set of rules with which TRIPS member states must comply. Thus, until the later harmonization at the EU level, the Austrian legislator was under no international obligation to enact a *droit de suite* on a national level.

This is not to say that there was no domestic interest in introducing a resale right. The collecting society of fine arts[13] issued an according draft and initiated public discussion on the introduction of a resale right as early as 1993. The draft was essentially based on the legal framework then in force in Germany and envisaged a compensation of five per cent of the sales price of every subsequent sale for a price exceeding €50.[14] These proposals were put aside under reference to the dawning European harmonization.[15]

European Harmonization of Resale Right through Directive 2001/84/EC

Legislative History and Background

In the wake of the "Phil Collins" decisions of the European Court of Justice,[16] it was established that the principle of non-discrimination

---

[11] World Intellectual Property Organization, *Guide to the Berne Convention for the Protection of Literary and Artistic Works* (1978), 14 *ter* 3.
[12] "In respect of Parts II, III and IV of this Agreement, Members shall comply with Articles 1 through 12, and Article 19, of the Paris Convention (1967)."
[13] VBK — *Verwertungsgesellschaft bildender Künstler*, later renamed "Bildrecht".
[14] Kovacs, "Kunstsachverständigentagung 2012: Das Folgerecht und seine Folgen", *Sachverständige* 4/2012, at pp. 227 *et seq.*
[15] Kovacs, "Kunstsachverständigentagung 2012: Das Folgerecht und seine Folgen", *Sachverständige* 4/2012, at p. 228.
[16] C-92/92 and C-326/92.

applied to copyright law. Reciprocity clauses could not be relied upon to deny nationals of other Member States rights that were conferred to national authors. At the time, the concept of a resale right was not uniformly embraced by all member states. Eleven of the then-fifteen Member States recognized the right in principle, and eight member states had already put it into practice. By admission of the Economic and Social Committee, "even there, implementation arrangements var(ied) widely".[17] Along with Austria, The Netherlands, Ireland, and the United Kingdom had no resale right regime in place at the time.

In April 1996, the European Commission presented the Council with a proposal for a European Parliament and Council Directive on the resale right for the benefit of the author of an original work of art.[18] The main motivation for the harmonization was the understanding that a non-uniform standard of *droit de suite* would lead to certain safe harbors within the EU and ultimately distort the internal market.[19] When faced with the choice between harmonizing a right and outlawing it, the European legislator chose to harmonize it. On 13 October 2001, European Resale Rights Directive 2001/84/EC came into force.[20]

Economic Considerations Leading to Resale Rights Directive

The Commission provided little economic information on its rationale for the Directive:

> "(3) The resale right is intended to ensure that authors of graphic and plastic works of art share in the economic success in their original works of art. It helps to redress the balance between the economic situation of the authors of graphic and plastic works of arts, and that of other creators who benefit from successive exploitations of their works."

The economic rationale, based solely on a comparison with artists who are able to benefit from successive exploitations, is inconsequent at best. While a good number of artists other than those of graphic and plastic works are able to commercialize successive exploitations, this does not

---

17 Opinion of the Economic and Social Committee on the "Proposal for a European Parliament and Council Directive on the resale right for the benefit of the author of an original work of art" (97/C 75/03), 10 March 1997, Paragraph 1.4.
18 *Official Journal*, C 178, 21 June 1996, at p.16.
19 Recital 13 of the Directive.
20 Directive 2001/84/EC of the European Parliament and of the Council of 27 September 2001 on the resale right for the benefit of the author of an original work of art.

hold true for all of them. Authors of actionist works of art come to mind as a category of artists that may not be able to profit from either. Furthermore, one may argue that authors of graphic and plastic works are able to work their neighboring rights more efficiently.

Most importantly, this recital alone barely provides a sufficient economic assessment of the legislation in question. The Directive again seems to have the stereotypical theme in mind where a young artist is forced to sell cheaply, and then becomes a world-reputed household name who still is barred from his profits. As implied above, this does not generally apply. Only a fraction of artists reach the degree of notoriety that is implicitly assumed by this theme. It seems unreasonable to make policy just in order to cater to this small minority, especially when this policy may be detrimental to others.

In addition, it must be kept in mind that artists have several other means of capitalizing from their works at their disposal, most importantly the vast array of rights provided by the European neighboring-rights doctrine. Partially overlapping is the European Court of Justice extensive interpretation of trade mark functions and trade mark use that allows artists to benefit from their works by ways of merchandising.[21] Commentators have argued that, when assessing the economic impact of a resale right, it must be borne in mind that, from a dealer's perspective, purchasing a work of art from an unknown is a tremendous risk. Only a fraction of the works lead to revenues.[22]

Reasonable dealers will take the resale right into account when buying works of art, which of course leads to a decrease in the initial market price. Commentators have argued that "the *droit de suite* shifts income from his youth to his older age. The artist is forced to accept a lower income now, in exchange for some uncertain future gain, shifting income to a perhaps more prosperous stage of his life. This transfer of a part of the artist's current income to the future may be harmful even if the present value of the lifetime income stream is increased".[23] Generating additional revenues in times of low income leads to more utility than having additional income in a phase where the income is already high.[24]

---

21 European Court of Justice, C-487/07, LOreal/Bellure.
22 Kirstein and Schmidtchen, *Do Artists Benefit from Resale Royalties? An Economic Analysis of a New EU Directive*, 24 April 2000, at p. 5.
23 Kirstein and Schmidtchen, *Do Artists Benefit from Resale Royalties? An Economic Analysis of a New EU Directive*, 24 April 2000, at p. 15.
24 Kirstein and Schmidtchen, *Do Artists Benefit from Resale Royalties? An Economic Analysis of a New EU Directive*, 24 April 2000, at p. 16.

If anything can be concluded from Recital 31, it must be that the European legislator saw the need for an additional source of income for the creators of certain categories of arts and the need to incentivize the creation of these categories, without spending much thought on what these categories are. While one may argue that, at the time, harmonization of the heterogeneous situation made sense in order to allow for a functioning Common Market, especially keeping in mind that the majority of Member States had a resale right in place, introducing a uniform European resale right might have been the simplest solution. However, while this author is not so naive to deny that the political process leading to such solution would have been profoundly complicated, it is to be pointed out that convenience should not replace economic analysis in legislation.

Infringement and Subject Matter of Resale Right

Subject Matter — Notion of Originality

In order to define the limits of infringement, the definition of the categories of works is of utmost importance. The scope of the Directive is defined in Article 2, titled "Works of art to which the resale right relates":

> "1. For the purposes of this Directive, 'original work of art' means works of graphic or plastic art such as pictures, collages, paintings, drawings, engravings, prints, lithographs, sculptures, tapestries, ceramics, glassware and photographs, provided they are made by the artist himself or are copies considered to be original works of art.

> "2. Copies of works of art covered by this Directive, which have been made in limited numbers by the artist himself or under his authority, shall be considered to be original works of art for the purposes of this Directive. Such copies will normally have been numbered, signed or otherwise duly authorized by the artist."

Further clarification can be found in the recitals:

> "(1) In the field of copyright, the resale right is an unassignable and inalienable right, enjoyed by the author of an original work of

graphic or plastic art, to an economic interest in successive sales of the work concerned.

"(4) The resale right forms an integral part of copyright and is an essential prerogative for authors. The imposition of such a right in all Member States meets the need for providing creators with an adequate and standard level of protection.

"(19) It should be made clear that the harmonization brought about by this Directive does not apply to original manuscripts of writers and composers.

"(21) The categories of works of art subject to the resale right should be harmonized."

Article 2 of the Directive thus essentially defines the scope of the resale right by applying two separate criteria, and both must be met in order for resale right to apply. A work must suit a certain category of works, and it either must be an original or considered an original.

Categories of Works Subject to Resale Right

As to the first criterion, the European legislator has restricted the scope to "works of graphic or plastic art". The legislator further provided a list of categories, apparently for demonstration purposes. That list provided some clarification, but it does not definitely define the subject matter.

The inclusion of glassware, for example, stems from the European Parliament's initiative,[25] as it was not part of the initial draft.[26] The Commission first rejected the proposal, arguing, "it is generally accepted, both under Article 14 *ter* of the Berne Convention and in the legislation of the Member States on resale right, that the applied arts are not included among works of art covered by resale right".[27]

Glassware appearing in the final version of the Directive, according to some commentators, is a reliable indicator of the intent to include works of applied arts in the subject matter of the resale right.[28] One may

---

25 Opinion of the Parliament of 9 April 1997, Amendment 69.
26 *Official Journal*, C 178, 21 June 1996, at p. 16.
27 Amended proposal for a European Parliament and Council Directive on the resale right for the benefit of the author of an original work of art, 12 March 1998, 96/0085 COD, I-4-e.
28 Walter, in Lewinski, Walter, Blocher, Dreier, Daum, and Dillenz, *Europäisches Urheberrecht, Folgerecht-RL*, Article 3, Paragraph 7.

argue that this understanding is not convincing in light of the fact that not all glassware is applied art. However, this interpretation would render the Commission's proposal contradictory.

The phrasing of the Directive does not mention applied arts, neither explicitly including nor explicitly excluding it from the subject matter of the resale right. It does, however, mention categories of works that regularly constitute works of applied arts, most importantly sculptures, ceramics, and glassware. Based on the phrasing itself, there is a case to be made that applied arts are to be included by the wide definition of the term "original work of art", especially since they were not explicitly excluded, as was the case with manuscripts in Recital (19).

The legislative history and the phrasing of the Directive do not provide an explicit solution to the dilemma of whether applied arts are to be subject of the resale right. The legislator's intention to "redress the balance between the economic situation of the authors of graphic and plastic works of arts, and that of other creators who benefit from successive exploitations of their works"[29] does not exclude authors of applied arts from benefiting from the resale right.

The fact that a work of art has a practical purpose does not automatically impact the artist's ability to successively exploit it. In light of this, the Directive offers sufficient grounds to include works of applied arts in the scope of the resale right.

The question of applicability with regards to works of applied arts is of utmost importance in practice, as the furniture example demonstrates. In general, furniture must be considered a work of applied arts. The legislative history as to whether works of applied arts are to be included in the subject matter of the resale right does not provide a clear-cut solution.

The two-step test, differentiating between the term "work of art", on the one side, and the "originality", on the other, allows for a broader application of the former criterion. Walter's argument hinting at the Commission's change in opinion as to applied arts is convincing enough to conclude that the European Commission has ultimately given up its resistance against the inclusion of applied arts. It will probably be up to the European Court of Justice to settle this question.

Considering the Directive's half-hearted attempt at providing an economic rationale, a case can be made for the inclusion of applied arts. The mere fact that a work of art also has a practical application does not automatically imply that it is produced in large quantities or that it even

---

[29] Recital 3 of the Directive.

can be produced in large quantities. This leads, according to the legislator, to the unsatisfactory situation in which an artist in unable to capitalize on his later rise in popularity and repute.

When compared to an artist who is able to capitalize from a high-volume reproduction of his works (e.g., a musician), the economic situation of a creator of a work of applied art is no different from that of a painter. Hence, one may conclude that works of applied arts cannot generally be excluded from the scope of the *droit de suite*. Serial works are not subject to limitation on this level. They typically must stand the test of originality. Nor does the Directive generally exclude works finished posthumously on this level. Again, this is a criterion that must be evaluated on the level of originality.

Originals

As to originality, the European legislator again introduced a standard that allowed for some leeway in its application by requiring works to be an original or to be considered an original. Some commentators have argued that "considered to be an original" points to the market's understanding of originality.[30] This is in line with the Commission's initial proposal that provided for the phrasing "copies considered to be original works of art according to professional usage in the Community".[31]

It is this vague phrasing that is perhaps the most troubling about the Directive's definition of scope. There is often no consensus as to what is to be considered an original. One would commonly construe the wording of the Directive as meaning a work is an original if experts knowledgeable of the matter would concur. However, this is not reconcilable with the practice of the art market.

According to experts on the art market, a work of art will be considered an original in the sense of the Directive so long as it is "authentic". The authentication process of works of art is imperfect, which is much due to the fact that it is not centralized and mostly in the hands of a stakeholder, most notably the artist or his estate.

While a limitation to a maximum of twelve copies was proposed by the European Parliament, the legislator made a deliberate choice not to

---

[30] Walter, in Lewinski, Walter, Blocher, Dreier, Daum, and Dillenz, *Europäisches Urheberrecht, Folgerecht-RL*, Article 3, Paragraph 5.
[31] OJ C 178, 21 June 1996, at p. 16, Article 2.

introduce such limitation.³² The legislator's reasoning not to include a limitation was to account for some categories of works, most notably photographs that are usually recreated in larger quantities, yet still considered originals. However, one may argue whether, in that case, the economic rationale stated above still applies.

As noted above, the resale right was introduced in order to "redress the balance between economic situation of authors of graphic and plastic words, and that of other creators who benefit from successive exploitations of their works".³³ A serially produced work clearly qualifies as such successive exploitation. Applying the resale right to such works would lead to the unfair situation of some artists benefitting from both the possibility to successively exploit and additionally to participate in later sales of the same works.

Since it was the legislator's self-proclaimed intent to redress the balance, the Directive cannot be construed in a way that is applicable to serial works. This understanding may not be clearly covered by the legislative materials.³⁴ The interpretation of the term "considered original" may further lead to large quantities of posthumously produced everyday objects being within the Directive's scope. In addition, economically, it is the most sensible approach not to include serial works. This becomes most striking when considering our furniture example, leading to a situation with a high volume of potential infringers (i.e., end-consumers reselling furniture, unaware of their infringement).

The phrasing "considered original" further leads to the inclusion of works that may not stem directly from the artist but are made under his supervision, or works whose concept was conceived by the artist, but that were finished without his participation. This may include works that are finished posthumously.

In this context, it is appropriate to base originality on the market's understanding of the authenticity of works finished *post mortem*. Such will be considered original if the work substantially is based on the late artist's plans or has been commenced by the artist or under his supervision. Within the Copyright Term Directive, the European legislator has

---

32 Amended proposal for a European Parliament and Council Directive on the resale right for the benefit of the author of an original work of art, 12 March 1998, 96/0085 COD, I-4-d.
33 Directive 2001/84/EC, Recital 3.
34 Amended proposal for a European Parliament and Council Directive on the resale right for the benefit of the author of an original work of art, 12 March 1998, 96/0085 COD, I-4-d.

made clear its general intent to grant protection to such works.[35] In this case, if the person finishing the work is expressing his own intellectual creation upon finishing the work, the rules of co-authorship apply.

Furthermore, finishing a work that has already been started is less problematic than serially reproducing a work *post mortem*. This justifies to treat works *post mortem* differently than serial works. As a result, posthumous works qualify for resale right protection. As to works of applied arts, the question of originality appears to be irrelevant. Works that possess practical value do not call for a different treatment than any other works in terms of originality.

De Minimis Standard or Fully Harmonized Legal Concept?

The scope and extent of harmonization remained somewhat contentious throughout the legislative process. Some commentators have argued that the scope defined in the Regulation is but a *de minimis* rule that may be exceeded by the national legislator[36] and that the subject matter of resale right may be extended to categories of works.

This reasoning cannot be upheld in light of the European Court of Justice case law concerning the autonomous definition of terms used in acts of EU legislation (recently confirmed in its *Padawan* decision[37]), as well as the Recitals of the Directive. The Court has consistently held that it follows from the need for uniform application of EU law and from the principle of equality that the terms of a provision of EU law that makes no express reference to the law of the Member States for the purpose of determining its meaning and scope must normally be given an autonomous and uniform interpretation throughout the EU, having regard to the context of the provision and the objective pursued by the legislation in question.[38]

While this in itself does not disprove the existence of a *de minimis* standard in the present case, Recital 21 of the Directive postulates that "[t]he categories of works of art subject to the resale right should be harmonized". The Commission has stated that discrepancies in the subject matter of the resale right may cause disruption in the common market, which was the reason why the Directive was enacted in the first place.[39]

---

35 Directive on the term of protection of copyright and certain related rights, 2006/116/EC.
36 Walter, in Lewinski, Walter, Blocher, Dreier, Daum, and Dillenz, *Europäisches Urheberrecht, Folgerecht-RL*, Article 2, Paragraph 2.
37 European Court of Justice, C-467/08.
38 European Court of Justice C-201/13, Paragraph 14, *Deckmyn*.
39 *Official Journal*, C 178, 21 June 1996.

This must hold true for national regulations that exceed the EU rules just as much as for such that fall short of them. In light of this, there is a case to be made that the concept of *droit de suite*, as well as its subject matter, must be understood as an autonomous EU law concept. This leaves no room for national legislators to exceed the Directive's scope. As a result, the central question must be answered uniformly in the entire EU.

Austrian Implementation of Directive

Throughout the European legislative process, Austria appeared not to embrace the resale right and voted against the Directive.[40] The Austrian legislator maximized waiting time, finally taking its first step into the unknown terrain of resale rights by amending the following rules into Section 16b of Austria's Copyright Act:

"(3) For the purposes of this law, the following are to be considered original works of art:

"1. Works that have been created by the artist himself,

"2. Works that have been created by the artist himself or under his authority in limited edition, and normally numbered as well as signed by the artist or otherwise duly authorized by the artist,

"3. Works that otherwise are to be considered original."[41]

It is evident that the Austrian legislator directly adopted a large part of the Directive's phrasing. The Austrian legislator implied its understanding of the key problem (an exceedingly broad scope of the resale right) by providing a limitation to works that have been made under the artist's authority, in limitation, signed, or otherwise duly authorized in Paragraph (3)2. This is a step in the right direction; however, it falls short of solving the problem, mostly due to it being relativized by the introductory phrasing "normally". Nor does this implementation or the parliamentary discussions that led to it shed additional light on the topics set forth above or provide any information useful for our furniture example.[42]

---

40 See http://europa.eu/rapid/press-release_PRES-01-288_en.htm?locale=en.
41 *Bundesgesetz über das Urheberrecht an Werken der Literatur und der Kunst und über verwandte Schutzrechte* (*Urheberrechtsgesetz*).
42 Protocol 869/A of the 24th legislative period, 18 November 2009.

Some commentators[43] have argued that the Austrian implementation includes serial works only in cases where they are limited. "As a general rule", these commentators claim, works must be created by the author himself. Walter, for example, concludes that works are to be considered originals when they are considered as such by the market and the relevant public.[44] He maintains the phrasing of the Directive to be construed as a special provision that shall extend to a single, original piece as well as to a small-batch series, however, he fails to cite a valid source for this understanding.[45] Walter appears to employ the market's understanding[46] as the prime criterion of originality in a legal sense, thus overlooking the dilemma his understanding entails.

Handig applies an even more reduced understanding of Section 16b, concluding that, in order for a work to qualify for resale right royalties, it must have been created under the artist's authority in limited edition and numbered as well as signed by the artist or otherwise duly authorized by the artist. This effectively ignores the word "normally" in the rule of law.[47] His understanding of the scope seems very narrow, and at least some form of participation is deemed required to qualify as an original.[48] Thus, according to Handig's understanding, posthumous works are not in the scope of the resale right. As to works of applied arts, Handig argues that one is to evaluate the artistic value of a work and compare that to its practical value. Only where the artistic value decisively outweighs its practical value is a work affected by *droit de suite*.

Conclusion

As indicated above, and in light of the economic motivation as stated by the European legislator, the notion that works of applied arts, as was the general understanding at the time of the conception of the resale right on the international stage,[49] can no longer be upheld. The legislative history and genesis of the Directive leaves enough leeway for the understanding

---

43 Walter, *Handbuch Österreichisches Urheberrecht, I.Teil*, III.9, Paragraph 860.
44 Walter, *Handbuch Österreichisches Urheberrecht, I.Teil*, III.9, Paragraph 860.
45 Walter, *Handbuch Österreichisches Urheberrecht, I.Teil*, III.9, Paragraph 863.
46 Walter, *Handbuch Österreichisches Urheberrecht, I.Teil*, III.9, Paragraphs 862, 863, and 864.
47 Handig, in *Urheberrecht*, Section 16b UrhG, Paragraph 22.
48 Handig, in *Urheberrecht*, Section 16b UrhG, Paragraph 22.
49 World Intellectual Property Organization, *Guide to the Berne Convention for the Protection of Literary and Artistic Works* (1978), 14 *ter* 2.

that works of applied arts are subject to resale right, and thus can be subject to its infringement. This is compatible with the Directive's economic rationale.

As to serial works, a delicate balance must be struck between those types of works that habitually or traditionally are reproduced in series yet still considered originals, and those that are being reproduced without being considered originals. The trouble is that the current definition of the term "original" is not sufficient to lead to fair results. One may hope that the European Court of Justice will clarify that the authentication of works, if customary in the market to define an original, should not factor into the question whether *droit de suite* applies. This is to keep stakeholders from defining their own legal position at will, at the cost of a functioning Common Market.

Considerations of fairness do not call for the additional remuneration of serial works, or posthumous works. Either they do not benefit the artist or they are inherently designed to generate additional profits for the artist without requiring further effort. There is no need to incentivize those two categories of works; one may even argue to the contrary. In light of this, it is suggested to exclude works commonly produced in series (e.g., photographs) from the scope of the resale right. This, of course, is a mere policy recommendation, not covered by Austria's or the EU's current legal framework.

There is no reason to generally exclude works that were finished after the passing of the artist from resale right royalties. A modern understanding of works of art should allow for cooperative creation, which should include posthumous completion of works. In addition, the rules set forth in connection with serial works, meaning a market-based, yet unbiased understanding, should apply.

Brazil

Ricardo Barretto Ferreira da Silva,
Camila Taliberti Ribeiro da Silva,
and Vitor Rodolfo Koketu da Cunha
Azevedo Sette Advogados
São Paulo, Brazil

Introduction

In general, copyright is the right of an author to prevent unauthorized productions of his work that is entitled to copyright. Copyright protects the author in his intellectual and personal relationship with his work and use of his work, and it serves to secure reasonable remuneration for use of the work.

Brazil follows the continental system of copyright. It differs from the Anglo-American system to the extent that it is addressed to protect creativity of the work to be copied and moral rights of its author. In turn, the Anglo-American system was built on the possibility of reproducing copies and focusing on protection of such right. The Constitution[1] has granted copyright the status of fundamental right. It establishes that the exclusive right of use, publication, or reproduction of works belongs to their authors and it is transmissible to their heirs for the time established by law; consequently, the author has the right to all benefits and economic income resulting from a work.

Law Number 9,610 of 19 February 1998 governs copyright in Brazil (the "Copyright Act").[2] The Law extends to rights of authors and neighboring rights. Software is subject to a specific provision, Law Number 9,609 of 19 February 1998, which regulates the protection of intellectual property in computer programs and commercialization in Brazil (the "Software Act").[3] The copyright laws apply to computer programs when suitable. Copyright also is mentioned in specific sectoral laws, which only apply to certain sectors and areas of activity, such as:

(1) Law Number 6,533 of 24 May 1978, which regulates the professions of artists and technicians in amusement shows;

---

[1] See http://www.stf.jus.br/repositorio/cms/portalStfInternacional/portalStfSobreCorte_en_us/anexo/Constitution_2013.pdf.
[2] See http://www.wipo.int/edocs/lexdocs/laws/en/br/br002en.pdf.
[3] See http://www.wipo.int/wipolex/en/text.jsp?file_id=125391.

(2) Law Number 6,615 of 16 December 1978, which regulates the radio broadcast profession; and
(3) Law Number 12,378 of 31 December 2010, which regulates architecture and urbanism.

In addition, Brazil is a signatory to the main treaties that protect copyright, such as:
(1) The Paris Convention for Protection of Industrial Property (as reviewed in Stockholm in 1967), incorporated into Brazilian law by Decree Number 75,572 of 8 April 1975;
(2) The Agreement on Trade-Related Aspects of Intellectual Property Rights (TRIPs), incorporated into Brazilian law by Decree Number 1,355 of 30 December 1994;
(3) The Berne Convention for Protection of Literary and Artistic Works, incorporated into Brazilian law by Decree Number 75,699 of 6 May 1975;
(4) The Washington Copyright Convention, incorporated into Brazilian law by Decree Number 26,675 of 18 May 1949;
(5) The Universal Copyright Convention, incorporated into Brazilian law by Decree Number 76,905 of 24 December 1975;
(6) The Rome Convention for Protection of Performers, Producers of Phonograms, and Broadcasting Organisations, incorporated into Brazilian law by Decree Number 57,125 of 19 October 1965; and
(7) The Geneva Convention for Protection of Producers of Phonograms against Unauthorised Duplication of Their Phonograms, incorporated into Brazilian law by Decree Number 76,906 of 24 December 1975.

Rights Protected by Copyright

In General

There are two types of rights covered by the Copyright Act, namely:
(1) Property rights that entitle the copyright owner to extract a financial advantage due to economic use and exploitation of his work by third parties; and
(2) Moral rights that are non-economic and non-transferrable and allow the author to adopt certain measures to preserve the personal connection between one and the work.

An individual may be held liable for copyright infringement if he is directly violating a copyright or contributes to, facilitates, or gains advantages from the copyright infringement.

Property Rights

According to the Copyright Act, Articles 28 and 29, an author has the exclusive right to use his literary, artistic, or scientific work, as well as to derive benefit from it and to dispose of it. The law states that property rights ensure the copyright owner financial benefits from exploitation of his work, and that express prior authorization shall be required for any kind of use, such as:

(1) Complete or partial reproduction;
(2) Publication;
(3) Adaptation, setting to music, or any other transformation;
(4) Translation into any language;
(5) Incorporation in a phonogram or in an audiovisual production;
(6) Distribution where it is not provided for in a contract signed by the author with third parties for the use or exploitation of the work;
(7) Distribution for the purposes of offering works or productions by cable, optic fiber, satellite, electromagnetic waves, or any other system enabling the user to select a work or production and to receive it at the time and place of his choice, provided that access to works or productions is made through any system requiring payment on the part of the user; and
(8) Direct or indirect use of literary, artistic, or scientific work in one of the following forms: (a) performance, recitation, or declamation; (b) musical performance; (c) use of loudspeaker or comparable systems; (d) radio or television broadcasting; (e) reception of a radio broadcast in places frequented by the public; (f) provision of background music; (g) audiovisual, cinematographic, or equivalent presentation; (h) use of man-made satellites; (i) use of optical systems, telephone or other lines, cables of all kinds, and comparable means of communication as may be devised in the future; (j) exhibition of works of three-dimensional and figurative art; (k) incorporation in databases, storage in a computer, microfilming, and any other means of archiving of that kind; (l) and any other form of use that exists at present or might be devised in the future.

Moral Rights

Moral rights are related to authorship of the work. These are the rights that bind the author to his creation, which belong exclusively to him. For that reason, moral rights are considered personal, unalienable, and non-transferable. Moral rights are mainly composed of two elements:

(1) The right to authorship, which entitles the author the right to claim authorship of the work at any time, so that even if the author assigns the rights to a third party, he still maintains the moral rights of the work and can demand at any time the status of author of the work, and have the authorship recognized; and

(2) The right to integrity of the work, which means the right to oppose any distortion, mutilation, or other modification of, or other derogatory action in relation to the work, which would be prejudicial to his honor or reputation.[4]

In other words, anything that may detract from the author's relationship with the work, even after it leaves the author's possession, may bring these moral rights into play. Thus, the author can oppose the use of his work in a context where there is a situation that will affect its cultural or artistic integrity. According to the Copyright Act, the moral rights of the author are understood as those to:

(1) Claim authorship of the work at any time;
(2) Cause his name, pseudonym, or conventional sign to appear or be announced as that of the author when the work is used;
(3) Keep the work unpublished;
(4) Ensure the integrity of the work by objecting to any modification or any act liable in any way to have an adverse effect on the work or to be detrimental to his reputation or honor as author;
(5) Amend the work either before or after it has been used;
(6) Withdraw the work from circulation or to suspend any kind of use that has already been authorized where the circulation or the use of the work is liable to have an adverse effect on the reputation or image of the author; and
(7) Have access to the single or rare copy of the work that is lawfully in a third party's possession with a view to preserving the memory thereof by means of a photographic or similar or an audiovisual process, in such a way that the least possible inconvenience is caused to its possessor who shall in any event be indemnified for any damage or loss suffered.[5]

---

[4] Bern Convention, Article 6. See http://www.wipo.int/treaties/en/text.jsp?file_id =283698#P123_20726.
[5] Copyright Act, Article 24.

Neighboring Rights

Neighboring or related rights protect the interests of those who contributed to reproduction of the works by providing public access to it, or in any way contributed artistically or technically to execution of the work. Related rights gained legal relevance with invention of the press, phonograms, and radio broadcasting. Now, with development of new reproduction and transmissions techniques through satellite and Internet, related rights are even more relevant.

Additionally, related rights are originated from works protected by copyright. Therefore, they will always be connected. However, because they are based on technical elements and creativity, related rights are linked to communication of the work to the public, not to the work itself. While not qualifying as works under the copyright systems of all countries, these works contain sufficient creativity or technical and organizational skill to justify recognition of a copyright-like property right.[6]

Thus, Brazilian law protects related rights of three categories: the right of artists and performers; the rights of phonogram producers; and the rights of broadcasting organizations.

Rights of performers are recognized because their creative intervention is necessary to give life to, for example, motion pictures or musical, dramatic, and choreographic works, and because they have a justifiable interest in the legal protection of their individual interpretations.[7] The Copyright Act provides that, either under payment or free of charge, performers enjoy the exclusive right to authorize or to prohibit:

(1) The fixing of performances;
(2) The reproduction, public performance, or rental of fixed performances;
(3) The broadcast of fixed or unfixed performances;
(4) The making available to the public of performances in such a way that any person may have access to them at the time and in the place of that person's choosing; and
(5) Any other form of use of performances.[8]

Rights of producers of sound recordings are recognized because their creative, financial, and organizational resources are necessary to make

---

[6] WIPO, *Understanding Copyright and Related Rights*. See http://www.wipo.int/edocs/pubdocs/en/ wipo_pub_909_2016.pdf.
[7] WIPO, *Understanding Copyright and Related Rights*, at p. 28.
[8] Copyright Act, Article 90.

sound recordings, often based on musical works, available to the public in commercial form, and because of their legitimate interest in having the legal resources to take action against unauthorized uses.[9] The Copyright Act provides that a phonogram producer has the exclusive right to authorize or prohibit, under payment or free of charge:

(1) Direct or indirect, total or partial reproduction of his phonograms;
(2) Distribution by sale or rental of copies of phonograms so reproduced;
(3) Communication of his phonograms to public-by-public performance, including broadcasting; and
(4) Any other form of use of his phonograms that exists at present or might be devised in the future.[10]

In the same way, broadcasting organizations have infrastructure costs to distribute audiovisual works to the public and have a legitimate interest in court protection of their transmission and retransmission rights. The Copyright Act establishes that broadcasting organizations have the exclusive right to authorize or prohibit retransmission, fixation, and reproduction of their broadcasts and communication of such broadcasts to the public by television in places attended by the said public, without prejudice to the rights of owners of the intellectual property embodied in the programs.[11]

Types of Copyrightable Works

Essentially, copyright protects creations of the human spirit. According to the Berne Convention, to which Brazil is a signatory, all artistic, literary, and scientific expressions are protected by copyright. Protected is the materialized and/or executed artistic expression; the idea *per se* of an intellectual work does not hold a copyright. Therefore, the Copyright Act recognizes intellectual works as creations of the mind, expressed or registered in any form or mean, whether tangible or intangible, known or susceptible of an invention in the future, such as:

(1) Texts of literary, artistic, or scientific works;
(2) Lectures, addresses, sermons, and other works of the same kind;
(3) Dramatic and dramatic-musical works;
(4) Choreographic and mimed works whose stage performance is set down either in writing or otherwise;

---

[9] WIPO, *Understanding Copyright and Related Rights*, at p. 30.
[10] Copyright Act, Article 93.
[11] Copyright Act, Article 95.

(5) Musical compositions with or without words;
(6) Audiovisual works, with or without accompanying sounds, including cinematographic works;
(7) Photographic works and other works produced by a process analogous to photography;
(8) Drawings, paintings, engravings, sculptures, lithographs, and works of kinetic art;
(9) Illustrations, maps, and other works of the same kind;
(10) Drafts, mock-ups, and three-dimensional works relating to geography, engineering, topography, architecture, park and garden planning, stage scenery, and science;
(11) Adaptations, translations, and other transformations of original works, presented as new intellectual creations;
(12) Computer programs that are complementarily subject to the Software Act; and
(13) Collections or compilations, anthologies, encyclopedias, dictionaries, databases, and other works that, by virtue of the selection, coordination, or arrangement of the subject matter, constitute intellectual creations.[12]

By virtue of Article 7, the law is concerned to protect works that belong to the domain of literacy, arts, and science; are original (i.e., can be differentiated from other works); and were made public, in any form and by any means. Article 8 of the Copyright Law establishes the exclusions of copyright protection for:
(1) Ideas, normative procedures, systems, methods, or mathematical projects or concepts as such;
(2) Diagrams, plans, or instructions for performing mental acts, playing games, or conducting business;
(3) Blank forms intended for completion with all types of scientific or other information and the instructions appearing thereon;
(4) Texts of treaties or conventions, laws, decrees, regulations, judicial decisions, and other official documents;
(5) Information of common use, such as that contained in calendars, diaries, registers, and legends;
(6) Names and titles in isolation; and
(7) Industrial or commercial exploitation of the ideas embodied in works.

---

12 Copyright Act, Article 7.

The Copyright Act also states that:
(1) A copy of a three-dimensional work made by the creator of such work will enjoy the same protection as the original;
(2) The protection of an intellectual work will extend to its title, provided that it is original and not liable to be confused with that of a work of the same nature disclosed earlier by another author; and
(3) The titles of periodical publications, including newspapers, will be protected for a period of one year from publication of the last issue, except in case of annual publications, in which case the period shall be two years.

Sectoral laws also protect copyright of architectural works and performance rights. Law Number 12,378 of 31 December 2010, which regulates the exercise of architecture and urbanism profession, ensures copyright protection of architectural works and technical collections.

Law Number 6,533 of 24 May 1978, which regulates the professions of artists and technician, in amusement shows, provides that copyright and neighboring rights of artists and technicians in amusement shows are protected for each exhibition of the work and may not be subject to assignment. Law Number 6,615 of 16 December 1978, which regulates the radio-broadcasting profession, provides that copyright and neighboring rights of radio broadcasters are ensured for each exhibition of the work and may not be subject to assignment.

Registration of Copyright

According to the Copyright Act, the rights provided for intellectual works do not depend on registration but are naturally granted as from the creation of the work. However, it is always advisable to register the work, as it is the best way to formalize protection of copyright. Registration of copyright depends on the nature of the work since there is no main agency to concentrate copyright in Brazil.

Musical works must be registered with the National School of Music of the Federal University of Rio de Janeiro. Literary works must be registered with the Copyright Office of the National Library Foundation. Audiovisual works must be registered with the National Cinema Agency (ANCINE). Visual art works must be registered with the School of Beaux-Arts of the Federal University of Rio de Janeiro. Computer software must be registered with the National Institute of Industrial Property (INPI). Architect projects and technical collections must be registered with the Brazilian Council of Architecture and Urbanism.

Length of Protection

Copyright starts with the creation of the intellectual work and generally lasts for seventy years following the author's death. There are some exemptions for photographic, audiovisual, and collective works, where copyright lasts for seventy years starting from their publication.

As regards neighboring rights, according to the Copyright Act, the term of protection is seventy years from 1 January of the year following fixation for phonograms, transmission of broadcasts by broadcasting organizations, and public performance in other cases.

Copyright Enforcement in Brazil

Enforcement Authorities

Enforcement of copyright involves relevant governs and sanctions under the Copyright Act, the Civil Proceeding Code, and the Criminal Code, as well as the coordination of several authorities in federal, state, and municipal levels, such as the Customs/Revenue Service, Police, Prosecution Service, and Judiciary.

In addition, since 2004, Brazil has a National Council against Piracy and Intellectual Property Crimes, a public/private body created within the framework of the Ministry of Justice. The Council's strategy and tactics are defined within the National Plan for Combating Piracy. The III National Plan for Combating Piracy (2013–2016) includes ninety-nine guidelines for short, medium, and long-term action. The National Plan defines the strategy of broadening and coordinating intelligence work within all the government departments involved in combating piracy, counterfeiting, and other intellectual property-related crime.

Educational programs have been designed not only to alert the public about the risks inherent in buying pirated goods but, more broadly, to promote an intellectual property culture in Brazil, encouraging consumers to privilege genuine products. In parallel with educational campaigns, the National Council against Piracy and Intellectual Property Crimes has set about dealing with pricing issues. The solution may be to promote creation of alternative lines of original products at more affordable prices. The National Council against Piracy and Intellectual Property Crimes is in charge of encouraging the public and private sectors to develop initiatives, offering producers and industry-free publicity and government incentives to develop inexpensive branded products.[13]

Legal enforcement is commonly supported by industry associations, which have strong influence over enforcement authorities and frequently denounce copyright infringements and file civil and criminal lawsuits. The most important associations are the Business Software Alliance, the Brazilian Association of Software Companies, the Entertainment Software Association, and the Motion Pictures Association.

Criminal Enforcement

Penalties for infringement of copyright include fines, seizure, and destruction of copied materials, and imprisonment for three months to four years. The key laws in this regard are the Software Law, Article 12, and the Criminal Code, Article 184, which apply to all copyrightable works rather than software.

Article 184 of the Criminal Code defines crimes against copyright. It states that an infringer of copyright and/or neighboring right is subject to imprisonment ranging from three months to one year or a fine. The penalty is raised from two to four years, plus a fine, when infringement consists of total or partial unauthorized reproduction with direct or indirect economic purposes.[14] The same penalty is applied to one who distributes, sells, offers for sale, rents, imports into Brazil, acquires, hides, or stores the original or copy of copyrighted work without the express authorization of the owner.[15]

If infringement consists of offering copyrighted work to the public, with direct or indirect economic purposes, by cable, fiber optic, satellite, radiofrequency, or any other means that allows the user to select the copyrighted work, the infringer is subject to imprisonment ranging from two to four years plus fine.[16] Article 184, Paragraph 4, provides an important exclusion of the criminal sanctions for cases of exception or limitation to copyright, or copying and intellectual or phonogram work into a single template, for private use of the copier, with no direct or indirect profit purpose. In principle, the rule does not incriminate an individual who obtains copyrighted works by peer-to-peer transactions.

---

13 WIPO, *Country Focus, Combating Piracy: Brazil Fights Back*, see http://www.wipo.int/wipo_magazine/en/2006/05/article_0003.html.
14 Criminal Code, Article 184, Paragraph 1.
15 Criminal Code, Article 184, Paragraph 2.
16 Criminal Code, Article 184, Paragraph 3.

Article 12 of the Software Act states that the infringement of software copyright is subject to imprisonment ranging from six months to two years and/or a fine. If the infringement consists of unauthorized full or partial reproduction, by any means, for commercial purposes, the infringer will incur a penalty of one to four years of imprisonment, plus a fine. The same penalty is applied when the infringer sells, acquires, imports, or stores software for a commercial purpose.

Criminal Enforcement Proceedings

Criminal proceedings concerning copyright infringement can initiate upon charges pressed by the copyright owner or public prosecutor acting *ex officio*. In the case of non-commercial infringement and software copyright infringement, the prosecution depends on the victim's initiative (private prosecution) and the Police have the duty to investigate the victim's charges.

Copyright infringement for commercial purposes is always investigated by the Police, and prosecution is initiated by the public prosecutor acting *ex officio* (public prosecution). Usually, before criminal prosecution begins, a preliminary investigation proceeds with a search-and-seizure action to collect samples of the products. A court-appointed expert will examine the samples and look for evidence of copyright infringement. If the infringement is confirmed, or if there is strong evidence that the infringement happened, the public prosecutor can ask the judge to file a criminal lawsuit. On the other hand, if there is a lack of evidence, the public prosecutor can choose not to proceed with the case.

In the specific case of software copyright infringement, criminal lawsuit and preliminary service of search and seizure will be preceded by an inspection, and the court may order seizure of the unlawful copies in possession of the infringer. In addition, the Police and administrative authorities have the power to conduct raids and seizures targeting piracy and counterfeiting activities. Following these actions, a final report is sent to the authorities of appropriate jurisdiction so they can proceed with the subsequent actions.

Civil Enforcement

The legal framework allows an aggrieved party to file a civil lawsuit in order to stop copyright infringement, prevent further infringement, and seek compensation for property and moral damages. Article 102 of the Copyright Act states that a copyright owner whose work is fraudulently reproduced, disclosed, or used can request seizure of the copies or originals made or stoppage of the disclosure, without prejudice to indemnification.

Article 103 states that a person who publishes a literary, artistic, or scientific work without authorization of the copyright owner must forfeit the copies that were seized and pay the cost of those items that have been sold. If the number of copies of the fraudulent edition is unknown, the offender must pay the value of 3,000 copies in addition to that of the copies seized.

Article 104 imposes joint liability to a person who, for the purposes of sale or the obtaining of direct or indirect gains, advantages, or profits for himself or for third parties, sells, displays for sale, receives and conceals, acquires, distributes, keeps on deposit, or uses a fraudulently reproduced work or phonogram. Article 108 establishes that, besides seizure of equipment used, a person will be liable for damages in an amount not less than 3,000 copies, if he:

(1) Alters, removes, modifies, or in any way disables technical devices that have been incorporated in copies of protected works and productions to prevent or restrict reproduction;
(2) Alters, removes, or in any way spoils the encrypted signals intended to restrict the communication to the public of protected works, productions, or broadcasts or to prevent the copying thereof;
(3) Without authorization, removes or alters any rights management information; or
(4) Without authorization, distributes, imports for distribution, broadcasts, communicates, or makes available to the public, works, performances, copies of performances fixed on phonograms, and broadcasts in the knowledge that the rights management information, encrypted signals, and technical devices have been removed or altered without authorization.

The court has discretion to evaluate case-by-case the economic and moral damages compensation based on the consequences of infringement, evaluating consequences of infringement, lost sales, intangible losses, moral harms, and benefits that accrued to the defendant, among other factors. In addition, to be entitled to moral damages, the plaintiff must prove that infringement caused more than property damages alone. The statute of limitation to file a lawsuit for civil damages is three years, if the unlawful act is not prohibited by contractual clause,[17] or ten years, if the unlawful act is similar to a contractual infringement.[18]

---

[17] Civil Code, Article 206, Paragraph 3, Item V.
[18] Civil Code, Article 205.

Civil Enforcement Proceedings

According to the Civil Procedure Code, the court may issue a preliminary injunction relief and/or precautionary measures to protect a plaintiff's status during the course of civil proceedings. The requisites for award of such measures are:
(1) Strong evidence of plaintiff's right;
(2) Substantial proof of infringement; and
(3) Risk of damage to the process without immediate injunction.

Based on Articles 105 and 106 of the Copyright Act, the court may grant injunctive relief, as follows:
(1) Seizure of infringing goods and cessation of infringement;
(2) Imposition of daily fines for continuing infringements;
(3) Suspension of offering and sale;
(4) In appropriate cases, seizure and destruction of the materials and equipment used in production of the goods;
(5) Immediate discontinuance of transmission or retransmission of copyrighted work; and
(6) Attribution of authorship.

As regards software copyright infringement, there is a special proceeding for civil lawsuits. The owner of the software copyright must file an injunction request for preliminary inspection, and court experts will search *in loco* for illegal licenses. Based on the finding, the plaintiff may apply for injunction measures to prevent the infringement. According to the Superior Court of Justice, compensation for software copyright infringement cannot be simply based on the product's market value, since that would actually stimulate this practice. Accordingly, the fine established for such infringement is usually ten times the market value of the products.

Piracy in Brazil

Due to Brazil's long border (23,102 kilometers) and frontiers with several countries, there are numerous points of entry for illegal products, and thus a variety of supply chains deliver goods for the informal market in Brazil. Most traffic is related to the shared border with Paraguay and Argentina, known as the "Tri-Border Area". It accounts for a large percentage of counterfeit hard goods distributed in Brazil. According to the National Forum against Piracy, counterfeit of hard goods represented losses of at least BRL 130-billion in 2016.[19]

Brazil is one of the largest online markets worldwide, behind only the United States, China, and India. Brazil had 115.64-million Internet users in 2016 and that is projected to grow to 134.91-million users by 2022.[20] The Internet user penetration in Brazil in 2016 was 55.6 per cent of the population. This was expected to grow to 61.89 per cent by 2022.[21]

According to the International Intellectual Property Alliance, in the 2016 Special 301 Report on Copyright Protection and Enforcement, digital piracy via peer-to-peer traffic in Brazil is part of the online cultural environment. The study ranked Brazil in first place of "non-monetized demand" reaching US $100-billion in value of content exchanged, mostly from copies of video games. The Entertainment Software Association ranked Brazil second in number of connections participating in illegal video game downloading via peer-to-peer traffic.[22]

Another important issue is software piracy. It is estimated that 56 per cent of all programs installed in Brazil are illegally obtained. While the legal acquisition of software produced BRL 2.53-billion in 2016, the illegal market causes estimated loses of BRL 2.84-billion per year to manufacturers.

Exemptions to Infringement of Copyright

The Copyright Act allows use of copyrighted works without owner authorization provided that it is made to further informational, educational, and social objectives and done for non-commercial purposes. Under the Copyright Act, the following reproductions will not constitute violation of copyright:

(1) Daily or periodical press of news or informative articles from newspapers or magazines, with a mention of the name of the author, if they are signed, and of the publication from which they have been taken; newspapers or magazines of speeches given at public meetings of any kind; portraits or other forms of representation of likeness, produced on commission, where reproduction is done by the owner of the commissioned subject matter and the person represented or his heirs have no objection to it; literary,

---

19 See http://www.justica.gov.br/noticias/protocolo-de-intencoes-une-setores-no-combate-ao-contrabando-e-a-pirataria.
20 See https://www.statista.com/statistics/255208/number-of-internet-users-in-brazil/.
21 See https://www.statista.com/statistics/292757/brazil-internet-user-penetration/.
22 See http://www.iipawebsite.com/rbc/2016/2016SPEC301BRAZIL.PDF.

artistic, or scientific works for the exclusive use of the visually handicapped, provided that the reproduction is done without gainful intent, either in Braille or by means of another process using a medium designed for such users; and one copy of short extracts from a work for the private use of the copier, provided that it is done by one and without gainful intent;

(2) Quotations in books, newspapers, magazines, or any other means of communication of excerpts of a work for the purposes of study, criticism, or debate, to the extent justified by the purpose, provided that the author is named and the source of the quotation is given;

(3) Notes taken in the course of lessons given in teaching establishments by the persons for whom they are intended, provided that their complete or partial publication is prohibited without the express prior authorization of the person who gave the lessons;

(4) Use of literary, artistic, or scientific works, phonograms, and radio and television broadcasts on commercial establishments for the sole purpose of demonstration to customers, provided that the said establishments market the materials or equipment that make such use possible;

(5) Stage and musical performances carried out in a family environment or exclusively for teaching purposes in educational establishments and where devoid of any profit-making purpose;

(6) Literary, artistic, or scientific works as proof in judicial or administrative proceedings; and

(7) Works of short extracts from existing works, regardless of nature, or of the whole work in the case of a work of three-dimensional art, on condition that the reproduction is not in itself the main subject matter of the new work and does not jeopardize the normal exploitation of the work reproduced or unjustifiably prejudice the author's legitimate interests.[23]

In addition, the Copyright Act states that:
(1) Paraphrases and parodies will be free where they are not actual reproductions of the original work and are not in any way derogatory to it; and
(2) Works permanently located under public places may be freely represented by painting, drawing, photography, and audiovisual processes.

---

[23] Copyright Act, Article 46.

Public Domain

According to the Copyright Act, Article 45, public domain is the condition of intellectual works whose property rights have expired or are non-existent (in Brazil, the works become public domain seventy years after the death of the author); a deceased author does not have successors; and works of unknown authors, with due regard to legal protection to ethnic and traditional knowledge.

Integrity and authorship of work under public domain will be assured by the State. Thus, the use of a work under public domain is not unrestricted. In November 2014, the government launched the "Public Domain Portal"[24] making accessible to the public a library with literary, artistic, and scientific works under public domain.

Conclusion

Brazil's 1998 Copyright Act is outdated and must reflect today's reality of copyright protection and enforcement in the digital era. At the same time, the current legislative framework is inadequate to support the sharing and innovation of works in the internet. There was an important legislative development in 2014, with the Civil Rights Framework for the Internet,[25] which establishes principles, guarantees, rights, and obligations on the use of the Internet in Brazil. However, the law does not regulate copyright on the Internet.

Proposed legislation to improve development of the copyright framework is in discussion in Congress, specifically, the Bill of Law Number 3,133 of 2012 that seeks to amend, update, and consolidate copyright legislation. The most important amendment is that of Article 46 of the current Copyright Act, establishing several cases that allow for use of a work without authorization by copyright owners or remuneration for such use. There is no schedule as to when the legislative process will be completed.

---

[24] Public Domain Portal, at http://www.dominiopublico.gov.br.
[25] Law Number 12,965 of 23 April 2014.

Germany

Ulrich Lohmann and Igor Barabash
Pinsent Masons
Munich, Germany

Introduction

Copyrighted Works

The Copyright Act protects "works in the literary, scientific, and artistic domain".[1] Only "the author's own intellectual creations" are considered works within the meaning of the Copyright Act.[2] Such works may constitute:

(1) Literary works, such as written works, speeches, and computer programs;
(2) Musical works;
(3) Pantomimic works, including works of dance;
(4) Artistic works, including works of architecture and applied art and drafts of such works;
(5) Photographic works, including works produced by processes similar to photography;
(6) Cinematographic works, including works produced by processes similar to cinematography; and
(7) Illustrations of a scientific or technical nature, such as drawings, plans, maps, sketches, tables, and three-dimensional representations.[3]

The Act also provides for "related rights" (*Verwandte Schutzrechte*) in works that could be regarded as being one step removed from an author's own intellectual creations, notably rights in scientific editions[4] and posthumous works;[5] in products manufactured in a similar manner

---

[1] Copyright Act (*Urheberrechtsgesetz*) of 9 September 1965, BGBl. I S. 1273, as amended, Section 1.
[2] Copyright Act, Section 2(2).
[3] Copyright Act, Section 2(1).
[4] Copyright Act, Section 70.
[5] Copyright Act, Section 71.

to photographs;[6] the rights of performing artists[7] and organizers;[8] and rights in audio recordings;[9] in broadcasting;[10] in data bases;[11] in newspapers and magazines;[12] and in cinematographic works and moving pictures.[13]

The related rights of the publishers of newspapers and magazines were introduced in 2013. This provoked a major public debate involving participants such as Google, who opposed a levy for the benefit of the publishers on articles copied from their newspapers and magazines to be distributed by news aggregators and similar services.

Works Not Covered by Copyright

The following works have been considered as "not worthy of protection" by the Act or by case law:
(1) Works produced by animals;[14]
(2) Works produced by chance or accident;[15]
(3) Mere ideas without perceptible form;[16]
(4) Works without individual intellectual performance;[17] and
(5) Works with very low individual characteristics (e.g., everyday products).[18]

Rights Emanating from Copyright

The author of a work protected by the Act has the exclusive right to exploit such work in tangible form,[19] including the following:
(1) Right of reproduction;[20]

---

6 Copyright Act, Section 72.
7 Copyright Act, Sections 73–80, 82, and 83.
8 Copyright Act, Section 81.
9 Copyright Act, Section 82.
10 Copyright Act, Section 87.
11 Copyright Act, Sections 87a–87e.
12 Copyright Act, Sections 87f *et seq.*
13 Copyright Act, Sections 88 *et seq*
14 LG München I, UFITA 54 (1969) 320 — *Tierdressur.*
15 Wandtke/Bullinger, *Praxiskommentar zum Urheberrecht, 4. Auflage 2014*, Section 2 Rz. 15.
16 Dreier/Schulze, *Urheberrechtsgesetz, 5. Auflage 2015*, Section 2 Rz. 37.
17 Wandtke/Bullinger, *Praxiskommentar zum Urheberrecht, 4. Auflage 2014*, Section 2 Rz. 21.
18 BGH, 27 January 1983, GRUR 1983, 377, 378 — *Brombeermuster.*
19 Copyright Act, Sections 15 *et seq.*
20 Copyright Act, Section 16.

(2) Right of distribution;[21] and
(3) Right of exhibition.[22]

The author also has the exclusive right to communicate his work to the public in non-tangible form, in particular including:
(1) Right of recitation, performance, and presentation;[23]
(2) Right of making the work available to the public;[24]
(3) Right of broadcasting;[25]
(4) Right of communication by video or audio recordings;[26] and
(5) Right of communication of broadcasts and of works made available to the public.[27]

Copyright in Computer Software

The Act regards computer software as a work of literature.[28] Software is, therefore, protected in the same fashion as all other works mentioned above. In addition, the Act contains specific provisions reflecting the characteristics of computer software.

Section 69a of the Act defines software as programs of any form, including drafts and their preparatory design material, and states that copyright will apply to any form of software, but not to ideas and principles underlying the software and its interfaces. The protection extends only to software that is the author's own intellectual creation; other criteria, in particular qualitative or aesthetic factors, are irrelevant for the eligibility of the software for protection.

The rights in computer software created by an employee as a part of his duties or following instructions given by his employer belong to the employer, unless agreed otherwise.[29] Under Section 69c of the Act, a copyright holder has the exclusive right to:
(1) Reproduce the code of the computer software permanently or temporarily, wholly or in part, by any means and in any form, including loading, displaying, running, transmitting or storing the software where this requires its reproduction;

---

[21] Copyright Act, Section 17.
[22] Copyright Act, Section 18.
[23] Copyright Act, Section 19.
[24] Copyright Act, Section 19a.
[25] Copyright Act, Section 20.
[26] Copyright Act, Section 21.
[27] Copyright Act, Section 22.
[28] Copyright Act, Section 69a(4).
[29] Copyright Act, Section 69b.

(2) Translate, adapt, arrange or otherwise modify the code software, as well as to reproduce the results, without limiting the rights of those individuals who adapted the program;

(3) Disseminate the source code of the software or copies thereof, but the right to disseminate a specific copy of the software will be deemed exhausted with respect to the European Economic Area (EEA) if such copy is brought into circulation (other than by rental) within the EEA; and

(4) Communicate the software to the public (by wire or wireless), including communicating the work in such a way that it is available to members of the public from places and at times individually chosen by them.

International Scope

Germany was one of the first countries to sign the Berne Convention for the Protection of Literary and Artistic Works (the "Berne Convention").[30]

The Berne Convention essentially provides that authors who enjoy copyright protection in their home country will enjoy the same degree of protection in the other member states of the Berne Convention, as well as the rights specially granted by the Berne Convention.[31] This is known as the "country of origin" concept.

Infringement

Types of Infringement

Infringements of rights granted by the Act are categorized as either direct or indirect infringements.

Direct Infringement

Direct infringement is an infringement of the rights of the author described above. When another author copies parts of a protected work,

---

[30] *Berner Übereinkommen zum Schutz von Werken der Literatur und Kunst, Pariser Fassung vom 24. Juli 1971*, BGBl. 1973 II S. 1071 and 1985 II S. 81; see http://www.wipo.int/export/sites/www/treaties/en/documents/pdf/berne.pdf.
[31] Berne Convention, Section 5.1.

a user reproduces a work, or a service provider disseminates a protected work, this constitutes direct infringement.

Indirect Infringement

A violation of a duty of care (*Störerhaftung*) that results in copyright infringement is indirect infringement. For instance, the provider of an Internet video platform (such as YouTube) would not be deemed to have infringed copyright if an infringing video popped up on the site, but the provider would have a duty to take the video down as soon as he is made aware that the video is infringing copyright.[32]

Non-Commercial File Sharing

Non-commercial sharing of copyrighted material has created a whole new industry of "bounty hunters", mostly law firms working together with technical investigation specialists to obtain proof of infringements — legally or not — and then to claim relatively small damages from a very large number of more or less unsuspecting consumers and businesses.

However, it seems that, in recent years, this "industry" has been experiencing a push back as the German courts now regard non-commercial streaming as non-infringing. However, uploading protected files for the use of others would normally be regarded as an infringement and raises the issue as to what extent the access providers[33] and the owners of devices[34] or the access points[35] are obligated to disclose the identity of third parties who may have committed infringement by means of such access or device.

---

[32] BGH, 17 May 2001, MMR 2001, 671 — *ambiente.de*; BGH, 11 March 2004, MMR 2004, 668 — *Internet-Versteigerung ROLEX*; OLG Hamburg, 1 July 2015, MMR 2016, 269 — *Störerhaftung von YouTube*.

[33] BGH, 11 June 2015, ZUM 2016, 173 — *Tauschbörse I*; BGH, 11 June 2015, ZUM 2016, 373 — *Tauschbörse III*; OLG Köln, 20 April 2016, ZUM-RD 2016, 467 — *The Walking Dead*.

[34] OLG München, 14 January 2016, ZUM 2016, 384 — *Loud*.

[35] BGH, 12 May 2016, ZUM 2017, 62 — *Everytime we touch*; BGH, 6 October 2016, I ZR 154/15 — *Afterlife* pursuant to which a husband cannot be requested to provide information about the use of, and content stored on, access devices used by his wife, and *vice versa*.

Online Intermediary Liability

Online intermediary liability has been a source of discussion in Germany for many years. The Telemedia Act[36] now provides for different levels of liability of intermediaries, as follows:

(1) Pursuant to Section 7 of the Telemedia Act, service providers are responsible for content that they themselves provide to other parties.

(2) Service providers are not responsible for third-party content that they transmit through a communication network or that they grant access to as long as they do not initiate the transfer, select the recipient of the content, or select or change the content, as stipulated by Section 8(1) of the Telemedia Act.

As of 2016, this provision also applies to service providers granting internet access via a local area network (WiFi). The enactment of Section 8(3) of the Telemedia Act has put an end to an extensive discussion as to whether WiFi providers should be held liable if unlawful content is channeled through their access point.[37] Nevertheless, there still are very few open WiFi access points in Germany, because it is still unclear whether Section 8(3) protects the provider against liability in damages only, or extends to protection against requests for injunctive relief. The courts must resolve this.

(3) Section 9(1) of the Telemedia Act provides that service providers are not responsible for third-party content that they store automatically and temporarily solely for the purpose of transmission, as long as the service providers refrain from altering the content; provide access to the content; update the content in accordance with industry standards; enable the capture of data concerning the use of such content in accordance with industry standards; and act without delay to take down or block such content as soon as they become aware that the content has been removed from the network at the place of origin or that access to it has been blocked or that a court or a government agency has ordered such content to be removed or blocked.

---

[36] *Telemediengesetz* of 26 February 2007 (BGBl. I S. 179), as amended.
[37] Gersdorf/Paal, *Informations- und Medienrecht*, 16. Aufl., Section 8 TMG Rz. 43.

(4) Under Section 10 of the Telemedia Act, service providers are not liable for third-party content that they store on behalf of a user, as long as *grosso modo* they did not know and could not have known of any unlawful act or unlawful content and they act without delay to take down or block such content as soon as they obtain such knowledge.

Piracy

Piracy of copyrighted material in Germany is (yet) mostly limited to cultural assets, such as music, and software.[38] Instructions and blueprints for manufacturing goods do not appear to be affected yet by digital piracy,[39] but this may change with the advance of additive manufacturing and third printing.

Limitations on Copyright

The Act sets forth, in Sections 44a–63a, several limitations[40] of copyright, including in particular the following acts that do not constitute an infringement:

(1) Acts of reproduction that are transient or incidental and constitute an integral and essential part of a technical process and whose sole purpose is for transmission or lawful use of a work and which have no independent economic significance;[41]

(2) Reproduction for the purpose of the administration of justice and public security;[42]

(3) Reproduction for non-commercial purposes to facilitate access by individuals with disabilities, subject to appropriate compensation of the author;[43]

---

[38] Business Software Alliance (BSA), "Unlicensed Software Use Still High Globally Despite Costly Cybersecurity Threats", see http://globalstudy.bsa.org/2016/index.html.

[39] Chamber of Industry and Commerce (Ihk) of Munich and Upper Bavaria, *Leitfaden zum Urheberrecht*, see https://www.ihk-muenchen.de/ihk/documents/Recht-Steuern/16-51-019_Broschuere-Urheberrecht_web.pdf.

[40] These limitations in effect permit the exploitation of works in a fashion that is comparable to the "fair use" doctrine in Common Law.

[41] Copyright Act, Section 44a.

[42] Copyright Act, Section 45.

[43] Copyright Act, Section 45a.

(4) Incorporation of small parts of works into an anthology of works intended exclusively for use in schools or churches, subject to appropriate compensation of the author;[44]
(5) Current events reporting, citations from works, or using works for research purposes;[45] and
(6) Personal use of works, with a number of additional limitations.[46]

With respect to computer software, the licensed user may do any of the following, even if the license prohibits such acts:
(1) Reproduce the code, in whole or in part, and also translate, adapt, arrange, and otherwise modify the code, in each case to the extent required for loading, displaying, running, transmitting, or storing the computer program in accordance with its intended purpose or for the correction of errors;
(2) Make a back-up copy;
(3) Observe, study, and test the functioning of the software to determine the underlying ideas and principles in the context of loading, displaying, running, transmitting, or storing the program; and
(4) Reproduce and translate the code to the extent this is indispensable to obtain the information required to achieve interoperability with other programs, provided such information has not previously been made readily available.[47]

Remedies

Injunction

Anyone who infringes the copyright or any other right protected under the Act, whether for reasons within or outside its control, may be required by the injured party to cease the infringement and, if there is any risk of repetition, to desist from such infringement in the future.[48]

---

44 Copyright Act, Section 46.
45 Copyright Act, Sections 50, 51, and 52a.
46 Copyright Act, Section 53.
47 Copyright Act, Section 69e.
48 Copyright Act, Section 97(1).

Damages

The injured party also may claim damages but only if the infringer committed the infringement for reasons within its control, i.e., either negligently or intentionally.[49] According to case law, the injured party may, at its discretion, claim the following:

(1) Damages equivalent to the actual loss suffered, including lost profits, which is often difficult to prove;
(2) Disgorgement of the profit generated by the infringement, which would also need to be proven by the injured party; or
(3) Constructive license fee, which is often easier to prove because the courts have developed benchmarks for the more frequent types of infringement.

Claim for Information and an Accounting

If a party can be shown to have infringed copyrights on a commercial scale and the injured party does not have sufficient information to calculate the damages due to it, the injured party may claim the requisite information and an accounting from the infringer.[50] Such information would, for example, include data on profits, turnover, and distribution channels.

Inspection

The injured party also may demand the permission to inspect codes, documents, or other objects in the infringing party's possession if it can show a probable infringement and the inspection is necessary to substantiate its claims under the Act.[51]

If the injured party can show that the infringement was committed on a commercial scale, it also could demand the presentation of banking, financial, or commercial documents. This provision would enable the injured party to request the source code of software that appears to be infringing and to inspect such source code for similarities with the original and to evaluate whether the source code is infringing.

---

[49] Copyright Act, Section 97(2).
[50] Copyright Act, Section 101.
[51] Copyright Act, Section 101a.

Recall and Destruction

The Act grants the infringed party several additional remedies in Section 98, including:
   (1) The right to claim destruction of the illegally produced or distributed copies and copies which are intended for illegal distribution in the infringing party's possession; and
   (2) The right to request a recall of the illegally produced or distributed copies and copies intended for illegal distribution or a definitive recall of such copies from the distribution channels.

Criminal Liability

Copyright infringement is a criminal offense under Sections 106–111a of the Act, as follows:
   (1) Unlawful exploitation of copyrighted works,[52] or infringement of related rights;[53]
   (2) Affixing unlawful copyright notices;[54] and
   (3) Interference with technical protective measures, and or with notices designed to protect copyrights except for personal use.[55]

The penalty may be a fine, but also could be imprisonment of up to three years, or five years if infringements have been committed on a commercial scale.

Procedural Law

Obtaining Judgment

Pleadings

The complaint should set forth all facts relevant to the alleged copyright infringement and the evidence offered to prove such facts (Section 253(1) of the Code of Civil Procedure).[56] The defense should likewise set forth

---

[52] Copyright Act, Section 106.
[53] Copyright Act, Section 108.
[54] Copyright Act, Section 107.
[55] Copyright Act, Section 108b.
[56] *Zivilprozessordnung* as restated on 5 December 2005 (BGBl. I S. 3202; 2006 I S. 431; 2007 I S. 1781), as amended.

all relevant facts and the evidence offered to disprove the facts alleged in the complaint, or to prove such facts as may be required to conclude that the alleged copyright infringement was justified or did not cause any loss on the part of the plaintiff.

More specifically, the plaintiff should identify the work at issue and show that it is protected by copyright, that it has all rights in and to such work, and that his copyright has been infringed as described above. The defendant should comment on the facts alleged by the plaintiff[57] and may allege other facts in support of the conclusion that the alleged infringement was justified or did not cause any loss on the part of the plaintiff. The comments on the facts alleged by the defendant may take three basic forms:

(1) If the defendant knows the alleged facts to be true, he need not comment on them;[58] if he admits certain facts, he will be bound by such admission.[59]

(2) If the defendant considers the alleged facts to be untrue, he should contest them. This will be accepted by the courts only if the defendant provides his own version of the story in full detail; merely stating that certain facts are contested will not suffice.[60]

(3) If the defendant does not know the alleged facts, he can and should plead ignorance.[61]

In all cases, the parties' statements of fact must be correct and complete.[62] Making false or incomplete statements of fact in submissions to the court will expose the party concerned to criminal fraud charges (*Prozessbetrug*).[63] Mere notice pleadings, as they are known in the Anglo-Saxon world, are not sufficient. Both parties should provide evidence for all alleged facts, except those they do not expect to be contested. In the pleading, each allegation that is likely to be contested should be followed by a separate reference labelled "Evidence" (*Beweis*) that indicates the specific means of evidence provided.

After receiving a complaint, the court will communicate a calendar for the proceedings. This will normally provide for two exchanges of briefs, whereby the Defendant will usually have the last word. The

---

[57] Code of Civil Procedure, Section 138(2).
[58] Code of Civil Procedure, Section 138(3).
[59] Code of Civil Procedure, Section 288.
[60] Code of Civil Procedure, Section 138(2).
[61] Code of Civil Procedure, Section 138(4).
[62] Code of Civil Procedure, Section 138(1).
[63] Criminal Code, Section 263, *Strafgesetzbuch* of 13 November 1998 (BGBl. I S. 3322), as amended.

parties are generally required to submit all relevant facts and evidence as soon as reasonably practicable.

If facts and evidence are submitted late, the court may disregard them in reaching its decision. There is no pre-trial discovery under German procedural law, with limited exceptions,[64] and no depositions. Consequently, the plaintiff should not rely, when preparing the complaint, on documents that he would have to obtain from the defendant, except as explained above.[65]

If the object of the complaint is a claim for the payment of money, such as a claim for damages, and documentary evidence is available for all facts required to support the claim, the plaintiff may choose to assert its claim in documentary proceedings (*Urkundsverfahren*).[66] In documentary proceedings, the court will consider only documentary evidence, which generally saves time. If the plaintiff cannot prove his case using documentary evidence, the complaint will be dismissed as inadmissible for documentary proceedings. The plaintiff then has the option of pursuing his claim in standard court proceedings, which may take longer as all types of evidence will then be taken into consideration.

Costs

The court fees for proceedings in copyright matters are regulated by statute and depend on the amount in dispute (*ad valorem* fees). The court fee must be paid in advance. Accordingly, before filing a complaint, the plaintiff should ask his lawyer to determine the amount in dispute, to calculate the corresponding court fee, and to arrange for payment in advance or — at the latest — upon receipt of an invoice for such fee from the court. Similar rules apply in case of an appeal.

Fees for legal representation also are regulated by statute and depend on the amount in dispute. However, the lawyers and their clients are free to agree on other methods to determine such fees — for example, hourly or fixed rates — as long as they are not lower than the statutory fees in contentious matters. It is unethical, with very few exceptions, for German lawyers to claim or agree on contingency fees or a *quota litis*. Third-party funding, however, can be obtained in Germany, which may help to manage the risk of complex or repeated litigation.

---

[64] Code of Civil Procedure, Section 142.
[65] Copyright Act, Sections 101 and 101a.
[66] Code of Civil Procedure, Section 592.

The losing party in civil or commercial litigation will be ordered to reimburse the winner for court costs, fees for legal representation, and incidental expenses. Fees follow the event. Fees for legal representation are assessed, for the purpose of reimbursement, on the basis of the statutory fee scale. Thus, if the lawyers are paid on an hourly basis, the reimbursement is normally lower than the fees actually paid by the client. If the complaint is successful in part, each party is ordered to reimburse the other for a part of the legal fees incurred by it, depending on the extent of the success, as assessed by the court.

A German defendant may request security for legal fees *grosso modo* if the plaintiff resides outside the European Economic Area (EEA), except if treaties expressly stipulate that no such security may be requested. Therefore, before filing a complaint or appeal, a plaintiff residing outside the EEA should ask his lawyer to determine whether or not he may be required to post security and, if so, prepare to meet a request to that effect if submitted by the defendant.

Jurisdiction

Copyright infringement may constitute a breach of a contract, e.g., a breach of a license agreement. If so, the courts specified in the contract, if any, would have jurisdiction to hear a dispute from such contract, or, alternatively, the courts having personal jurisdiction over the defendant.

Copyright infringement would also constitute a tort. If any element of the alleged tort is located in Germany, the German courts will assume jurisdiction. However, if non-German copyrights are infringed, the jurisdiction of German courts may not be based merely on tort; in such cases, the plaintiff should ask his lawyer to determine whether the German courts have personal jurisdiction over the defendant.

Service of Process

Service of process must be made through the courts. If the defendant resides outside Germany, the plaintiff should provide a translation of the complaint into the language of the defendant and apply to the court to effect service through the courts of the country of the defendant.

Hearings

Hearings are scheduled when the judges decide to hold a hearing; normally, one to three hearings per case in first instance, depending on the complexity of the case, and one hearing per appeal. The hearings are led by the judge. They are usually relatively brief, except if witnesses or experts are being heard. Hearings are held in German. Non-German-speaking individuals wishing to attend court hearings should arrange for capable interpreters to be present.

Litigation in civil and commercial matters before German courts never involves a jury. There are lay judges in commercial matters, but the procedure is dominated by professional judges. As a consequence, the hearing gives less opportunity for oratory talent than trials in Anglo-Saxon countries. German judges often open the hearing with settlement discussions. They may attempt to facilitate settlement discussions and even make settlement proposals.

Evidence

Judges are expected to use a specific methodology, referred to as relational methodology (*Relationstechnik*), to resolve their cases. In essence, such methodology requires the judge to:
(1) Distill from the parties' submissions all statements of fact that are undisputed and those that are disputed and to discard those that are irrelevant;
(2) Check whether evidence has been provided for the disputed statements of fact and to discard those statements of fact that are disputed but are not backed by evidence;
(3) Make a preliminary assessment of the case assuming that all evidence will be presented and will convince the court;
(4) Dismiss the case without hearing evidence if, on the basis of such preliminary assessment, the plaintiff did not have a case even if he could prove all of its disputed statements of fact;
(5) Grant the complaint without hearing evidence if the plaintiff's statements of fact are undisputed while, on the basis of the preliminary assessment, the defendant would not have a defense even if he could prove all of his disputed statements of fact; and
(6) In all other cases, issue an order specifying which evidence is to be heard.

There are generally four means of evidence, namely:
(1) Witnesses (*Zeugen*);
(2) Documentary evidence (*Urkunden*);
(3) Expert opinions *(Sachverständigengutachten)*; and
(4) On-site verification (*Augenschein*).

In addition, facts may be deemed proven if the court itself is aware of them. Parties and their representatives cannot be heard as witnesses, but the court may hear them anyway to supplement the party's allegations. Experts are appointed by the court rather than the parties. Nevertheless, in complex cases it is not uncommon for parties to submit expert reports that they have commissioned themselves. These would not be considered evidence but may give more weight to their statements of fact.

After the hearing, the court will decide whether or not it has been convinced that a certain statement of fact made by the parties is true, based on the entire content of the hearings and on the result of the taking of evidence, if any.[67] The court is not bound by any particular rules as how to evaluate the evidence except if and to the extent that such rules are specifically set out in the Code.[68]

An exception applies to the determination of liability for, and the quantum of, a loss.[69] In these cases, the court may decide whether or not it has been convinced based on the preponderance of probabilities.[70] In practice, this means that the court has discretion as to whether liability exists and what the quantum is. Also, in such cases, the court may decide in its discretion whether or not to hear evidence at all, and may hear the party bearing the burden of proof.

Judgment

If a copyright infringement complaint is successful, the judgment normally orders the defendant to cease and desist from the copyright infringement and, if the infringement was committed negligently or intentionally, to pay damages to the plaintiff. Damages could be assessed on the basis of actual loss or of constructive license fees, as explained above, but a German court could not award punitive damages.

In addition, the court may order that any copies that have been, or that are intended to be, unlawfully made or distributed, as well as the means to circumvent or eliminate any technical mechanisms designed to prevent unauthorized copying, be destroyed or, alternatively, be delivered to the plaintiff against payment of reasonable compensation.[71]

---

[67] Code of Civil Procedure, Section 286(1).
[68] Code of Civil Procedure, Section 286(2).
[69] Code of Civil Procedure, Section 287.
[70] Prütting in *Münchener Kommentar zur ZPO*, 5. Aufl. Band 1, Section 287, Anm. 17.
[71] Copyright Act, Sections 69f and 98.

Duration

Civil and commercial proceedings in Germany may be completed in less than a year[72] but they can take several years, particularly if complex expert opinions are required or in case of an appeal.

Provisional Measures

Provisional measures to fight copyright infringement are important because most plaintiffs do not want to wait for the duration of a full court procedure.

Warning Letters

Plaintiffs can — and often will — challenge (alleged) copyright infringements by dispatching a warning letter (*Abmahnung*). Normally written by an attorney, this letter describes the (alleged) copyright infringement and requests a written undertaking *(Unterlassungsverpflichtungserklärung)* to the effect that the recipient (the defendant) will cease and, in the future, desist from committing the copyright infringement at issue and promise to pay to the plaintiff a penalty for future violation of the undertaking.

This is done because the defendant is expected to continue the (allegedly) unlawful practices, and therefore may need to be restrained by the court, unless he provides an undertaking that unequivocally states his willingness to stop. The promise to pay a penalty is required to be included in the undertaking because without it, the undertaking would not be regarded as sufficiently strong. The amount of the penalty claimed is normally between €5,000 and €20,000, or is alternatively left to the discretion of one of the parties, subject to review by the court.

The warning letter will normally provide a tight deadline for providing the undertaking. This is because the plaintiff will not be able to obtain a temporary restraining order (*einstweilige Verfügung*) from the court unless he proves urgency. It is difficult, if not impossible, to prove urgency unless the plaintiff applies for a temporary restraining order within one month from the day on which he became aware of the

---

[72] According to recent statistics, 65 per cent of the proceedings initiated before the district courts (*Landgerichte*), which deal with most commercial disputes, will be completed within six months, and 85 per cent within twelve months. Appeals may be completed within six months, but complex proceedings of course, can take many years as well.

(alleged) infringement. Therefore, the plaintiff will ask for a response from the defendant within a few days, and the defendant should take the deadline seriously.

If the undertaking is provided and accepted by the plaintiff, the matter is closed. The plaintiff is then entitled to statutory attorney's fees on the theory that he provided a service to the defendant by asking him to stop the (allegedly) unlawful practices.

If the defendant fails to provide the undertaking before expiry of the deadline, he should expect the plaintiff to apply for a temporary restraining order. If the defendant provides the undertaking, he will be considered to have given up on the (alleged) infringement whether or not the plaintiff accepts the undertaking. If the plaintiff fails to accept the undertaking, he will not be able to claim the penalty promised by the defendant if the undertaking is violated.

Users of copyrighted material should be aware that the warning-letter procedure described here is sometimes abused by "bounty hunters" who allege copyright infringements to claim relatively small damages from a very large number of more or less unsuspecting consumers and businesses.[73]

Temporary Restraining Orders

A temporary restraining order in copyright infringement matters would normally provisionally enjoin the defendant from continuing and repeating the infringement, but it may not be used to obtain more permanent relief, such as damages. As an exception, in copyright infringement matters, a temporary restraining order may order the defendant to disclose information about the infringement or to permit the inspection of the infringing works.[74]

In the temporary restraining order proceedings, offering *prima facie* evidence (*Glaubhaftmachung*) is sufficient. Such *prima facie* evidence can be, and often is, offered in the form of affidavits (*eidesstattliche Versicherungen*). A temporary restraining order may be issued, or an application for a temporary restraining order rejected, *ex parte* (i.e., without a hearing), which could happen within a day. If the judge is unsure whether to grant the application for a temporary restraining

---

73 *Lohmann*, Companies warned to avoid German "bounty hunter" schemes, see http://www.out-law.com/en/articles/2016/march/ german-companies-should-not-get-involved-in-bounty-hunter-schemes/.
74 Copyright Act, Sections 101(7), 101a(3), and 101b(3).

order, he will normally schedule a hearing and decide thereafter. In those cases, it may take a week, a month, or longer until the decision is made.

To defend against an application for a temporary restraining order, the defendant may submit to the court a pre-emptive response (*Schutzschrift*). This submission should have the effect that the court will schedule a hearing if the plaintiff applies for a temporary restraining order, rather than issuing the temporary restraining order *ex parte*. If a temporary restraining order is issued *ex parte*, it must be served upon the defendant within one month; otherwise, it will lapse.

If a temporary restraining order is issued, the defendant may object (*Widerspruch*) by submitting a substantiated application to the court and request an oral hearing, which will normally be granted. After the hearing, the court must decide whether to uphold or set aside the temporary restraining order. Temporary restraining orders and orders rejecting an application for a temporary restraining order also may be appealed.

Making Temporary Restraining Orders Permanent

The temporary restraining order is, as its name suggests, only temporary. Many claims based on copyright law are subject to statutory limitation periods (time bars) of three full calendar years. As the temporary restraining order, as such, does not suspend the limitation period, in order to keep its claims from becoming time-barred, the plaintiff normally requests that the defendant formally acknowledge the temporary restraining order as final and binding (*Abschlussschreiben*).

If the defendant fails to provide such acknowledgement, he should expect the plaintiff to sue for a permanent injunction. These proceedings, often referred to as main proceedings (*Hauptverfahren*), are separate from the temporary restraining order proceedings. In the main proceedings, affidavits are not admissible.

Appeals

In copyright infringement matters, the complaint will normally be filed with, and decided by, the Regional Courts (*Landgerichte*). The judgments of the Regional Courts can be appealed to the Higher Regional Courts (*Oberlandesgerichte*). Only under limited circumstances may the statement of facts be amended before the Higher Regional Court.[75]

---

75 Code of Civil Procedure, Section 529.

In particular, if the Regional Court ordered certain facts to be disregarded because a party missed a deadline set by the Regional Court — or was otherwise late in submitting such facts — such facts will remain excluded also before the Higher Regional Court. In any event, the Higher Regional Court will assess the judgment of the Regional Court on points of law. Appeals to the Higher Regional Courts are fairly common. If a large amount is at issue, one or perhaps even both parties will normally appeal.

In certain more important cases, the judgment of the Higher Regional Court may be appealed to the Federal Court of Justice (*Bundesgerichtshof*), which will assess the judgment of the Higher Regional Court on certain points of law only.

Arbitration and Alternative Dispute Resolution

Arbitration, mediation, and other alternative dispute resolution mechanisms are generally available and used in Germany. In copyright infringement scenarios, this applies only if the parties are already bound by a contract, such as a license agreement, that provides for arbitration or mediation or both.

When negotiating a license agreement, the parties should consider commercial arbitration for dispute resolution, as it would give a foreign licensor the opportunity to have the dispute decided in privacy by arbitrators who understand his business and who speak his language. Arbitration also provides investors good prospects for enforcing the resulting award around the world in accordance with the New York Convention of 1958. Mediation should also be considered as it is rapidly gaining in importance for German businesses. This may have to do with the Germans' preference for consensus. To the foreign licensor, mediation provides an opportunity to address the dispute without damaging the relationship with the licensee.

Criminal Investigations

Copyright infringement constitutes a criminal offense, as explained in the first part of this article. Therefore, a plaintiff may want to consider filing a criminal complaint. Doing so might help in cases where the plaintiff is not aware of the identity of the infringer, particularly where there is reason to believe that the copyright infringement has been committed by professional criminals.

On the other hand, when filing a criminal complaint, the plaintiff hands control of the case over to the prosecutor, which may result in delays and may sometimes make it more difficult to recover damages.

Italy

Riccardo G. Cajola
Cajola & Associati
Milan, Italy

Introduction

Territoriality was once a main feature copyright. This is no longer the case. During the last couple of decades, the internet age and rising of the new digital technologies have led copyright to lose its characteristic of territoriality. The on-going globalization process has progressively eliminated distances among countries, and several former geographic and economic obstacles to the cross-border movement of original intellectual works are no longer an issue. Original works need not be physically placed at specific venues, if the work is available on the web.

In addition, texts, images, and multimedia content can be published, divulged, and played online, without resorting to intermediaries. These aspects have rendered copyright protection more complex and the enforcement actions aiming at tracking down infringements less efficient. If the analysis is focused only on the recent wide dissemination of the "file sharing", i.e., the file exchange and sharing of copyrighted material, the changes during the last decades have made it necessary to review the statutory regulations aiming at copyright protection, to the extent of bringing regulations up to speed in the new global scenario.

Copyright arises through the creation of an original work. That means copyright is automatically available to its author, on condition that the work is original. The author therefore gets the exclusive right over the use of the original work and may authorize or refuse its duplication, distribution, performance, or content display.

Unless expressly authorized to do so by its author, using or disseminating an original work is forbidden, even if the work exists on the Internet. In case of written work, copying or reproducing a written text (or a part of it) is prohibited in general terms.

As exceptions to this rule, briefing works for citation purposes or reproducing parts of literary original works aiming at their studying, discussion, teaching, or scientific research is allowed, provided the original author is cited and the use is not for profit.[1] If an infringement

---

1 Act Number 633 of 22 April 1941, the "Copyright Act".

occurs in Italy, different remedies and sanctions may apply, both under civil and criminal statutory law, depending on the kind of infringement carried out. These sanctions are stricter if the infringer is using the unauthorized original work for profit.

Rights Covered by Copyright

In General

Copyright does not protect a simple idea. The idea is just a beginning; developing it into a work having both novelty and originality characteristics is necessary. Many original works may be protected through copyright. Among these are:
(1) Literary works, such as novels, poetry, essays, and articles;
(2) Visual works, such as paintings, drawings, photographs, and sculptures;
(3) Audiovisual works, such as television programs, movies, and videos;
(4) Theatre and musical works;
(5) Musical works and audio recordings; and
(6) Software and databases.

Copyright protects creative works. Article 1 of the Copyright Act provides that protection should concern all the intellectual creative works belonging to literature, music, figurative arts, architecture, theatre and cinematography, no matter the way and the type of expression. Computer programs also are deemed literary works and belong to the field of protection of the Copyright Act. The list provided is not exhaustive, and protection can be extended to works different from those explicitly indicated.

Creativity Requirement

The creativity standard is not considered in absolute terms, as it refers to a subjective, individual expression of an objectiveness. Even a work that is the product of a "creative act", also a minimum one, reflecting itself in the external world, can be copyrighted. This means that not only "literary" works *per se* (e.g., poetry, narrative, and essay writing), but also texts that communicate information created and organized in a subjective and independent way by the author, are protected.[2]

Form of Expression

In order to be protected, the work must have a form of expression. The protected forms are the "external" one, like the text of a book or the realization of a painting, but also the "internal" one, considered as the structured organization of some ideas, the plot of a book, and the relation among the subjects of an image. Simple ideas instead are not protected. Ideas are freely appropriable, as a teaching from a book, and there is no need for asking the permission of the author.

Presumption of Authorship or Ownership

The holder of the copyright is the one who created the work. According to the Copyright Act, the author of an intellectual work is, unless it is proven otherwise, the one who is indicated as such in the forms of use, or is announced as such in the acting, performance, representation, or radio broadcast of the intellectual work.[3]

In the absence of evidence to the contrary, the owner of copyright is who is presented as such in the usual manner on the protected materials, or is indicated as such in the acting, execution, performance, or announcement to the public.[4] If a work is created by more than one person, copyright lies with them all.

Employers and Projects

In some cases, copyright does not belong to the author. Unless a different agreement exists, the employer owns the exclusive right to benefit from the computer program or the database created by the employee during the fulfilment of his tasks or upon instruction given by the employer himself.[5]

Similarly, with regard to photography, if the intellectual work was created during the fulfillment of the photographic contract, subject to contract terms and conditions, the exclusive copyright lies with the

---

[2] Court of Cassation, Case Number Civ. 11953/1993.
[3] Copyright Act, Article 8.
[4] Copyright Act, Article 99 *bis*.
[5] Copyright Act, Article 12 *bis*.

employer.[6] A particular rule applies to public administrations that hold the copyright for all the works created and published in their name, on their behalf, and at their expenses.[7] Non-profit private organizations, academies, and other cultural organizations enjoy the same rights, with reference to their records and publications.

Copyright Protection and Soundreef Judgment

In General

Copyright arises with the creation of the intellectual work. Different from patents and trade marks, there is no need of filing a record to obtain copyright. Proof of being the author of the work, e.g., having created it in the presence of other people, is the standard for according copyright protection. In order to facilitate evidence about the work paternity, filing the work with an entity able to certify its creation date is possible. This role has been exclusively performed in Italy by the Italian Society of Authors and Publishers (*Società Italiana degli Autori ed Editori*, SIAE), where a number of works, also unpublished, can be filed.

SIAE certifies the filing, through a number and a filing date; however, no searches about the filed content are carried out. Hence, if a work is not worthy of protection based on the Copyright Act, a filing does not acquire rights even if the filing was performed with SIAE. The legitimacy of the exclusive mandate granted to SIAE has been challenged several times; the Italian courts have constantly reiterated that it is fully compatible with the rules and the purposes set out by law. The Constitutional Court stated that SIAE would not operate in the monopoly regime as the Copyright Act, Article 180, does not prevent the authors from directly protecting or exercising their rights (i.e., without the intermediation of SIAE).

On 12 September 2014, the Court of Milan held that the service offered by Soundreef, a small start-up carrying out a rights management and royalty collecting service, is legitimate and it does not infringe any provision of law. In addition, its activity does not constitute unfair competition against the role assigned by the Copyright Act to SIAE,

---

6 Copyright Act, Article 88 *bis*.
7 Copyright Act, Article 11.

particularly by Article 180 of the Copyright Act, which provides that "the intermediation activity [omitted] is reserved on an exclusive basis to SIAE".[8]

The Court of Milan observed that there is not a competitive relationship between the claimant and the defendant. It stated that the claimant cannot be deemed as an entrepreneur as it does not carry out organized activity for the purpose of the production or the exchange of goods and/or services. On the other hand, Soundreef is not a mere phonogram producer as it manages the rights of tracks produced by third parties. Hence, according to the Court of Milan, there is no basis to consider the activity of Soundreef unlawful pursuant to Article 180 of the Copyright Act.

Soundreef manages musical compositions that are mainly owned by foreign composers and performers. This argument would imply that there is no violation of the prerogative of SIAE. The judge clarified that, in accordance with the territorial principle, the exclusivity recognized for SIAE by the Copyright Act applies to musical compositions composed by Italian authors or by foreign authors domiciled in Italy and published for the first time in Italy.[9]

Moreover, pursuant to international conventions,[10] including the Berne Convention, the enjoyment and the exercise of the rights should not be subject to any formality, including the association to a collecting society such as SIAE. Eventually, after a long debate and jurisprudence on the topic, the Italian government passed a Legislative Decree in March 2017 that opens the possibility that management collective bodies other than SIAE may act as intermediaries and perform the copyright filing work that SIAE does.[11] This provision was to be in force as of January 2018.

Protected Works

The Copyright Act sets out the following list of protected works:
(1) Literary, dramatic, scientific, didactic, and religious works, whether in written or oral form;

---

[8] Tribunal of Milan, Court Order of 12 September 2014, Case Number 48903/2014.
[9] Copyright Act, Article 185.
[10] Copyright Act, Article 186.
[11] Legislative Decree of 15 March 2017, Number 35, amending Copyright Act, Article 180.

(2) Musical works and compositions, with or without words, dramatic musical works, and musical variations constituting original works;
(3) Choreographic works and works of dumb show, the form of which is fixed in writing or otherwise;
(4) Works of sculpture, painting, drawing, engraving, and similar figurative arts, including scenic art, even where such works are applied to industrial products, if their artistic value is distinct from the industrial character of the product with which they are associated;
(5) Architectural plans and works;
(6) Works of cinematographic art, whether silent or with sound, provided they are not mere documentaries otherwise protected;
(7) Works of photographic art and works expressed with processes analogous to photography provided they are not simple photographs otherwise protected; and
(8) Computer programs, in whatever form, provided they are original and result from the author's own intellectual creation.[12]

Rights Enjoyed by Author

The rights given by the law are divided into those of economic usage and moral rights. With regard to economic rights, the law makes a distinction between primary rights and secondary or related rights, depending on the type of work concerned. Primary rights are granted to works that benefit from full protection of copyright.

Related rights instead are "added" to primary rights and have less relevance and a shorter duration. Finally, there are *sui generis* rights concerning certain types of works, in particular databases. Primary rights give the work's author the right to:
(1) Publish and use the work in any form and by any method;
(2) Reproduce the work, multiplying it by all means;
(3) Perform, represent, or act out the work in public;
(4) Divulge the work by using broadcasting media;
(5) Distribute and sell the work by any means;
(6) Translate, elaborate, and transform the work; and
(7) Rent and lend the work.

---

12 Copyright Act, Article 2. Ideas and principles underlying any element of a computer program, including those underlying its interfaces, are excluded from the protection afforded by the Copyright Act. The term "computer program" includes preparatory design materials.

The fact that these rights are reserved to the author means that no one else may perform one or more of the mentioned actions without the consent of the author and without paying him compensation.

Next to rights regulating the economic aspects of the utilization of the work, moral rights involve the entitlement to be recognized as the author of a work and to prevent others from modifying it without his consent. The author preserves the right to claim the paternity of the work and to oppose any deformation, mutilation, or other modification, as well as any other act that may damage the work itself, or effect its honor or its reputation.[13]

A recent noteworthy court case in this respect involved Roger Waters, a former member of the band Pink Floyd and now a solo performer. During the spring of 2017, Rogers Waters returned with his first solo album in 25 years, *Is This the Life We Really Want?*.

The Court of Milan blocked all sales of the record, both physical and digital, due to copyright infringement concerns. The pending dispute centers on the artwork for the album, which bears a strong resemblance to the conceptual work of Emilio Isgrò, an Italian artist famous for his usage of the "erasure technique".[14]

Copyright Assignment and License

The economic rights of the author may be assigned or licensed upon payment or for free. The courts distinguish between the assignment of the work (*corpus mechanicum*) and the author's rights on the work (*corpus mistycum*). This latter belongs to the author even after the assignment, unless otherwise provided. According to the Copyright Act, the assignment of one or more samples of a work does not imply, unless agreed otherwise, the transfer of the rights to use.[15] A written contract is necessary for transferring the proprietary rights of the author to the purchaser.[16]

A license contract instead is a contract with which the author allows a third party the right to use his work for a precise period or purpose, but the author maintains full ownership. Once the license contract elapses, the author receives back all the rights on the work. Both the assignment

---

13 Copyright Act, Article 20.
14 Tribunal of Milan, Court Order of 24 July 2017 (*Emilio Isgrò* vs. *Sony Music Entertainment Italy spa*).
15 Copyright Act, Article 109.
16 Copyright Act, Article 110.

and the license can concern all or part of the rights. A license may be exclusive or not exclusive.

Duration

The right of economic use of a work lasts for the author's whole life and for the 70 years following his death.[17] After this period, works are in the "public domain". Therefore, works belonging to authors who died 70 or more years ago can be freely published.

The Copyright Act protects the author's moral right exercised by the heirs without time limits.[18] Hence, the publication of an out-of-copyright work is possible if the honor of the artist is respected or if prejudice does not arise against the author. Here, the heirs may speak out in defense of the deceased author.

Exhaustion Principle

A basic principle is that copyright ends with the first sale. This means that, once the author puts a work on sale, he cannot oppose the subsequent circulation of that work which could be sold or gifted to third parties without his consent.[19]

While the selling of the work legitimately bought is permitted, copying, duplicating, or renting are not. Thus, if someone buys a DVD that contains an opera, the purchaser may sell the DVD but not duplicate it or transfer the file containing the music recorded on the DVD.

Territoriality

The Copyright Act applies to all works made by Italian authors, published anywhere for the first time, and to all works of foreign authors, domiciled in Italy, published in Italy for the first time.[20]

International conventions regulate the protection area of the Copyright Act regarding foreign authors and, specifically, the 1866 Bern Convention provides that all citizens of the member states acceding to the Convention benefit from a similar protection offered by the state to its citizens and that this protection must include minimum

---

17 Copyright Act, Article 25.
18 Copyright Act, Articles 20 and 23.
19 Copyright Act, Article 17.
20 Copyright Act, Article 185.

guarantees.[21] Therefore, the citizens of the states acceding to the Convention who use their works in Italy benefit from the protection of the Copyright Act. Rights concerning intangible assets are regulated by the law of the state where their use takes place.[22] Therefore, the Copyright Act applies to works used in Italy.

Special Copyrights

In General

Neighboring areas of copyright involve the rights of phonogram producers, movie producers, radio or television stations, artists and producers, and rights on photographs, engineering works, databases, and titles of books and magazines.

Rights of Phonogram Producer

A producer who produces and supports a phonogram track is entitled to the exclusive right to authorize:
(1) The direct or indirect, temporary or permanent, reproduction of his phonograms by any process of duplication;
(2) The distribution of copies of his phonograms;
(3) The rental and lending of copies of his phonograms; and
(4) The making them available to the public.

The duration of the right is fifty years from the recording.[23]

Rights of Movie Producer

A producer who produces and supports the work itself is entitled to the exclusive right to authorize:
(1) The direct, indirect, permanent, or temporary reproduction of originals and copies of the work;
(2) The distribution of the work by any means, including sale;
(3) The rental and lending of the work;
(4) The making of the original and copies available to the public.[24]

The duration of these rights is fifty years since the recording.

---

21 Berne Convention for the Protection of Literary and Artistic Works of 9 September 1886, Article 5.
22 Act Number 218/95, Article 54.
23 Copyright Act, Article 72.
24 Copyright Act, Article 78 *ter*.

Rights of Radio and Television Stations

Further rights are added to rights due primarily to the author of a work and secondarily to producers, artists, and performers, as regards those engaged in radio or television broadcasting activity. They are entitled to the exclusive right to authorize:

(1) The recording of its own wireless transmissions or by wire;
(2) The direct, indirect, temporary, or permanent broadcasting of their recordings in any manner or form, in whole or in part;
(3) The retransmission of the work;
(4) The making of them available to the public; and
(5) The distribution of the work.[25]

In addition, radio and television broadcasters are entitled to the exclusive right to use the recording of their emissions for new programs or new recordings. The duration of these rights is fifty years from the first publication.[26]

Rights of Artists and Performers

Actors, singers, musicians, dancers, and other persons who play, sing, recite, or perform in any manner intellectual works, whether protected or in the public domain, are considered performers.[27] Regardless of any remuneration to which they may be entitled for their live performances, performers have the exclusive right to:

(1) Authorize the recording of their performances;
(2) Authorize the direct or indirect reproduction of recordings of their performances;
(3) Authorize the broadcasting over the air and the communication to the public, in any form or manner, including by satellite, of their live performances, unless the latter are intended for broadcasting by radio or television or are already the subject of a recording for broadcasting purposes;
(4) Authorize the distribution of recordings of their performances;[28] and

---

[25] Copyright Act, Article 79.
[26] Copyright Act, Article 79.
[27] Copyright Act, Article 80.
[28] The right may not be exhausted within the European Union unless the first marketing was made in a European Union member state by the right holder or with his authorization.

(8) Authorize the rental or lending of recordings of their performances and of the reproductions thereof.[29]

Performers are entitled to oppose dissemination, transmission, or reproduction of their performances that might be prejudicial to their honor or reputation. The duration of these rights is fifty years from the first performance or representation.[30]

Rights on Photographs

The Copyright Act provides for three categories of photographs, namely:
(1) Photographic works having such creative features as to easily recognize they come from the author;
(2) Simple photographs, as images of persons or aspects, elements, or events of natural and social life, acquired by photographic or equivalent process; and
(3) Photographic reproductions, i.e., simple reproductions of written papers, business documents, material items, technical drawings, and similar products.

Photographic works possess both moral and economic rights.[31] The use of a photographic work, like any other work, is subject to the author's permission or his heirs and possibly upon a payment. The economic rights last for the author's life and 70 years after his death. Simple photographs, on the other hand, grant a number of "minor" rights. The author has the exclusive right of reproduction and distribution and sale in addition to the right of an appropriate payment for the use of the photographs, providing they display the following details:
(1) The photographer's name;
(2) The date when the photograph was taken; and
(3) The author's name of the photographic work of art.

These rights have a validity of twenty years from the creation of the photograph.[32] Aside from the above, photographic reproductions do not have any particular protection and can freely be used.

---

[29] Performers retain the right to equitable remuneration in the event of rental agreed by the producer with third parties, even if they are assigned. A contrary arrangement is null and void.
[30] Copyright Act, Article 85.
[31] Copyright Act, Articles 12–19.
[32] Copyright Act, Article 92.

Rights on Engineering Works

Engineering works that do not have a real artistic feature or that cannot be patented are subject to special protection. The author of engineering projects, or similar works constituting original solutions to technical problems, is eligible, besides the exclusive right to reproduce the same plans and projects, to receive compensation from those who use the technical project for profit without authorization.

In order to apply this kind of protection, it is necessary to add, on the project or drawing, a reserve declaration over the right of use, and file it at the Presidency of the Ministers Advisory Council. The duration of these rights is twenty years from the filing of the work.[33]

Rights on Databases

The term "database" means an electronic or paper gathering of works or other independent elements, systematically or methodically arranged and individually accessible by electronic means or in another way.[34] Independence of the individual components of a database is necessary.

Hence, the necessary arrangement in a systematic or methodical way results in the exclusion from protection of all the works generally classified as "collections of elements", where these elements constitute a single body, losing their independent accessibility. A book, therefore, is not deemed a database.

The law provides for two forms of protection of the database, depending on whether it is a database with creative feature, or a database without particular creativity. The first case occurs when the database has a particularly original way of compilation, due to the choice of materials and to the collection process or the data organization. The author of a creative database is entitled to the full rights under the law on copyright and to the exclusive right to perform or authorize:

(1) Permanent, temporary, total, or partial reproduction, by any means and in any form;
(2) Translation, adaptation, arrangement, and any other modification;
(3) Any form of distribution to the public of the original or copies of the database;
(4) Any presentation, demonstration, or communication in public; and

---

[33] Copyright Act, Article 99.
[34] Copyright Act, Article 2, Number 9.

(5) Any reproduction, distribution, communication, display, or performance to the public of the results of operations performed on the database.³⁵

When the database does not have its own creative feature but is of commercial importance for investments made for its implementation, the law recognizes for the "establisher" certain rights, although these are less broad than authors' rights. An "establisher" is who makes significant investment for the establishment of a database or for its verification or presentation, such as financial means, time, or work.³⁶

Therefore, evidence of the existence of "significant investment" must be offered to claim copyright protection. A database establisher has the right to prevent the extraction or re-utilization of all or a substantial part of the data by third parties. The duration of the right of the establisher is fifteen years from the database completion or at least from the date the database was first made available to the public.³⁷

Rights on Titles of Books or Magazines

The title of a work, e.g., a book or another publishing work, is protected by the Copyright Law, but with some limits. Copying of another work of the same kind with the same title without the author's consent is forbidden. The same principle applies to section titles. Titles of newspapers, magazines, and periodicals cannot be used until two years have passed after suspension of the original periodical publication.

Website Copyright

In General

A website is a virtual place where any kind of contents can be included. There are informative sites, mainly containing texts; figurative sites with photographs; commercial sites; or any other kind. The author of the website enjoys the protection provided by the Copyright Act, which covers every part of the site, e.g., a text, image, music, film, or photograph.³⁸

---

35 Copyright Act, Article 64 *quinquies*.
36 Copyright Act, Article 102 *bis*.
37 Copyright Act, Article 102 *bis*.
38 Copyright Act, Article 1, provides: "Intellectual works having a creative character (. . .) whatever their way or form of expression, are protected by this law".

Site as Author's Work

In contrast, issues have arisen when the site is considered as a single independent work, bearing a higher and different creative character, in respect to that obtained through the mere sum of the various components. Different opinions still exist on this subject matter. Upon specific circumstances, the imitation of a web page by a competitor may represent a hypothetical unfair competition. The site is protectable in its entirety as a structure, upon condition that Copyright Act standards are met.

The Court of Bari held, in 1998, that a data transmission work is worth protection if the access process, the information types, and the manners of consultation are original and the result of a creative and intellectual activity.[39] Copyright protection is not granted for the idea itself as to a site realization and its content, rather for the concrete way it has been realized.

File Sharing

Online sharing of files is not *per se* considered unlawful in Italy, as long as sharing is not meant for lucrative purposes. The domestic courts follow the principles set out in this respect on 5 June 2014 by the Court of Justice of the European Union (EU).[40] The Court of Justice ruled that making temporary copies on the user's screen or in the user's cache is not, in itself, illegal:

> "Article 5 of Directive 2001/29/EC of the European Parliament and of the Council of 22 May 2001 on the harmonization of certain aspects of copyright and related rights in the information society must be interpreted as meaning that the copies on the user's computer screen and the copies in the internet 'cache' of that computer's hard disk, made by an end-user in the course of viewing a website, satisfy the conditions that those copies must be temporary, that they must be transient or incidental in nature and that they must constitute an integral and essential part of a technological process, as well as the conditions laid down in Article 5(5) of that Directive, and that they may therefore be made without the authorization of the copyright holders."

---

[39] Tribunal of Bari, Court Order of 21 June 1998.
[40] European Court of Justice, Case Number C-360/13 (*Public Relations Consultants Association Ltd.* vs. *Newspaper Licensing Agency Ltd. and Others*).

The domestic courts then established that criminal liability does not extend to file sharing copyrighted material, as long as it is not performed for commercial gain. In a case involving a copyright holder who employed a third party to collect Internet protocol addresses of suspected copyright infringers, the Italian Data Protection Authority ruled in February 2008 that the systematic monitoring of peer-to-peer activities for the purpose of detecting copyright infringers and suing them is prohibited.[41]

Online Intermediary Liability and Hyperlinks to Pirated Copies

In a 2017 judgment, the Tribunal of Frosinone held that a link or a banner on a website routing to another website where film downloading is possible is not *per se* illegal, unless it is performed for economic gain.[42] The Tribunal held that "uploading online files protected by copyright is not the same as sharing, through a link, the original works".

Due to the judgment, a fine of €546,000 that had been issued by the Fiscal Police against the owner of the websites filmsmakers.biz, filmaker.me, filmakerz.org, and cineteka.org was set aside. Based on the court's decision, those who upload files for economic purposes, not those who share a link or banner to those sites, are liable for copyright piracy.

In 2016, the *Tribunale del Riesame* of Rome overturned one of the 152 website blocks imposed by a court in Rome and ruled that embedding does not constitute copyright infringement.[43] The order against the Italian site Kisstube was set aside, while the other websites remained blocked. Kisstube is a YouTube channel, which also exists as a standalone website that does not host content itself, linking instead to YouTube. Both the channel and website arrange content by categories for the convenience of users.

The Italian court's decision was influenced by a ruling by the European Court of Justice.[44] In the *BestWater* case, the European Court of Justice held that embedding or framing a video or image from another website is not copyright infringement if the latter is already accessible to the public. The Court of Justice also held in a subsequent case that posting hyperlinks to pirated copies of material is only legal if it is done

---

41 Personal Data Protection Authority, Resolution of 28 February 2008 (*Peppermint Jam Records GmbH, Techland sp. z. o.o. e Logistep AG*).
42 Tribunal of Frosinone, Judgment of 7 February 2017, Case Number 1766/2015.
43 Tribunal of Rome, *Sezione Speciale del Riesame*, Court Order of 30 Number 2016.
44 European Court of Justice, Order of the Court (Ninth Chamber), 21 October 2014, *BestWater International GmbH* vs. *Michael Mebes and Stefan Potsch*.

without knowledge that they are unauthorized versions and is not carried out for financial gain.[45]

Copyright on Apps and Facebook Ruling

Facebook was held responsible in March 2016, for the first time, for breach of copyright and unfair competition toward a client company. According to the first instance judgment, Facebook took advantage of the knowledge it acquired of the Faround product, designed by the Italian company Business Competence SRL, through unlawful conduct and then promoted and made available to its users "its own" application called Nearby with the same characteristics.[46]

The Faround application allowed users to see, using a geolocation system, all nearby venues and places of interest to users, together with promotions and discounts offered by those venues. Nearby, the Facebook product that was launched on Facebook's social network in December 2012, four months after the Faround product, worked the same way, except for the coupons and discount system offered by Faround.

Facebook Inc., the parent company, Facebook Srl, the Italian subsidiary, and Facebook Ireland were ordered to not use, distribute, or exploit the application. In addition, they were ordered to withdraw it from the market for Italy. Moreover, it was ordered that they:

(1) Pay a fine of €5,000 for each day of further use of the application after 60 days following the judgment;
(2) Publish the judgment in two Italian national daily newspapers and for fifteen days on www.facebook.com; and
(3) Pay damages to the Italian company and return undue profit obtained from Nearby.

Enforcement

In General

Italian legislation provides for the necessary measures, procedures, and remedies to ensure the enforcement of copyrighted intellectual property

---

[45] European Court of Justice, Case Number C-160/15, 8 September 2016, *GS Media BV* vs. *Sanoma Media Netherlands BV, Playboy Enterprises International Inc., Britt Geertruida Dekker.*
[46] Tribunal of Milan, Judgment of 10 March 2016, Case Number 68360/2013.

rights. Those measures, procedures, and remedies are effective and applied in such a way as to avoid the creation of barriers to legitimate trade.

In general, an author or the holders of copyright, and all other persons authorized to use those rights, in particular licensees, are recognized as persons entitled to seek application of the measures, procedures, and remedies referred to in the Copyright Act. In order to be entitled to initiate a court action, the plaintiff must have an "interest to carry on the action", which (with reference to intellectual property claims) must be identified with the actual intellectual property right or priority right claimed.[47]

Cease and Desist Proceedings

In General

A person having reason to believe the infringement of a copyright belonging to him occurred, or who is seeking to prevent the continuation or repetition of an infringement that has already occurred, may institute legal proceedings to ensure that his right is recognized and the infringement forbidden.[48] There are two possible judicial initiatives under this provision.

Prevention of Threatened Infringement

The first is meant to acknowledge who is the holder of the economic rights when such rights have not yet been infringed, but the claimant has reason to believe infringement may occur. The second can be used when an infringement has occurred, and it is aimed at preventing repetition of the illicit behavior.

Protection of Public Performances

A person who is entitled to exercise the rights of public performance of a work intended for such performance, including a cinematographic work or a work of musical composition, may request the Prefect of the province to prohibit any performance for which written proof of his consent is not produced.[49]

The Prefect must, upon request and based on the notices and documents submitted to him, authorize or forbid the performance,

---

47 Civil Procedure Code, Article 100.
48 Copyright Act, Article 156.
49 Copyright Act, Article 157.

subject to the right of the interested party to have recourse to the judicial authority for final decision within its competence.

Destruction or Removal of Result of Infringement

A person damaged through infringement of copyright belonging to him is entitled to institute legal proceedings for the destruction or removal of the goods constituting the infringement and for damages compensation.[50] The removal or destruction is possible only in respect of specimens or copies illegally reproduced or disseminated, and devices employed for reproduction or dissemination that, by their nature, are not capable of use for the reproduction or dissemination of other matter.

If a part of the specimen, copy, or device in question is capable of use for the reproduction or dissemination of other matter, the interested party may, at his expense, request the separation, in his interest, of such part. If the specimen, copy, or device of which the removal or destruction is requested has special artistic or scientific value, the court may order *ex officio* its deposit in a public museum.

The injured party may, at any time, plea that the specimens, copies, and devices to destroy be delivered to him and their estimated value set off against the damages due to him. The provisions for destruction and delivery may not apply to infringing specimens or copies acquired in good faith for personal use.

Removal or destruction cannot be pleaded in the last year of the term of the right. Seizure of the work or of the product may be ordered in such case at any time up to the end of the term. If the damages arising from the infringement of the right have been paid, seizure may be authorized even before the abovementioned date.[51]

Proceedings in Respect of Moral Rights

The above provisions also apply to proceedings concerning the exercise of moral rights, insofar as the nature of such rights permits, subject to the application of the following provisions.[52] Copyright claims relating to the authorship of a work can lead to removal or destruction, if the infringement cannot be eliminated by, e.g., adding or suppressing information on the work, which refers to its authorship, or by other means of publicity.

---

50 Copyright Act, Article 158.
51 Copyright Act, Article 160.
52 Copyright Act, Article 168.

Actions in defense of the rights relating to the integrity of a work give rise to removal or destruction of the deformed, mutilated, or otherwise modified copy of the work only when it is not possible to restore such copy to its original form at the expense of the party wishing to avoid removal or destruction.

Interim Remedies, Inventories, and Expert Appraisals

The Copyright Act provides for several interim measures in order to facilitate the above civil proceedings.

In copyright claims, the plaintiff is entitled to plead the judge for interim measures in order to preserve relevant evidence before the beginning of the proceedings on the merits of the case.

Ex parte remedies also can be pleaded upon existence of the above-mentioned risk that a defendant may conceal or remove evidence of the allegedly infringing products. A court may order an inventory report (*Descrizione*), an expert appraisal, or the seizure of all matter constituting an infringement of the exploitation right. In copyright interim proceedings, if the judge does not set a deadline for commencement of proceedings on the merits of the case, it must begin within twenty working days or thirty-one calendar days, whatever period is longer.[53]

Description

Description is an order granted by the President of the court having jurisdiction over the claim, by which the plaintiff is authorized (with the assistance of a bailiff, possibly a court expert, and usually a photographer) to inspect and describe the allegedly infringing products and the means used to manufacture them.

A detailed description of the operations and any evidence collected must be recorded in a written report. The aim of the procedure, frequently used in patent claims, is to collect evidence of infringement to be used during the trial. Upon specific motion, the order can be granted *ex parte*, i.e., without the opposing party being heard, if there is a risk that the defendant may conceal or remove evidence of the allegedly infringing products. Usually, no bond is requested. Requests for description are usually made during trade fairs or expositions, since no remedy of civil seizure is possible during these events.

---

[53] Copyright Act, Article 162 *bis*.

Seizure

Seizure is an order granted by the judge having jurisdiction to entertain the claim by which the plaintiff is authorized to search and seize, through the assistance of a bailiff, all the allegedly infringing products and all the means of their manufacture.

A seizure can be enforced several times in different places within a period of thirty days from being granted. The seizure also can be directed against third parties in possession of the allegedly infringing products, unless they are meant for private use only. This order can be granted *ex parte*, whereupon the judge must call a hearing within fifteen days from the date the order of seizure was granted, and the counterparty must be served with notice of the hearing. After having heard the parties at this hearing, the judge confirms, amends, or sets the remedy aside.

In granting both of the above remedies, the judge can specify the necessary measures to be employed to ensure protection of confidential information. The goods constituting copyright infringement, as well as the means used for their manufacture, and any relevant evidence concerning the alleged infringement can be seized, following the ordinary rules of civil procedure on interim seizure proceedings. Seizure may not be effected in the case of works resulting from the collaboration of two or more persons, except in particularly serious cases or where the infringement is imputable to all joint authors.

Cease and Desist

A judge can issue a preliminary cease-and-desist injunction aiming at termination of any copyright infringement and specifically of any manufacturing trade and use of what constitutes intellectual property right infringement. A judge can set a bond upon the claimant.

In addition, a judge can order recall from the channels of commerce of any infringing goods. This order can be directed to the owner of the goods and/or those to whom these goods are available. Cease-and-desist injunctions may be directed against those intermediaries whose services are being used by a third party to infringe copyright.[54] Interim provisional seizures and cease-and-desist orders may be pleaded as well, and a penalty may be imposed on the infringer for subsequent eventual infringement actions.

---

54 Copyright Act, Article 162, paragraph 6.

In particularly serious cases, a court also may order the seizure of profits due to the author of the disputed work or product. Finally, a court may order publication of its decision in one or more national newspapers as additional punishment for the infringer.[55] These provisions also apply to any person putting into circulation, in whatever manner, or possessing for commercial purposes, unauthorized copies of computer programs and any means the sole intended purpose of which is to facilitate the unauthorized removal or circumvention of any device applied to protect a computer program.

The above measures must be authorized, at request of the interested party, by an order of the magistrate of the district in which they are to be executed, whatever the value involved. However, if litigation is pending between the parties, the measure in question must be authorized by an order of the magistrate or, if the suit is pending before a collegiate court, by the examining judge.[56]

In cases of urgency, the measures also may be authorized by the magistrate of the district in which they are to be enforced. The same order may require the claimant to deposit adequate security. Except in cases of imminent danger, the judicial authority, before ruling upon the pleading, must summon to chambers the party against whom the measure would be executed and the party making the plea. Notice of a court order must be filed, before its execution or simultaneously therewith, with the party against whom it is to be executed. Execution must be effected by a judicial official and, where necessary, with the assistance of one or more experts named in the order.

In the case of public performances, the limitations of days and hours specified by the Code of Civil Procedure for measures of such nature may not apply to the execution of orders described here. Unless otherwise provided through a court order of seizure for purposes of penal justice, the measures referred to in the preceding paragraphs have no effect if, within eight days following their execution, no action has been taken before the competent court to confirm the measures in relation to the person against whom they were taken.[57] The author of a copyrighted work, even after the assignment of economic rights, may intervene at any time, to protect his interests, in proceedings instituted by the assignee.

---

[55] Copyright Act, Article 166.
[56] Copyright Act, Article 162.
[57] Copyright Act, Article 163.

Injunctions

As seen above, a court may provide an order for the immediate halt of manufacturing, and trading and use of the infringing goods can be included in a judgment that ascertains and declares that a copyright infringement has occurred. A penalty for delay in complying with the order, as well as an injunction of definitive removal of the same goods from the channels of the market, also can be issued.

Evidence

When a party has provided serious circumstantial evidence to lay the ground of his claim and has individuated documents, elements, or information available to his counterpart confirming the circumstantial evidence, the party can obtain that the judge order the counterpart to exhibit them or to provide information about them.

In addition, a party can obtain that the judge orders the counterpart to supply the information for the identification of those involved in the manufacturing and distribution of the products or services constituting infringement of an intellectual property right. A judge also can order the counterparty, upon request, to provide banking, financial, and commercial documentation in the case of an infringement committed on a commercial scale through piracy actions.[58] Administrative sanctions may apply in event of non-compliance.

Damages

Compensation for damages arising from copyright infringement shall be determined in accordance with the relevant provisions of the Civil Code referring to contractual breaches and defaults.[59] These provisions of the Civil Code establish that:

(1) The measure of damages arising from non-performance or delay must include the loss sustained by the creditor and lost profit as long as they are a direct and immediate consequence of the non-performance or delay;
(2) If the amount of damages cannot be proved in court, damages will be equitably liquidated by the court; and
(3) If any negligence by the creditor has contributed to cause the damage, compensation will be reduced accordingly.

---

[58] Copyright Act, Articles 156 *bis* and 156 *ter*.
[59] Civil Code, Articles 1223, 1226, and 1227.

The amount of damages must take into account not only the economic aspects, such as the loss of profit of the injured copyright holder or the economic benefits for the infringer but, as well, in the appropriate cases, non-economic elements, such as moral damage suffered by the right holder due to the infringement. Upon motion, liquidation for damages also may be fixed in a total amount, taking into account the pleadings and the proceedings and the presumptions arising therefrom. In such case, the missing profit will amount to a sum not less than the royalties for a fictitious license. A copyright holder can always plead that the profit gained by the infringer be disgorged, as an alternative to the compensation of his loss of profit or limited to the amount of profit of the infringer exceeding such compensation.

Legal Costs

As a rule, legal costs and other expenses in a trial are to be borne by the unsuccessful party. However, if the parties were both unsuccessful in their claims or just reasons exist for the partial or entire payment of the costs among the parties, the judge can hold that each party is partially or entirely liable for costs.[60]

Publication of Judicial Decisions

As noted above, following the acknowledgment during ordinary or interim proceedings of a copyright infringement, the judge can order publication, in one or more newspapers, of the judgment or the interim judgment at the expense of the unsuccessful party.

Penal Remedies and Sanctions

Sanctions under criminal law regulations for copyright infringement are primarily those that the Copyright Act provides and can involve imprisonment of the infringer or monetary fines. Intermediaries are liable to the same penal sanctions as infringers. The penalties hereunder apply in all instances where the acts in question do not constitute a more serious offense under the Penal Code or other laws. Based on the Copyright Act, a fine applies to any person who, without having the right thereto, and for any purpose and in any form:

(1) Reproduces, transcribes, recites in public, disseminates, sells or offers for sale, or otherwise commercially distributes the work of

---

60 Civil Procedure Code, Articles 91 and 92.

another person, or reveals the contents of such work before it is made public, or introduces or circulates within Italy copies produced abroad contrary to Italian law;

(2) Performs or recites in public or disseminates, with or without variations or additions, the work of another person intended for public performance, or a musical composition;[61]
(3) Commits the acts referred to in the preceding items by means of any form of transformation referred to in the Copyright Act;
(4) Reproduces copies or gives performances in excess of the number which he has the right to reproduce or perform; or
(5) In an unauthorized manner, retransmits by wire or by radio, or records on phonograph records or other like devices, radiophonic transmissions or retransmissions, or sells the unlawfully recorded phonograph records or other devices.[62]

The penalty will be imprisonment of up to one year or a higher monetary fine if the acts referred to above are committed in relation to a work of another person not intended for public disclosure or by usurpation of the authorship of a work or with deformation, mutilation, or other modification of a work, and such acts constitute an offense against the honor or reputation of the author.

Software

A person who unlawfully duplicates computer programs with gainful intent, or who imports, distributes, sells, holds for commercial purposes, or rents such programs, being aware or having reason to believe that the copies are not authorized, will be liable to imprisonment of between three months and three years and to a monetary fine.

The same penalty will apply if the act concerns any means the sole intended purpose of which is to facilitate the unauthorized removal or circumvention of any technical device applied to protect a computer program. The penalty will be imprisonment of not less than six months and a higher monetary fine if the offense is serious or if the program that is unlawfully duplicated, imported, distributed, sold, held for commercial purposes, or rented has been previously distributed, sold, or rented on media bearing the mark of SIAE.[63] Conviction for any of the

---

[61] "Performance" includes the public showing of a cinematographic work, the performance in public of musical compositions included in cinematographic works, and broadcasting by means of a loudspeaker operated in public.
[62] Copyright Act, Article 170.
[63] Copyright Act, Article 171 *bis*.

above offenses will include publication of the sentence in one or more news-papers and in one or more specialized magazines.

Audiovisual Works

Imprisonment of between three months and three years and a monetary fine applies on any person who:
(1) Unlawfully duplicates or reproduces, with gainful intent and by whatever means, works intended for cinematographic or television distribution, records, tapes, or like media as well as any other media containing phonograms or video of cinematographic or audiovisual works or sequences of moving images;
(2) Without having participated in the duplication or reproduction, offers for sale, rents, or in any manner permits use, with gainful intent, introduces with gainful intent into Italy, performs a public showing of, or broadcasts by television the unlawful duplications or reproductions; or
(3) Sells or leases videotapes, music tapes, or any other media containing phonograms or video of cinematographic or audiovisual works or sequences of motion pictures, which do not bear the SIAE mark.

The penalty shall be not less than imprisonment for six months, plus a higher fine in the case of grave offenses. Conviction for any of these offenses will include publication of the sentence in one or more newspapers and in one or more specialized magazines. The amounts derived from the application of the monetary fines are devoted to the National Providence and Assistance Agency for Painters and Sculptors, Musicians, Writers, and Playwrights.

Unauthorized Rentals and Records

Imprisonment of up to one year or a monetary fine applies to any person who, without being authorized to do so and with gainful intent:
(1) Rents or in any manner permits the use, for whatever purpose, of original specimens or copies of media, obtained lawfully, of copyrighted works; or
(2) Records live performances on audio, video, or audiovisual media.

If the acts are committed with negligence, only a monetary fine will apply.

Public Enforcement

On 30 March 2017, the Regional Administrative Court of Lazio ("TAR Lazio") ruled on the validity of the Italian Communication Authority (AGCOM) Regulation on copyright enforcement in electronic communications networks (the "AGCOM Regulation"). TAR Lazio held that the legal basis for its ruling is found in various laws.

The Law of 21 July 1997, Law Number 249, entitles AGCOM to regulatory power over the relationship between operators in the telecommunication sector, for the implementation of laws on the access to network infrastructures, and attributes to AGCOM the powers under Article 182 *bis* of the Copyright Act:

(1) Article 182 *bis* of the Copyright Act assigns AGCOM (and SIAE) a surveillance role in order to prevent and verify possible copyright infringements;

(2) Legislative Decree Number 70/2003 states that Internet service providers (ISPs) are not under a general obligation of verification of the information and data transmitted by their means, but Legislative Decree Number 70/2003 does introduce some duties of collaboration for the ISPs with the judiciary and public authorities and requests that ISPs respect the orders of such authorities to remove infringing content; and

(3) Article 156 of the Copyright Act, regarding private enforcement, and notably allowing right holders to be granted injunctions in case of copyright infringement, does not prejudice the provisions of Legislative Decree Number 70/2003 (this should mean that the Italian legal system allows a binary system consisting of both private and public enforcement).

The finding of validity was the final step in a long process, which started in 2010, included three public consultations conducted by AGCOM (in 2010, 2011, and 2013), continued with the observations of the European Commission within the framework of the so-called Transparency Directive (98/34/EC), and arrived at the final approval on 12 December 2013. The resulting Regulation allows AGCOM to demand, following a short administrative procedure, that:

(1) Internet service providers selectively remove or block access to websites hosting allegedly copyright infringing materials; and

(2) Audiovisual media services (AVMS) providers and on-demand providers remove illegal content from their catalogues and refrain from retransmitting illegal works in their future schedules.

In cases of non-compliance with the orders, AGCOM can impose fines. The targets of AGCOM's intervention, in cases of online copyright infringement, are service providers, uploaders of the infringing content, and website operators hosting infringing material rather than users. Right holders are entitled to file, through online forms, complaints of online copyright infringement with AGCOM. The administrative procedure before AGCOM includes notice to the relevant parties that a procedure has started against them and the possibilities to:

(1) Immediately comply with the right holders' request by removing or blocking access to the infringing materials or in the case of objections; or
(2) File counterarguments within five days of receiving the notice.

An AGCOM collegial body, after investigation and within 35 days from the filing of the initial complaint, will determine whether the alleged infringement has occurred and will adopt, in the case of actual online infringement, various measures, depending on the location of the server hosting the content. If the server is located in Italy, AGCOM may order the hosting provider to selectively remove the infringing digital work from the website. If the server is located outside Italy, AGCOM will order the ISP to disable the access to the infringing website.

The AGCOM Regulation has the aim of boosting development and protection of legal provision of digital works, by promoting education of users and encouraging the legal fruition of online content. The Regional Administrative Court has raised concerns as to the constitutionality of the Regulation but has decided not to make a referral to the European Court of Justice regarding consistency with EU laws. However, it is possible that, in the future, the European Court of Justice will have the opportunity to rule on the Regulation.

Conclusion

The exclusive mandate granted to SIAE has been challenged several times. Italian courts have constantly reiterated that the mandate is fully compatible with the rules and the purposes set out by the Italian legislator. In light of globalization, however, it should be recognized that the SIAE role cannot be viewed as a monopoly, and it should be accepted that other players might operate within the local territory.

The recent intervention of the Italian government through the Legislative Decree in March 2017 has been welcomed by the music industry. The reform opens the possibility that management collective bodies other than SIAE act as intermediaries and perform the copyright filing work SIAE does. The provision, in force from January 2018, constitutes a major change for domestic copyright.

Likewise, the on-going discussion of the role of AGCOM in combating piracy does not imply that, under certain conditions, public enforcement will not also result in an improvement of the system for combating online copyright infringement.

The AGCOM Regulation has introduced effective means for reacting, especially for small copyright claims that probably would not otherwise have arrived before a court. It is nevertheless crucial that public enforcement on copyright matters be clearly included into the EU copyright framework and assure a fair balance between protection of proprietary rights and fundamental rights.

Mexico

Alfredo Pineda N. and Edgar Mata
Hogan Lovells
Mexico City, Mexico

Introduction

The most recent changes to the Mexican legal framework occurred on 10 June 2013, when amendments related to enforcement matters passed. The National Copyright Institute, which is the government agency responsible for the enforcement of the Federal Copyright Law,[1] was granted the authority to carry out infringement investigations, inspection visits, and requests of information and data.

For more than ten years, authors and right owners were not allowed to initiate damage claims without a final and non-appealable decision on an alleged copyright infringement. Copyright infringement actions in Mexico are administrative proceedings. Depending on the nature of the infringed right, the allegation will be resolved by the National Copyright Institute (as to moral rights) or the Mexican Institute of Industrial Property (as to economic rights). In addition, the legal framework provides three additional levels of appeal. Obtaining a final and non-appealable decision and the possibility of initiating damages actions was subject to a tortuous legal path and a considerable investment of time.

Only when the author or rights owner secured a non-appealable decision could a civil action for damages be filed through a separate and independent proceeding with a civil court. By the time civil action could be brought, authors or rights owners could be discouraged from seeking damages. The amendments of 2013 secure the right of authors and copyright owners to bring civil claims for damages without the necessity of securing a final and non-appealable decision in an infringement action.

Mexico is a member of the main intellectual property international treaties, as well as those related to copyrights and free trade agreements in which specific regulations for the latter, including prosecution and

---

[1] Civil courts and the Mexican Institute of Industrial Property are other government entities responsible for the enforcement of copyright and copyright-related legal provision.

enforcement, are provided. The hierarchy between national and international law does not represent a conflict.

The Mexican Supreme Court has resolved the conflict related to precedence between national law and international treaties. International treaties now are considered superior to internal law. In Mexico, case law does not prevail over statutory law, unless the latter becomes "jurisprudence".[2] Case law is used for the interpretation and determination of the scope of particular statutory law provisions.

Mexico recognizes moral rights of an author and, under the Berne Convention,[3] does not require compliance with any formality, such as registration, to recognize and protect copyright in favor of the author or the rights owner; the work need only be fixed in a material form.[4]

Copyright (*derecho de autor*) is regulated in Mexico by the Federal Copyright Law (*Ley Federal del Derecho de Autor*)[5] and its implementing regulations and the international treaties to which Mexico is a party. Other copyright-related provisions are included in various regulations, such as the Industrial Property Law (*Ley de la Propiedad Industrial*)[6] related to infringement proceedings.

Rights Covered by Copyright

In General

The Federal Copyright Law recognizes rights and grants protection of copyrights, neighboring rights, and the "reserve of rights for exclusive use".

Copyrights and Protected Works

The following definition is provided by the Federal Copyright Law:

> "Copyright is the recognition given by the State to an author of any of the literary and Artistic works specified in Article 13 of this law,

---

[2] Jurisprudence is created, as a general rule, when five non-contestable decisions in similar cases are issued in the same direction without a contrary decision in between.
[3] Berne Convention for the Protection of Literary and Artistic Works of 9 September 1886.
[4] Berne Convention for the Protection of Literary and Artistic Works, Article 2(2).
[5] *Official Gazette*, 24 December 1996.
[6] *Official Gazette*, 27 June 1991.

by virtue of which it grants its protection to the author to enjoy exclusive prerogatives and privileges of personal and economic nature. The former constitute moral rights and the latter economic rights."[7]

Works that are protected by the Federal Copyright Law are those of original creation and susceptible of being disclosed or reproduced in any form or medium. The works referred to in the definition above and provided by Article 13 of the Federal Copyright Law are:

(1) Literary works;
(2) Musical works with or without lyrics;
(3) Dramatic works;
(4) Dances;
(5) Pictorial works or works of drawing;
(6) Sculptures and works of three-dimensional art;
(7) Works of caricature and short stories;
(8) Architectural works;
(9) Cinematographic and other audiovisual works;
(10) Radio and television programs;
(11) Computer programs;
(12) Photographic works;
(13) Works of applied art, including works of graphic or textile design; and
(14) Works of compilation, consisting of collections of works such as encyclopedias, anthologies, and works or other elements such as databases, provided that the collections constitute intellectual creations by reason of the selection or arrangement of their contents or subject matter.

Works are protected if they are fixed in any type of material support, regardless of their registration or artistic merit, use, or means of expression. Even if no formality is required for copyright protection, it is possible to register works with the National Copyright Institute and obtain a registration certificate.

Moral Rights

As mentioned, Mexico fully recognizes moral rights of authors, considering them as individuals, as opposed to entities. Authors are considered

---

[7] Federal Copyright Law, Article 11.

the exclusive, original, and perpetual owners of moral rights.[8] Due to the importance of moral rights, they are inalienable and may not be encumbered.[9] As a consequence of moral rights, authors, and in some cases their heirs, are entitled to:

(1) Determine whether their work is to be disclosed and in which manner, or to be kept unpublished;
(2) Demand the recognition of author status with respect to the work created by them and to provide that its disclosure should be made as an anonymous or pseudonymous work;
(3) Demand respect for the work, opposing any deformation, mutilation, or other modification of it, as well as any action or attack that causes demerit of the work or prejudice to the reputation of the author;
(4) Modify the work;
(5) Withdraw the work from trade; and
(6) Oppose attribution to the author of a work that is not of his creation.[10]

Economic Rights

Rights related to the exclusive use and exploitation of works are considered economic rights that are part of copyright. Authors and their heirs or assignees can exercise economic rights, including the possibility to authorize third-party use and/or exploitation. Unlike other countries,[11] Mexico grants protection for a term that comprises the life of the author or of the last surviving co-author, plus one-hundred years. Owners of economic rights are entitled to authorize or prohibit the following conduct:

(1) Reproduction, publication, editing, or material fixation of the work in copies or copies made by any means, whether printed, phonographic, graphic, plastic, audiovisual, electronic, or similar;
(2) Public communication of the work;
(3) Public transmission or broadcasting of the work, in any form, including transmission or retransmission of the work;
(4) Distribution of the work, including the sale or other forms of transmission of the property or the material supports containing it, as well as any form of transmission of use or exploitation, including digital media;

---

[8] Federal Copyright Law, Article 18.
[9] Federal Copyright Law, Article 19.
[10] Heirs are not entitled to modify the work or to withdraw it from trade.
[11] Fifty or seventy-five years, fifty being the standard provided by the Berne Convention for the Protection of Literary and Artistic Works of 9 September 1886, Article 7(1).

(5) Importation into Mexico of copies of the work done without authorization;
(6) Dissemination of derivative works, in any form, such as translation, adaptation, paraphrasing, arrangements, and transformations; and
(7) Public use of the work, except as expressed under the Federal Copyright Law, its regulations, or international treaties to which Mexico is a party.[12]

Neighboring Rights

The Federal Copyright Law[13] also governs neighboring rights, which are those granted to performers,[14] broadcasters, book publishers, producers of phonograms, and producers of videos. Additionally, the Federal Copyright Law regulates the reserve of rights, which grants to its owners the exclusive right to use and exploit:
(1) Names of periodical publications;
(2) Periodical distribution;
(3) Characters;
(4) Artistic names; and
(5) Advertising.[15]

Infringement

Moral Rights Infringement

The following conduct[16] is considered as an administrative infringement to moral rights:
(1) Termination, in a manner contrary to the Federal Copyright Law, by a publisher, entrepreneur, producer, employer, broadcasting

---

12 Federal Copyright Law, Article 27.
13 Federal Copyright Law, Chapter II, Article 115.
14 An actor, narrator, declaimer, singer, musician, dancer, or any other individual who performs or executes a literary or artistic work or an expression of folklore, or performs an activity similar to the above if there is no previous text or script leading to its development.
15 Federal Copyright Law, Article 173. The period of protection is one year for periodical publications and broadcasts and five years for other works. The term of protection may be renewed for similar periods, except for advertising promotions.
16 Federal Copyright Law, Article 229.

organization, or licensee of a contract whose purpose is the transmission of copyright;

(2) Breach by a licensee of the terms of a compulsory license executed according to the Federal Copyright Law;

(3) Purporting to be a collecting society without having secured the appropriate registration with the National Copyright Institute;

(4) Failure, without just cause, to supply to the National Copyright Institute, when serving as a director of a collecting society, information and documents for management and administration duties;

(5) Failure to insert a copyright notice as provided by the Federal Copyright Law;[17]

(6) Failure to include information or including false information regarding an editor (name, domicile, and edition number and, if possible, ISSN or ISBN number) or the publisher (name, domicile, and date of last printing);[18]

(7) Failure to fix on a phonogram the (P) symbol and the year of first publication;

(8) Authorized publication of a work without indicating in copies of work the name of the author, translator, compiler, adapter, or arranger;

(9) Authorized publication of a work in a manner that harms an author's reputation and, where applicable, that of the translator, compiler, arranger, or adapter;

(10) The unauthorized publication of works created in the course of official duties on behalf of government agencies;

(11) Fraudulent use in a work of a title that causes confusion with a previously published work;

(12) Fixation, performance, publication, and communication in any manner or use in any form of a literary or artistic work protected under the Federal Copyright Law without mentioning the community or ethnic group or, if applicable, the region of Mexico to which it is specific; and

---

[17] "Works protected by this Law that are published shall display the notice *Derechos Reservados* (reserved rights) or the abbreviation *D.R.*, followed by the © symbol, the full name and address of the owner of the copyright, and the year of first publication. These particulars shall be displayed in a visible place. Failure to meet these requirements shall not cause loss of copyright, but shall make the licensee or publisher liable to the sanctions laid down in this Law." Federal Copyright Law, Article 17.

[18] Federal Copyright Law, Articles 53 and 54.

(15) Other infringement conduct deriving from interpretation of the Federal Copyright Law and its implementing regulations.

The above conduct is punishable by monetary fines. Infringement of moral rights is not prosecuted under criminal law.

Economic Rights Infringement

The National Copyright Law also provides a list of conduct that is considered as an administrative infringement of economic rights. Such conduct is known as "trade-related infringements". Certain conduct is considered to be trade-related infringement when they are related to direct or indirect profit-taking purposes; these include the following:

(1) Communication to the public or public use of a protected work by any means and in any form without the express prior authorization of the author, his lawful heirs, or the owner of the economic rights;
(2) Use of the likeness of a person without authorization or that of his successors in title;
(3) Production, manufacture, stocking, distribution, transportation, or marketing of unlawful copies of protected works;
(4) Offering for sale, stocking, transporting, or distribution of works protected by law that have been distorted, altered, or mutilated without the permission of the owner of the copyright;
(5) Importation, sale, rental, or conduct that affords possession of a device or system whose purpose is to deactivate electronic devices for the protection of a computer program;
(6) Retransmission, fixation, reproduction, and dissemination to the public, without due authorization, of the broadcasts of broadcasting organizations;
(7) Use of protected literary or artistic works with respect to popular cultures in a manner contrary to the provisions applicable to such type of works;[19] and
(8) Other infringements of the provisions of the Law that involve action on a commercial or industrial scale in relation to works protected by the Federal Copyright Law.

The above conduct also is punished by fines. Fines are not intended to benefit the author or economic rights owner but accrue the government.

---

19 Federal Copyright Law, Article 157.

If the author or economic rights owner wishes to claim compensation for damages, a separate civil action must be brought. In a civil action, the author or economic rights holder is entitled to request at least forty per cent of the public sale price of each original product or service rendered under the infringement.[20] Authors or economic rights owners may claim a compensatory consideration for a copy[21] or reproduction done without their authorization and not covered by any of the limitations on economic rights provided by the Federal Copyright Law (see text, above).

Criminal Infringement

While administrative infringement is dealt with in the Federal Copyright Law, conduct considered as criminal infringement is dealt with in the Federal Criminal Code.[22] Only conduct related to economic rights, consisting of producing, reproducing, introducing into Mexico, storage, distributing, selling, or renting copies of works, phonograms, videos, or books protected by the Federal Copyright law, in a willful misconduct manner, with commercial speculation purposes and without the authorization required from the owner of the economic rights is subject to criminal prosecution.

This conduct is punished with imprisonment from three to ten years and applicable fines. In addition, the manufacture, importation, sale, or rental of a system or device intended to decode a coded satellite signal carrying programs, without authorization of the legitimate distributor for such signal, constitutes criminal conduct and, carrying out any conduct, intended for profit, with the purpose of decoding a coded satellite signal carrying programs and without authorization of the legitimate distributor for such signal, are considered as criminal conduct.[23]

Infringement Proceedings

One of the peculiarities of the Mexican legal framework related to copyright infringements is that different authorities prosecute and enforce, through different proceedings, the corresponding rights, particularly those

---

20 Federal Copyright Law, Article 216 *bis*.
21 The Federal Copyright Law does not provide a specific definition of "copy"; however, the concept of "copy" is understood from the definition of "reproduction" in the Law.
22 Federal Criminal Code, Article 242 *bis*, Section I.
23 Federal Criminal Code, Article 426, Sections I and II.

related to administrative infringements, having one authority prosecuting and enforcing moral rights, and a different one attending to those related to economic rights.

Successful prosecution may result in the seizure and destruction of counterfeited goods, and the infringer will be punished with fines and when applicable with imprisonment, being subject also to the payment of damages.

Administrative Proceedings for Economic Rights

Additionally, in the event of trade-related copyright infringements, competent courts and the Mexican Institute of Industrial Property (*Instituto Mexicano de la Propiedad Industrial*) authority responsible for proceedings will be entitled to order border precautionary measures in order to suspend the free trade of foreign goods.

For administrative actions, the good faith of the offender is irrelevant; under criminal law, the bad faith of the offender (i.e., the intentional character of the offence) must be established. As an average, infringement in first-instance actions may require 18 to 24 months. A decision by the Mexican Institute of Industrial Property may be appealed through an optional revision recourse before the Mexican Institute of Industrial Property or challenged through petition for annulment with the Federal Court for Administrative Justice. Decisions by the Federal Court for Administrative Justice may be challenged through a constitutional appeal (*Amparo*) before the Federal Collegiate Circuit Court. Obtaining a final decision could require three to five years.

Customs Enforcement

The Customs Division of the Tax Administration System, part of the Treasury Ministry, has implemented a watch program over imports. The program was originally developed for trade mark rights; however, it has been expended to copyright and certain types of patents. A request must be made by a written petition in which the list of the intellectual property rights and related information is provided.

There is no cost for entering into the program. A Customs watch application may be implemented at any time and will last as long as the intellectual property rights remain valid and in full force. When Customs reports on finding offending goods, the products will be held for three to five days, during which the owner or licensee of the intellectual property right must file a request for enforcement of precautionary measures and/or infringement actions, or file a criminal complaint. The former must be filed with the Institute of Industrial Property, and the latter with the Attorney General's Office, requesting seizure of the counterfeited goods. Otherwise, goods will be released.

Damages

As noted, with respect to copyright, it is not necessary to bring an infringement action or secure an infringement decision in order to initiate a civil action in which damages are claimed. This differs from other types of intellectual property rights, such as trade marks, for which it is necessary to secure a final infringement decision before claiming damages.

Material and/or moral damages, as well as compensation for damages and lost profits, may not be less than forty per cent of the public sale price of the original product or of the original rendering of service that involves infringement of one or more of the rights protected by law. If the amount of the indemnification cannot be determined, a court will fix the amount of compensation.

It is not that clear whether the minimum forty per cent rule for damages in the Federal Copyright Law is considered to be statutory or punitive damages as there are no published precedents about the enforcement of the rule. The rule was introduced in 2003 but, due to a Supreme Court's decision that it is necessary to secure a final ruling in administrative infringement proceedings stating that a copyright infringement was committed prior to bringing a civil suit for damages, few cases have emerged.

Non-Commercial File Sharing

Unauthorized downloading is a criminal infringement when it is carried out as willful misconduct and with commercial purposes. If the conduct does not comply with these requirements, the rules for administrative infringement apply, and it will be necessary to determine whether rules for economic rights apply to the conduct.

Intermediary Liability

Certain conduct considered by the Federal Criminal Code as a felony is related to intermediary liability.[24] Whoever produces, reproduces, introduces to Mexico, stores, transports, distributes, sells, or leases copies of works, phonograms, videos, or books protected by the Federal Copyright Law, in willful manner, with commercial purpose, and without authorization, may be punished with imprisonment and fine. The same penalty will be imposed on those who knowingly contribute or provide raw materials or input intended for the production or reproduction of works, phonograms, videos, or books referred to above.

Piracy

Counterfeiting or "piracy" is a serious problem in Mexico. Piracy is prosecuted through criminal proceedings as a general rule. Lookalikes or similarities are subject to administrative rather than criminal proceedings. Criminal proceedings may be initiated *ex officio* or *ex parte*, depending on the nature of the infringement. To initiate an anti-piracy action, it is necessary to demonstrate ownership or legal standing with respect to the corresponding right.

For criminal proceedings, the complaint is filed with the Attorney General's Office, as counterfeiting is considered a federal felony. In such proceedings, it is possible to reach an out-of-court settlement and grant pardons to alleged offenders, with criminal action dismissed. Proceedings initiated *ex officio* cannot be dismissed or abandoned by granting a pardon or entering into a settlement. In an *ex officio* proceeding, the case may be dismissed or abandoned if it is considered that no right has been affected, but not as a consequence of pardons or settlements.

For criminal actions, one of the most relevant elements is the commercial scale of the conduct. The validity of the intellectual property right is a preliminary condition to a criminal action. Criminal courts do not have authority to determine the validity of an intellectual property right. A defendant who claims that an intellectual property right is invalid must initiate an action with the administrative authority or with a competent civil court to have the intellectual property right annulled or declared invalid.

---

24 Federal Criminal Code, Article 424 *bis*.

Remedies

A common remedy with respect to copyright infringement is injunction, among others. Unfortunately, injunction or preliminary relief is not regulated by the Mexican legal framework; notwithstanding, with respect to copyright infringement, other remedies are available.

One of the most common uses in administrative infringement proceedings with the Institute of Industrial Property, and in certain manner similar to injunction, is the enforcement of precautionary measures. Precautionary measures can be requested prior to filing an infringement action or within the proceeding. If precautionary measures are requested prior to the filing of an infringement action, and are effectively applied, twenty business days are granted to the plaintiff to formalize the proceedings against the infringer. Precautionary measures may consist of:

(1) Ordering prohibition of sale or distribution of the infringing merchandise; and
(2) Ordering the withdrawal from circulation or seizure of objects manufactured or used illegally; objects, wrappers, containers, packaging, paperwork, advertising material, and similar articles that infringe protected rights; signs, labels, tags, paperwork, and similar articles that infringe the rights protected by the Industrial Property Law; and implements or instruments intended or used for the manufacture, preparation, or production of any of the articles specified in the items above.

When the enforcement of precautionary measures is requested, a bond to guarantee possible damages and lost profits that the enforcement of such measures may cause to the alleged infringer should be provided by the plaintiff. The enforcement of precautionary measures must be made in writing and is subject to *periculum in mora* and *bonus fumi iuris* principles, including:

(1) The existence of infringement of rights;
(2) The imminence of infringement of rights;
(3) The existence of the possibility of irreparable damage;
(4) The existence of a justified fear that evidence might be destroyed, concealed, lost, or altered; and
(5) The information necessary for the identification of the goods, services, or establishments with which or in which the infringement of rights has been committed.

In the proceedings, any type of evidence to demonstrate the mentioned circumstances is accepted. Witnesses and expert witnesses are accepted only when their statements are included in documentary evidence. Obtaining enforcement of precautionary measures can take from three to fifteen business days. The imposition of precautionary measures cannot extend beyond the resolution of the proceedings. However, in the corresponding decision, an order may prevent future commercialization of goods, services, or use of related intellectual property rights.

The common result for infringing goods is destruction. The cost for destruction of goods is the responsibility of the owner of the infringed rights, as no order from the authority will be issued requiring the losing party to carry out destruction. Monetary remedies are only considered at first-instance proceedings. These remedies include fines that are to the benefit of the government, not the rights holder. As noted above, owners of rights have the possibility of bringing a civil action for damages.

Economic Impact

Making an accurate estimate of the economic impact from copyright infringement is difficult. In 2015, a study was commissioned by the American Chamber of Commerce of Mexico through the *Centro de Investigación para el Desarrollo, A.C.* (CIDAC).[25] The study was published under the title "Understanding the Shadow Market in Mexico".[26] The study focused on the following topics:

(1) Scale of consumption of illicit products in Mexico;
(2) Examination of spending habits and consumer profiles; and
(3) Ways to combat piracy in Mexico.

The findings, limited to 2014, showed that the shadow market in Mexico amounted to more than MXP 43-billion. The total does not include the value of seized merchandise, job losses, taxes, income, and the impact on the health and safety of consumers.

---

25 The *Centro de Investigación para el Desarrollo, A.C.* is an independent, non-profit think tank that conducts research and presents proposals for Mexico's medium and long-term development.
26 See http://www.wipo.int/edocs/mdocs/enforcement/en/wipo_ace_10/wipo_ace_10_12_ppt.pdf.

Exemptions from Copyright Infringement

Limitations on Economic Rights

The limitations on economic rights are similar to "fair use rules" as understood in other jurisdictions. The limitations are exceptions to specific conduct considered as infringement relating to non-authorized or non-compensated use or works, and are subject to requirements that the regular exploitation of the work is not adversely affected, the source of the work must be cited without exception, and the work is not modified. The limitations are:

(1) Quotation of texts, provided that the amount quoted may not be considered a substantial, simulated reproduction of the contents of the work;

(2) Reproduction of articles, photographs, illustrations, and commentaries relating to current events that have been published in the press or broadcast by radio or television, or any other medium of communication, if this has not been expressly prohibited by the owner of the rights;

(3) Reproduction of parts of the work for the purposes of scientific, literary, or artistic criticism and research;

(4) Single reproduction of a single copy of a literary or artistic work for the personal and private use of the person doing it, without gainful intent; a legal entity may not avail itself of this exception unless it is an educational or research institution or is not devoted to trading activities;

(5) Reproduction of a single copy by archives or a library for reasons of security and preservation where the work is out of print, no longer catalogued, and liable to disappear;

(6) Reproduction for the purposes of evidence in judicial or administrative proceedings; and

(7) Reproduction, communication, and distribution in drawings, paintings, photographs, and audiovisual processes of works that are visible from public places.[27]

In addition, the Federal Copyright Law[28] provides that certain conduct may be done without authorization of the owner of economic rights.

---

[27] Federal Copyright Law, Article 148.
[28] Federal Copyright Law, Article 149.

Literary and artistic works may be used in shops or establishments open to the public that trade in copies of the said works, provided that no charge is made for admission and that the use does not go beyond the place in which the sale is effected and serves the sole purpose of promoting the sale of copies of the works.

Ephemeral recordings may be made, subject to requirements that the transmission must take place within the period agreed for the purpose; no related or simultaneous broadcast or communication may be made of the recording; and the recording is subject to only one broadcast. The recording and fixation of images and sounds, carried out in the manner described above, does not require additional payment other than that due for use of the works.

Conclusion

There is no doubt about the seriousness of copyright infringement and its social, cultural, and economic consequences. Mexico provides a proper legal framework for protection of intellectual property rights, however, many things can be improved.

Portugal

Vasco Stilwell d'Andrade
Morais Leitão, Galvão Teles, Soares da Silva & Associados
Lisbon, Portugal

Introduction

The origin of Portuguese copyright law[1] is generally considered to date to 1851, although authors of literary works were recognized as having certain rights already from the 1820s onwards. Thus, it is possible to state that Portugal awoke late to the issue of copyright in relation to some other European nations (the Statute of Queen Anne[2] having been enacted in 1710).

Since the mid-19th century, Portugal has developed its domestic copyright law in line with the continental European tradition, drawing particular influence from the laws of France, Germany, and Italy. Current Portuguese substantive copyright law is, therefore, highly harmonized with that of other continental European countries.

Copyright is considered a fundamental right in the Portuguese legal system, and this naturally has an impact on the way copyright infringement is dealt with in the national legal system. Indeed, the right to the protection of one's literary and artistic works has been present in the various Portuguese constitutions, both during the constitutional monarchy period (19th century) and during the First and Second Republics (early 20th century).

In 1974, Portugal underwent a revolution that overthrew the *Estado Novo* dictatorship and gave rise to the current Third Republic and the creation of a modern constitutional democracy. Interestingly, the constituent assembly that drafted the (current) 1976 Portuguese Constitution did not forget copyright in the "highest law of the land". Article 42 of the Constitution states that everyone is free to invent, produce, and disclose scientific, literary, or artistic works, and this includes the legal protection of copyright.

---

1 Portuguese copyright and procedural law is complex and has many exceptions. The information provided in this chapter has been summarized for ease of comprehension and does not constitute legal advice. A Portuguese attorney should be retained to analyze a case of copyright infringement before initiating litigation.
2 Copyright Act of 1710.

Portugal is a Civil Law jurisdiction with codified legislation. At the center of this codified law system is the Civil Code, which contains some brief references to copyright. Article 1303 states that copyright is subject to special legislation and that the Civil Code is applicable on a subsidiary basis. The special legislation that the Civil Code speaks of is mostly contained in the Copyright and Related Rights Code (*Código do Direito de Autor e dos Direitos Conexos*, CDADC). The Copyright and Related Rights Code is the central legislation that regulates the majority of copyright matters. Additional laws exist in order to regulate specific areas or activities. For example, the protection of software and databases by copyright is regulated by two separate laws.[3]

Portugal is a contracting party to most of the major international treaties that deal with copyright and related rights, including the Berne,[4] Rome,[5] and Brussels[6] Conventions, the World Intellectual Property Organization (WIPO) Performances and Phonograms Treaty WPPT,[7] and the Agreement on Trade-Related Aspects of Intellectual Property Rights (TRIPS).[8] Consequently, copyright law in Portugal is shaped by the rules of these international treaties. Furthermore, in light of Portugal's inclusion in the European Union (EU) since the 1980s, the substantive copyright legislation that exists in Portugal is harmonized with that of other EU Member States.

In short, Portugal has essentially the same substantive copyright rules that can be found in other European countries but it also shares many of the same problems and challenges. Since the spread of high-speed broadband Internet, smartphones, and other fast copying technologies, copyright infringement has become so prevalent in Portugal that many people are not even aware of any wrongdoing. Some pedagogical initiatives have been undertaken to seek to curb the level of copyright

---

[3] Law-Decree Number 252/94 of 20 October 1994 (as amended); Law-Decree Number 122/2000 of 4 July 2000.

[4] Berne Convention for the Protection of Literary and Artistic Works (1886). Portugal ratified the Convention on 29 March 1911.

[5] Rome Convention for the Protection of Performers, Producers of Phonograms and Broadcasting Organizations (1961). Portugal ratified the Convention on 17 July 2002.

[6] Brussels Convention relating to the Distribution of Program Carrying Signals Transmitted by Satellite (1974). Portugal ratified the Convention on 11 March 1996.

[7] WIPO Performances and Phonograms Treaty (1996). Portugal ratified the Convention on 14 March 2010.

[8] The Agreement on Trade-Related Aspects of Intellectual Property Rights (TRIPS) is an international legal agreement between all the member nations of the World Trade Organization (WTO). The Agreement was negotiated in 1994 and came into effect on 1 January 1995.

infringement of musical and audiovisual works but, mostly, these have been timid and underfunded.

This chapter seeks to provide an overview of the current legal situation regarding copyright infringement in the Portuguese jurisdiction, including its triumphs and present shortcomings. The English term "copyright" is used throughout this chapter for ease of comprehension. However, Portuguese legislation uses the broader expression "author's rights" (*direitos de autor*). In the continental European tradition, this expression is used because it encompasses far more than a mere right to authorize reproductions of the work. Indeed, it includes the right to exploit the intellectual work in all its economic dimensions and the author's moral rights.

Works Protected by Copyright Law

Under Portuguese law, copyright protects "works" of a literary, scientific or artistic nature. In order to merit protection, the works must be incorporated into some medium. As a rule, protection is afforded to the intellectual work irrespective of the genre, the manner in which it is expressed or communicated, its merit, and its objective. Thus, the scope of protection is broad and, in practice, most intellectual creations by natural persons are covered by copyright law in Portugal.

In order to assist in the interpretation of the law, Article 2(1) of the Copyright and Related Rights Code contains a non-limiting list of the type of original intellectual creations that are protected by copyright. The list indicates the following types of works:

(1) Books, booklets, magazines, newspapers, and other writings;
(2) Conferences, lessons, speeches, and sermons;
(3) Dramatic works (with or without music) and their staging;
(4) Choreographic works and pantomimes that are recorded in writing or through some other medium;
(5) Musical compositions, with or without words;
(6) Cinematographic, televised, phonographic, video graphic, or radio works;
(7) Drawings, tapestries, paintings, sculptures, ceramics, tiles, engravings, lithography, and architecture;
(8) Photographs works and other works produced through analogous processes;

(9) Applied arts, industrial drawings and models, and designs that involve an artistic creation, notwithstanding the protection also afforded by industrial property rights;
(10) Illustrations and geographic charts;
(11) Projects, sketches, and models related to urbanism, geography, and other sciences;
(12) Slogans and sayings, provided they are original and irrespectively of whether they are used for advertising; and
(13) Parodies and other musical and literary compositions, even if they are inspired by other works.[9]

In addition to providing examples of works that may be protected by copyright, the Portuguese legislator also provides guidance on works that do not benefit from any protection under copyright law. First, the Copyright and Related Rights Code excludes abstract ideas, processes, concepts, principles, discoveries, and operational methods, as such. By clarifying that they are excluded as such, the Portuguese legislator indicates that it may be possible to protect these types of works if they are fixed (materialized) in some way and include some creative elements.

Exclusions from copyright protection are found throughout the Copyright and Related Rights Code. For example, Article 4(2) excludes titles that are generic, common, or necessary for the theme or type of work. Similarly, Article 7 excludes from copyright protection certain intellectual creations deemed not to have sufficient creative merit or that are excluded for other philosophical or sociological grounds. Examples of this are daily news snippets and other accounts of events that do not go beyond a simple communication of information, political speeches, public debates, and submissions made to judicial and administrative authorities.

This creativity threshold also can be found in the special regime that the Copyright and Related Rights Code contains for photographs. Article 164 states that for a photograph to be protected, it is necessary that it reveal a personal artistic creation of the author, namely, through the choice of the photographed object or the manner in which the photograph

---

9 Aside from these original works, the Copyright and Related Rights Code lists types of works that are classified as non-original works but that are deemed equivalent to originals. In this category, the Portuguese legislator included works such as translations, adaptations, instrumentals, and summaries. These so-called non-original works also are considered to be protected by copyright without prejudice to the protection also granted to the original works upon which they are based.

was taken.[10] In short, Portuguese copyright law covers various realities, but it also sets, in some cases, certain minimum criteria for copyright protection to be claimed. In practice, the creativity threshold is often subjective and hard to determine, but Portuguese case law has tended to set the bar rather low.

Following the principle set out by Article 5(2) of the Berne Convention, Portuguese copyright law does not, as a rule, require any formality for copyright to be recognized.[11] In other words, unlike the system that exists for industrial property rights (i.e., patents, trademarks, and registered designs), there is no need for the author to record his intellectual creation with any public office in order for protection to be afforded to the work.

Nevertheless, registration is possible at the *Inspecção-Geral das Actividades Culturais* (IGAC) should there be an interest in obtaining evidence of the date of filing and a legal presumption of ownership.[12] In addition, there are a few exceptional situations expressly provided in the Copyright and Related Rights Code that require mandatory registration in order for copyright protection to exist, namely, the title of unpublished works, the title and name of newspapers and other periodic publications, and the mandate of a collective rights management entity.[13] For these situations, the Portuguese legislator felt it was necessary to impose mandatory registration in the interest of legal security and to avoid an increase in potential conflicts.

There also has been a recent controversy regarding the registration of facts, court actions, or decisions that determine the creation, recognition, assignment, encumbrance, modification, or extinction of copyright or the pledging or seizing of copyrights. It was understood that these facts mentioned in Article 215 of the Copyright and Related Rights Code could be registered at the discretion of the copyright owner or of an interested third party/entity.

However, in 2014, the Government passed Law-Decree Number 143/2014, of 26 September 2014, which approved the Regulation for the Registration of Literary and Artistic Works. The main objective of the Regulation was to consolidate in a single legislation all the rules

---

10 Article 164(2) gives the examples of photographs of writings, documents, business papers, technical drawings, and other such things as photographic works that do not merit protection.
11 Copyright and Related Rights Code, Article 213.
12 The information contained in the registration can be challenged. The registration process consists of a mere statement and deposit of a copy of the work.
13 Copyright and Related Rights Code, Articles 4, 5, and 214.

regarding the registration of literary and artistic works that were dispersed through various other laws.

However, many scholars have spoken out against the Regulation given that it appears to create mandatory registration of some possibilities that were understood not to be obligatory. Therefore, the Regulation has been criticized as being technically inadequate and contrary to other national laws and international commitments.

Author's Rights

To fully understand copyright infringement in Portugal, it is necessary to have a grasp of the rights that Portuguese law grants to those who create literary, artistic, and scientific works. Article 67 of the Copyright and Related Rights Code states that the author[14] has the exclusive right to use and exploit the work, either wholly or partially, the right encompassing the ability to disclose, publish, and exploit economically the work in any manner, directly or indirectly, within the limits of the law.

In essence, Portuguese law provides the intellectual creator of the work with a temporary (but lengthy[15]) legal monopoly to exploit the literary, scientific, or artistic work. Such a legal monopoly (or exclusive right) is akin to the concept of property; hence, copyright falls under the umbrella expression of "intellectual property".

In addition to Article 67 defining the limits of the exclusive right in very broad terms, the law[16] also exemplifies in a quite detailed manner the type of concrete uses and rights that belong to the copyright owner. The specific sub-rights that derive from the exclusive right to the economic exploitation of the work include the right to publish; the right to recite, exhibit, and perform in public; the right to reproduce, adapt, and distribute; the right to broadcast and communicate to the public; the right to incorporate, translate, and arrange; and the right to make available on demand through wire or wireless means.

Naturally, as proprietor of an exclusive right, the copyright owner can assign and license the respective economic rights to third parties or, alternatively, provide a mere authorization for the works to be used for certain purposes. Like other economic assets, copyright can be pledged as

---

14 The law mentions the "author", but this must be read as the "copyright owner".
15 For the majority of works, it is 70 years from the death of the author.
16 Copyright and Related Rights Code, Article 68.

a security, or seized as collateral. In the continental tradition, Portuguese copyright law recognizes "moral rights", i.e., the right to claim authorship of the work and the right to object to any mutilation, deformation, or other modification of, or other derogatory action in relation to, the work that would be prejudicial to the author's honor or reputation.

Copyright Infringement

Copyright Infringement as Crime

In General

Under Portuguese law, copyright infringement is a crime. The criminalization of copyright infringement, with the possibility of prison terms, has been criticized by various scholars as being too excessive when one takes into consideration the level of harm that it causes to the copyright owner.

However, others point to the need to have a serious deterrent for this type of illicit behavior. The latter have, to date, won the argument with the Portuguese legislator, and there are no major pushes to de-criminalize copyright infringement. The Copyright and Related Rights Code sets out several crimes.

Usurpation (*usurpação*) occurs when someone, without the authorization of the author, uses the copyright-protected work in one of the ways cited in the Copyright and Related Rights Code. The concept of *usurpação* is identical to the notion of copyright piracy in other jurisdictions, and it applies to the unauthorized use of related rights or the unauthorized compilation of published or unpublished works.

The crime also is committed when someone willingly and abusively discloses or publishes a work that the author maintained undisclosed or unpublished or had intended to remain undisclosed or unpublished, even if the author is correctly identified and irrespectively of whether an economic gain is sought.[17] *Usurpação* also may occur when someone that is authorized to use the work or performance goes beyond the limits of the authorization. For example, if a person is authorized to recite a poem in a theatre, the intentional broadcasting of the recitation may lead to a crime of *usurpação*.

---

17 The crime of usurpation also is committed by those who compile published or unpublished works without the copyright owner's authorization.

If the rights are assigned to a third party (i.e., not the intellectual creator), the author is considered to commit the crime of *usurpação* if he continues to use and exploit the works, and by doing so disrespects the assignment agreement that was entered into.

Counterfeiting (*contrafacção*) occurs when someone uses someone else's work or performance as one's own creation. The Portuguese legal concept of *contrafacção* is equivalent to "plagiarism" or "passing off". It is not necessary for the infringer to use (plagiarize) the entire work. Indeed, *contrafacção* can occur when just a portion of someone else's work is used as one's own. Furthermore, it is not essential that the infringer use the same medium as the original work.

It also is a crime to claim authorship of a work when the infringer knows such a claim to be false. Similarly, if someone disrespects the authenticity or integrity of a work or otherwise affects the honor or reputation of the author, he may be found to infringe a third party's moral rights.

The law also punishes those that sell, offer for sale, import, export, or distribute to the public a usurped or counterfeit work or performance. These copyright infringement crimes laid out in the Copyright and Related Rights Code are considered mere activity crimes. In other words, the crime is committed when the infringer commits the illicit act and there is no need to take into consideration the consequences of the crime (i.e., harm, offense, and damages).

By opting for this legal solution, the Portuguese legislator has sent a clear signal that it wishes to facilitate the process of proving infringement and convicting infringers. In other words, the Portuguese lawmaker has sought to base the crime of copyright infringement on immoral or unethical behavior and not necessarily on the economic harm it causes.

Misdemeanors

The Copyright and Related Rights Code also establishes certain misdemeanors for some situations of non-compliance with Portuguese copyright law. For example, an editor's failure to identify the author of a literary work constitutes a misdemeanor that carries a monetary penalty of €99.76 to €997.60.

Civil Liability

Portuguese law makes it plainly clear that the criminal liability of the infringer does not exclude or preclude civil liability as well. Indeed, civil liability can be assessed in the criminal proceedings or, alternatively, they can run independently of each other in separate procedures.[18]

It also is possible, and common in Portugal, for copyright infringement to be dealt with solely in the civil courts. In accordance with Article 483 of the Civil Code, the illegal violation, with willful or negligent conduct, of someone else's right or a legal provision aimed at protection of third-party interests shall result in the obligation to indemnify the harmed party of the damages caused as a result of the infringement. The Copyright and Related Rights Code contains an almost identical provision in Article 211(1), although specifically directed to copyright infringement.

Based on these two separate (general and specific) legal provisions, copyright owners in Portugal frequently limit their enforcement efforts to civil liability proceedings.

The reasons behind this decision are varied. First, copyright owners often believe that criminal proceedings are too severe for the type of harm that has been caused or the conduct they are trying to prevent or stop. Criminal proceedings have a certain psychological weight that is often deemed too severe for something that is many times seen as a mere commercial issue.

On the other hand, civil proceedings allow the copyright owner to have a greater degree of control over the evidence that is produced, how it is presented to the court, and how the arguments are formulated. In criminal proceedings, it is the Public Prosecutor's Office that truly controls the proceedings, leaving the copyright owner much more in the "back seat".

Sanctions and Remedies

Criminal Sanctions

The punishment for the above crimes is three years' imprisonment or a fine ranging from 150 to 250 days,[19] depending on the gravity. If the infringer is a recidivist, the penalties can double and the infringer loses the ability to have the right to a suspended sentence.

Software and databases are regulated by specific legislation and are not covered by the Copyright and Related Rights Code. However, the unlawful copying, disclosing, or communicating to the public of software

---

18 Copyright and Related Rights Code, Article 203.
19 Penal law establishes a monetary penalty that is considered a day for the purposes of applying the fine.

and databases is punished with a penalty of up to three years' imprisonment or a fine.[20] If someone commits these crimes out of negligence, that circumstance does not prevent the infringer from being punished. The punishment is a fine ranging from 50 to 150 days in the case of *usurpação* and *contrafacção* and 50 days where someone takes advantage of the illegal works.

Accessory Sanctions

In addition to criminal sanctions, the Copyright and Related Rights Code also provides a set of additional punitive measures that seek to prevent future infringements. When applied, the measures must be adequate, necessary, and proportional to the gravity of the infringement. They also must take into consideration the legitimate interests of third parties, i.e., the consumers.

For example, the court can order, at the infringed party's request and at the infringer's expense, that the infringing objects be removed from the market, destroyed, be given to charities, or deemed forfeited to the State.[21] The same rules and principles apply to the instruments, tools, and equipment used in the production of the infringing articles. These also can be seized and forfeited to the State or transferred to some other institution. The court judgment can equally impose measures directly on the convicted infringer in order to attempt to prevent the reoccurrence of infringing conduct. These are fixed in Article 210-J(2) as follows:

(1) The temporary prohibition of exercising certain activities and professions;
(2) The cancellation of the right to participate in fairs or markets; and
(3) The temporary or permanent closing of a commercial establishment.

In order to ensure compliance with the measures, the court can impose, upon its own volition or at the request of the infringed party, a monetary sanction applicable to the infringer for each day until the measures are fully implemented. Moreover, the measures can be applied not only to the infringer, but also to intermediaries that are involved in the course of the infringing conduct. This is one way in which Portuguese law has recognized, to a certain extent, the concept of contributory infringement.

---

[20] Software Law, Article 14; Databases Law, Article 11; Cyber Crime Law, Article 8.
[21] Copyright and Related Rights Code, Article 210-I.

Lastly, following the implementation of the EU Enforcement Directive,[22] Article 211-A was introduced into the Copyright and Related Rights Code, allowing a court to order an infringer to pay for the publication of the final judgment in a newspaper if the claimant so requests it. This measure serves to dissuade other potential infringers and to inform the public of the gravity of copyright infringement.

Indemnification

Under civil procedural law, the court may only sentence the defendant based on what has been requested by the claimant. A judge cannot sanction the losing party for something that has not been claimed or require financial compensation higher than that which the plaintiff has requested (although a judge may impose a lesser amount and is sometimes asked to decide based merely on reasons of equity).

The Civil Code stipulates that indemnities are the means by which a party that has suffered damages is restored to the situation it would have been in had the illegal action not occurred. Financial remedies are calculated by taking into consideration direct economic losses, lost income, and moral damages. Punitive or exemplary damages are not accepted in Portugal. Therefore, as a rule, only those losses that can actually be proved will be taken into consideration.

The implementation of the Enforcement Directive in Portugal brought about new and specific indemnification rules for intellectual property infringement cases that deviate somewhat from the classic general rule described above. Under these specific rules, in determining the amount of compensation for damages, the court may take into account, in particular, the profit obtained by the infringer and the resulting damages and lost profits suffered by the injured party (as well as the costs borne by the right holder in the investigation and termination of the infringement and moral damages).

If it is impossible to quantify the losses suffered by the injured party based on these criteria, the law states that a court may define a fixed amount with a minimum value corresponding to the remuneration that the injured party would have received if the infringer had requested authorization to use the exclusive right and the expenses incurred for the enforcement actions. Finally, when the infringer's conduct constitutes a repeated practice or proves to be particularly harmful, a court may determine the compensation by cumulatively applying all the above criteria.

---

22 Directive 2004/48/EC of the European Parliament and of the Council of 29 April 2004 on the enforcement of intellectual property rights.

Unfortunately, the issues as to the application of the above criteria (damages, lost profits, infringer's profits, and license analogy) and their nature (notably in terms of whether they should be applied autonomously or cumulatively) have not been firmly tested in Portuguese case law, and many questions continue to arise when copyright owners attempt to apply these rules.

Copyright Infringement Defense Strategies

Lack of Legitimacy of Claimant

As in most countries that are members of the Berne Convention, there is no obligatory formal registration for copyright protection to exist and be recognized in Portugal (save the exceptions mentioned above). Indeed, copyright protection exists automatically as soon as the work is "fixed".

The ease in obtaining copyright protection has the downside that it is often difficult for the copyright owner to prove authorship and/or ownership. In order to assist the copyright owner, Article 27(2) establishes a legal presumption that the author is the person whose name is placed on the work in accordance with customary practice. This legal presumption does help in many cases where the work has been published with the author's name, but there are many cases in which no name is associated with the work (e.g., photographs).

In addition, there are cases in which discrepancies arise between the person indicated on the work and the owners of the copyright identified in other records. In light of situations in which the copyright ownership is not clear, a typical defense strategy in copyright infringement cases is to question the legitimacy of the claimant in the proceedings.[23] Often, if the claimant cannot firmly establish legitimacy, the proceedings are terminated, and the defendant is acquitted.

Absence of Protection

As described above, not every literary or artistic work meets the threshold of creativity and originality that is necessary for copyright

---

[23] Precisely to avoid these types of legitimacy issues, some copyright owners record their works with the General Inspection of Cultural Activities (IGAC) or secure some other sort of proof of authorship and/or ownership.

protection to be afforded to it. In some circumstances, a defense strategy can be based on the absence of copyright protection and, therefore, the lack of an exclusive right.

This is particularly common in copyright infringement cases involving the unauthorized use of photographs or short news reports since the Copyright and Related Rights Code has specific provisions that deal with the lack of protection for works that do not reveal enough creative merit.

Expiry of Protection

The duration of copyrights has varied in Portuguese legislation throughout the 20th and early 21st centuries. A particularly notable example is the duration of the protection afforded to photographs that, in the 1980s, was as short as 25 years from first publication.

In light of the changes in the duration of copyright protection over the decades, when the copyright infringement case involves works of a more historical nature, it may on occasion be possible to argue the expiry of the copyright protection.

Private Use Exception

Private use is a classic copyright infringement defense that is often used by natural persons accused of pirating works, in particular on the Internet. Portuguese law, like the legislation of many other EU Member States, provides that it is possible to use a copyright-protected work without the authorization of the copyright owner if it is for personal use and the criteria of the three-step test are met.

Limitations of Copyright Protection

Similar to the private use exception, Portuguese law also includes several limitations of copyright protection that are called "free uses" (*utilizações livres*). These are situations in which the Portuguese legislator has decided that the exclusive right afforded to the copyright owner should be limited or restricted.

Depending of the type of work and manner in which it has been used, it is sometimes possible to build a defense on free uses and, consequently, argue that there was no infringing activity since no authorization was required and authorship was duly recognized. Examples of *utilizações livres* are the right to include quotations or summaries of third-party works in order to support one's own opinions or for the purpose of critique; the use of a selection of news articles in order to review the day's press; the copying of broadcast works by not-for-profit institutions such as hospitals and prisons; and the use of architectural plans for the purpose of retrofitting works.

Dissimilarities between Original Work and Plagiarized Work

In cases of *contrafacção* (plagiarism), the allegedly infringing work is often not identical to the original but rather an imitation. The classic defense in these cases is to highlight the dissimilarities of the later work and the fact that it has its own individuality and creativity. In other words, the defense stresses the existence of inspiration (which is permitted) rather than an imitation (which is not).

There is a substantial amount of case law analyzing the criteria that, from a Portuguese perspective, must be met in order for *contrafacção* to be proven. In a well-known 2010 decision, the Supreme Court concluded that, to prove *contrafacção*, it is necessary to show that the following criteria are all met:

(1) Someone undertakes a fraudulent use;
(2) The person claims the third party's work to be his own;
(3) The work is a mere reproduction of the third-party work; and
(4) The reproduction is so similar that it does not have its own individuality.

If both works have their own individuality, the similarity between the works is not sufficient to constitute *contrafacção* because the individuality criterion prevails over objective similarities. Indeed, *contrafacção* is a situation in which one has not added anything substantial to a third party's creation. In light of these demanding and subjective requisites, *contrafacção* cases are often hard to prove in court.

Choice of Venue

Court System

In General

Portugal has a complex court system that is divided into two separate and independent structures, i.e., the judicial courts and the administrative courts. Outside these two structures are other quasi-courts, the most important being the Constitutional Court, which deals with constitutional matters. Administrative courts essentially follow the French model and deal above all with disputes arising out of the exercise of public power and prerogatives (*ius imperii*), such as taxation, building licenses, and public contracts.

Judicial courts are the default courts that deal with most private law issues. Within the judicial court structure, there are general courts and courts specializing in certain matters of law (e.g., employment law, criminal law, family law, and intellectual property law). Both the administrative and civil judicial courts are organized into hierarchical three-tier pyramids, albeit the administrative structure has far fewer courts in the middle and lower tiers.

In the judicial court structure, particularly at the first instance level, the courts can be divided into generic or specialized sections and divisions. Above the first-instance courts, there are five district courts[24] (second-instance or appeal courts) and, at the pinnacle of this structure, stands the Supreme Court of Justice. Other than in exceptional circumstances, all cases must be tried first in a lower or first-instance court before being heard in a higher instance court.

Courts with Jurisdiction over Civil Copyright Infringement Cases

Non-criminal copyright infringement cases in Portugal fall under the jurisdiction of the Intellectual Property Court that covers all of Portugal and has its seat in Lisbon. The Court was established in 2012 by Law Number 46/2011 of 24 June 2011 and is divided into two subdivisions (*juízos*).

Courts with Jurisdiction over Criminal Copyright Infringement Cases

As mentioned above, copyright infringement is a crime in Portugal. The general rule regarding jurisdiction in criminal cases is that the court of the area where the crime took place will be competent to judge the case. This can be particularly challenging in cases when copyright infringement is committed over the Internet.

---

24 Technically, there are six district courts in Portugal: Lisbon, Porto, Coimbra, Évora, Guimarães, and Faro. However, the Faro court has never been implemented, and the Évora district court continues to have jurisdiction over the Algarve region.

Dispute Resolution Alternatives

As an alternative to the judicial courts, it is possible to litigate copyright infringement within the context of an arbitration. Law Number 63/2011 of 14 December 2011, which approved the Law on Voluntary Arbitration, states that is possible to submit litigation to an arbitral court to decide upon economic matters when the law does not require the litigation to be subject to the State courts or mandatory arbitration.

It is possible to establish an *ad hoc* arbitral tribunal under the Law on Voluntary Arbitration, with procedural rules approved by the parties, or attempt to establish an arbitral tribunal in accordance with the pre-established rules of an arbitration center. In 2004, the Portuguese Bar Association and the Portuguese Intellectual Property Association (*Associação Portuguesa de Direito Intelectual*) established an arbitration center for copyright disputes but, largely, this initiative has failed.

Indeed, one of the main difficulties has been obtaining the consent of the alleged infringer to submit to arbitration. In situations of copyright infringement, there is typically little or no cooperation between the parties and, therefore, it is typically difficult to establish an arbitral tribunal to judge the case. The number of copyright infringement cases (excluding breach of contract) that have been resolved through the arbitration mechanism are, consequently, limited.

Civil Copyright Infringement Proceedings in Judicial Courts

Civil Court Proceedings Related to Copyright Infringement

In General

If it is not possible to reach an amicable extra-judicial settlement of the dispute, the copyright owner is left with the choice of not pursuing the issue further, filing a complaint (criminal or with some other authority), or initiating civil court proceedings. The latter typically unfold as described below.

Who Can Be Party to Proceedings?

In civil copyright infringement cases, the claimant must be a party with legitimacy to claim the violation of their copyright and, if applicable, damages. In the overwhelming majority of cases, the claimant will be the copyright owner. In addition to the copyright owner, it is possible for a collective rights management entity to initiate proceedings in representation and on behalf of the copyright owner/author.

Article 73(2) of the Copyright and Related Rights Code expressly states that these entities, that are considered to have public utility and are regulated by IGAC, have the legal capacity to intervene in civil and criminal proceedings related to matters of copyright on behalf of their members. Given their public utility status, the collective rights management entities are exempt from court fees.

When collective rights management entities seek to enforce the rights of one particular author/copyright owner, they must show that they represent the latter by presenting evidence (a power of attorney or a registered mandate). Often, the collective rights management entities seek to enforce the rights of an unknown number of different copyright owners/authors. Such is the case when, for example, a discotheque or a radio station does not have the necessary blanket license to communicate or broadcast musical works to the public.

In such cases, Portuguese case law has allowed collective rights management entities to show their legitimacy by "sampling",[25] i.e., by showing that they represent certain portfolios and that at least some of those works were used by the alleged infringer, the collective rights management entity shows it has legitimacy to intervene in the proceedings.

The issue of whether a licensee has legitimacy to enforce copyright in the Portuguese courts is an interesting and controversial point of law. With the implementation of the Enforcement Directive, the Portuguese legislator changed the Industrial Property Code (applicable to patents, trade marks, and designs) in order to expressly allow licensees to enforce the licensed rights but, strangely, did not change the Copyright and Related Rights Code in a similar manner.

There are scholars who argue that, despite this gap, it is possible to interpret the law in a way that would allow a copyright licensee to file a

---

25 Decisions of the Tribunal da Relação de Évora — 2ª Secção Cível, 29 September 2009, Case Number 1115/09.5TBABF.E1; Tribunal da Relação de Évora — 2ª Secção Cível, 6 October 2011, Case Number 2670/09.5TBAF; Tribunal da Relação do Porto — Secção Cível, 18 September 2008, Case Number 3543/08.3.

judicial copyright infringement action unless the license agreement expressly prohibited that possibility. Nevertheless, the case law of the higher instance courts has not confirmed this interpretation at this stage and, therefore, as a matter of caution it is still advisable to have the copyright owner or a collective rights management entity in representation of the copyright owner as a party to the proceedings.

Initial Claims and Counterarguments

Civil court proceedings will begin with the filing of the claimant's initial pleadings (*petição inicial*), which consists of a written document in which the claimant will state his version of the facts, the legal rules that are considered applicable, and the claims upon which the court is asked to decide upon. As discussed below, all of the claimant's documentary evidence should be presented at this stage.

The defendant (i.e., alleged copyright infringer) will have 30 days[26] as of the date in which he is served to reply, and he can do so either by refuting the claimant's arguments or by presenting defense exceptions as to why the case should not proceed. The defendant, in some circumstances, also may file a counter-claim.

Since the revision of the Civil Procedure Code in 2013, the general rule is that the claimant may only respond to the statement of defence if there is a counter-claim. This initial stage of the proceedings is known as the "group of articles" (*articulados*) because the petitions filed by the parties must typically be structured into numbered articles. Once this phase is over, the case will be delivered to a judge so that he may begin the proceedings.

Summarization and Improvement

Once the *articulado* stage has finished and both parties have provided their written versions of the facts and their interpretations of the law, the case is put before a judge whose first task will be to eliminate all issues that are irrelevant to the case. The judge also will resolve any procedural or jurisdictional questions that have been raised.

---

26 The general rule is 30 days. However, some extensions may be available, depending on who is served, where the defendant resides or is based, whether the defendant is a foreign citizen or entity, and whether the defendant requests an extension on account of the case being very complex.

After conclusion of the summarization and improvement of the case, the judge may schedule a preliminary hearing with the objective of reaching a mutual understanding and, if that is not possible, decide on things such as the scope of the issues and the evidence that will be discussed in trial. The judge may choose to skip this preliminary hearing phase if he believes it is unnecessary or there are other legal reasons for doing so. This stage of the proceedings ends with the issuance of an "improvement decision" (*despacho saneador*).

Final Hearing and Judgment

It is during the final hearing that the evidence is discussed and both parties present their closing statements. The proceedings end with the issuance of the court's ruling. If the judgment is not given orally by the judge at the end of the trial, it should be issued within 30 days but, as in other areas, this deadline must be interpreted as indicative and not binding on the judge.

The judgment must be structured in a specific way and the grounds for the decision must be clearly disclosed, indicating what evidence was taken into consideration. The court ruling also will decide on court fees, namely, which of the parties should bear them and whether they are to be divided among the parties (i.e., what proportions will be borne by each of the parties). The judgment will be recorded in the court's archives and may serve as the basis for an enforcement action, should the losing party fail to comply.

Appeals

Appealing first-instance court decisions is not an absolute right. Portuguese civil procedural law establishes a fairly wide range of restrictions regarding appeals, namely, limiting this right to a 30-day deadline (as a general rule) and only for cases over a certain value, and in which there has been a substantial difference between that which was claimed and that which was awarded by the court.

With only a few exceptions, appeals to the Portuguese Supreme Court of Justice are restricted to questions of law. It is possible to "leapfrog" a second-instance court directly to the Supreme Court when a set of specific conditions are met and where the issue appealed is strictly a matter of law. The general rule is that appeals do not affect (i.e., suspend) enforcement. However, it is possible to request a suspension of enforcement when it is argued that it will cause the losing party grave harm and some collateral is given until the decision of the appeal is known.

According to the Civil Procedural Code, court actions that deal with intangible interests are considered to have a value that enables them to be appealed to the second instance court. Since copyrights are intangible assets, an appeal to a second instance court will usually be possible. A further appeal to the Supreme Court of Justice is possible if there is a matter of law that must be clarified. An appeal is a review of a previous decision, but it can order a re-trial if the higher court believes that there were points of fact that were not properly discussed.

Length of Civil Copyright Infringement Proceeding

Prior to the creation of the Intellectual Property Court in 2012, civil copyright infringement cases were typically heard in the judicial court of the area where the alleged infringer resided or was based. Consequently, no real pattern or averages could be drawn from that period. Since the setting up of the Intellectual Property Court, it is now possible to start having some notion of the time copyright infringement cases take.

Preliminary injunction proceedings are normally dealt with quite swiftly in a matter of four to six months, although there are several cases in which it has been less than that. In relation to main actions, the Intellectual Property Court was unfortunately flooded with many cases from all around the country and it already shows many signs of strain. A main action currently takes anywhere from one to two years to be decided, although it can naturally be more or less than this.

Evidence

In General

The provision of evidence is generally done at two stages in the proceedings, namely at the beginning in the *articulados* phase and during the final hearing. One fundamental characteristic of Portuguese civil procedural law that must be kept in mind is that the facts presented by the claimant must be refuted by the defendant if they are untrue.

Should these facts not be expressly or implicitly rejected by the defendant, there is a considerable risk that those facts will automatically be considered proven. There are a few important exceptions to this rule, such as those facts that the law requires to be proven by documentary evidence. Nevertheless, the rule of thumb is that the defendant should always contest.

Documentary Evidence

Another basic overall rule is that documentary evidence must be presented at the *articulado* stage of the proceedings. Additional documentation may be presented until the end of the discussion of the facts during trial, but the party may be liable to pay a fine unless it can prove that it was not possible to present the documents at the earlier stage.

It is possible to obtain documents held by a third party, although it is necessary to provide convincing evidence or arguments that those documents exist. The implementation of the Enforcement Directive greatly reinforced the means by which copyright owners can request documentary evidence from opposing parties. Should the document not be delivered, there are several means that a copyright owner may attempt to force compliance. However, "automatic disclosure" does not exist in Portugal. Each party is responsible for presenting the facts and documents that support their case and position or, at the very least, requesting documents from the other side.

Relevant foreign documents should be translated into Portuguese and, if they are official documents, it is wise to have them legalized and authenticated by the competent consular bodies. Electronic documents with some form of digital certification are considered equivalent to signed private documents.

Written Expert Opinions

Written expert opinions can be presented at any phase of the proceedings, except when they are clearly untimely. In Portuguese copyright litigation cases, written opinions (*pareceres*) are frequently presented, although there have been some well-known cases in which the process of identifying adequate experts was problematic.[27] The written opinions issued by experts are not binding on the judges, and the court has total freedom to interpret and assess the expert findings as it sees fit.

Experts are sometimes appointed by the court to provide specialized assistance, although the parties may, at times, have some input in suggesting and deciding who the experts should be. The parties or the judge also may request that a team of experts be appointed. Normally, one is appointed by each party and a third by the court.

---

27 In a case involving the well-known Portuguese singer Tony Carreira, it took approximately two years to find an expert on musical compositions to compare some allegedly plagiarized musical works.

When an expert opinion is requested by one of the parties, it is necessary to indicate precisely the scope of the matter that will be subject to expert analysis; otherwise, the request will be dismissed. The judge can refuse to hear experts requested by the parties if he feels it is unnecessary, or he believes the request has been made merely to delay proceedings.

The conclusions of the experts appointed by the court are written in a report. The parties and the judge have an opportunity to object, or request that the expert report be perfected in some way. Cross-examination (as such) of experts is not provided in Portuguese civil procedural law but they can and do often go to court to clarify their report. A second expert opinion also may be requested by the court or by the parties within ten days of being notified of the conclusions of the first opinion.

Witness Evidence

Witness evidence is a fundamental aspect of copyright infringement cases, particularly expert witnesses on the issue of proving infringement and damages caused. The rules regarding witness evidence are generally the same as those in other EU jurisdictions although, in civil actions, there is a limit to the number of witnesses that can be presented, and there are other situations where witness evidence can be denied.

Portuguese procedural law accepts witnesses to provide testimony through video calls if done through equipment in another court closer to the residence of the witness. Cross-examination is possible, as is hearsay. According to the rules of the Portuguese Bar Association, coaching witnesses is expressly prohibited.

Confessions and Other Forms of Evidence

In addition to the forms described above, other types of evidence are accepted in the civil courts. These include confessions, depositions, court inspections, and legal presumptions that shift the burden of proof from one party to the other. Foreign court decisions on the same matter are useful as an influence on the Portuguese court, but they carry no official value.

There are some legal presumptions that are central to copyright infringement cases, such as the presumption that the author of a work is the person whose name is placed on the work in the customary manner.[28]

---

[28] Copyright and Related Rights Code, Article 27(1).

In light of the fact that copyright registration is not mandatory in Portugal, this legal presumption allows the author to establish legitimacy in the proceedings simply by showing that his name was placed on the work in the customary way. If the opposing party wishes to dispute authorship of the work or the ownership of the copyright, the burden of proof falls on it.

Evidence-Gathering Measures

Since the implementation of the Enforcement Directive by Law Number 16/2008, of 1 April 2008, Portuguese copyright law has contained several legal provisions aimed at facilitating the gathering and preservation of evidence.

Indeed, given the intangible nature of intellectual property rights, one of the difficulties that copyright owners have always had is the gathering of evidence of the infringing actions. The evidence- gathering measures that were implemented into the law in 2008 seek to fill this gap.

Interim Relief and Other Measures

Cease-and-Desist Letters

Experience has shown that the overwhelming majority of copyright infringement cases in Portugal result from a lack of knowledge of the law. There are many that assume that by owning the tangible object in which a work is incorporated (i.e., a book, a music CD, a newspaper, or other such works), they are allowed to make an unlimited number of copies, place the content on the Internet, or exploit the work in some other way.

Given the general ignorance of the law, it is often advisable, but not mandatory, to send an initial warning cease-and-desist letter. In many cases, by pointing out the legal provisions that the recipient of the letter has infringed with his actions, it is possible to cease the unlawful use in a fast and inexpensive manner.

Notwithstanding the above, when planning to proceed with such a cease and desist letter it is always advisable to obtain as much evidence as possible before contacting or alerting the infringer. Taking simple precautions such as having a public notary certify that on a certain date a specific website had certain content can sometimes make the difference if the case goes to court.

Contrary to what occurs in some other European countries, it is not customary practice in Portugal to request compensation in a cease-and-desist letter, although some attempts are sporadically made. It is, therefore, important to remember that, when deciding to engage an attorney to draft and send a cease and desist letter, those costs of enforcement will, in the majority of the cases, have to be borne by the copyright owner.

Preliminary Injunctions

Preliminary injunctions (*providências cautelares*) are provided in general procedural law and in legislation specific to copyright law. Until April 2008, preliminary injunctions followed the normal non-specific procedural rules established under the Civil Procedure Code. As mentioned, the Parliament passed legislation implementing the Enforcement Directive, thus bringing about a new reform of the Copyright and Related Rights Code.

Because of the implementation of this Directive, Portuguese intellectual property enforcement procedures were substantially reinforced and harmonized with those of its European partners. The preliminary injunction regime included in article 210-G of the Copyright and Related Rights Code provides two scenarios, the first being a situation in which the copyright owner wishes to prevent an imminent infringement of his copyright and the second being a situation where the copyright owner wishes to stop the continuance of the alleged ongoing infringement. The criteria for the issuance of a preliminary injunction are different based on the scenario in question.

For the issuance of an *inter partes* preliminary injunction based on the imminent infringement of copyright, the applicant must demonstrate to the court that there is *fumus boni iuris* (i.e., *prima facie* evidence of the existence of the right and its infringement) and *periculum in mora* (i.e., fear of suffering irreparable or serious damage in case the preliminary injunction is not granted).

These requirements are the same as those that would be necessary for the grant of an *ex parte* preliminary injunction. The temporal urgency requirement is usually assessed under the *periculum in mora*; however, there is no set rule or standard on the temporal urgency requirement and each court is entitled to come to its own conclusions regarding whether this urgency criterion has been met based on the facts presented to it.

In the second scenario, i.e., in which the copyright owner requests a preliminary injunction in order to stop the continuance of an alleged ongoing infringement, it emerges from the law (followed by case law) that it is not necessary to assert *periculum in mora*. In other words, the copyright owner need not demonstrate the risk of suffering irreparable or serious damage in case the preliminary injunction is not granted. It is, therefore, established practice to grant preliminary injunctions when it is demonstrated, on a prima *facie basis*, that there is a valid and existing copyright and an actual ongoing infringement of that right.

There is case law that also states that, since there is no need to show *periculum in mora*, the court is not required to assess urgency or consider arguments of proportionality (meaning that the court cannot refuse to grant a preliminary injunction when the harm resulting to the defendant exceeds the injury that the claimant intends to avoid through that same preliminary injunction).

An *ex parte* injunction can be authorized by a judge when there are convincing arguments or proof that it would not be effective if the defendant were previously warned. There also have been various cases in which the Intellectual Property Court has granted a preliminary injunction when the infringement was clear but it was not possible to identify the infringer (e.g., illegal film or sports streaming sites).

To a certain degree, it is up to the court's discretion to grant a preliminary injunction. Weak evidence of infringement or threatened infringement, problems with the evidence of authorship or ownership, the time taken by the preliminary injunction applicant to react, lack of use of the work in the market, and other such factors may all contribute towards the rejection of a preliminary injunction application.

Administrative Injunctions

Without prejudice to normal preliminary injunctions (described above), the copyright owner can request that the police and administrative authorities provide the location where the copyright infringement is taking place to immediately suspend the use or reproduction of the protected works and, in addition, the seizure of all the revenue of the event.[29]

Although difficult to apply in practice, this is a powerful tool for copyright owners in the cinema, theatre, and music fields. This legal provision allows, for example, for the police authorities to close down a café, music concert, and other establishments while the infringement is occurring.

---

[29] Copyright and Related Rights Code, Article 209.

Seizure of Assets

Another main type of interim relief provided in the Copyright and Related Rights Code and civil procedural law is the seizure of assets (*arresto*).

The purpose of such seizure is to provide some sort of guarantee for the payment of damages should the final court ruling be in favor of the plaintiff and to seize infringing goods or instruments and machines that can only be used for producing the infringing products. In general, the *arresto* is authorized without prior notice to the infringer, provided sufficient evidence is given as to the infringement and the existence of valid copyrights.

Seizure of Evidence

The Copyright and Related Rights Code specifically provides the possibility of requesting urgent seizure of evidence. This can include a detailed description of the products made available at a certain location, or the collection of samples and physical evidence to present in court at a later date. When appropriate, this procedure also can be used to seize the materials, instruments, and documents used in the infringement of copyrights.

Border Control Measures

Portuguese customs (*alfândega*) may, on their own initiative or at the general or specific request of a right holder, suspend the release of or detain all products that are believed to infringe intellectual property rights. In order for the procedure to be effective, it is essential to provide customs with the necessary information regarding the copyright protected works and, when notified of the customs action, act in accordance with the procedures provided in EU Regulation 608/2013, which came into force on 1 January 2014 and revoked Regulation 1383/2003.

As mentioned above, Portugal does not have a system of mandatory registration for copyright-protected works. However, in order to file a customs action with the Portuguese customs authorities, it is necessary to deposit the works with IGAC and obtain a certificate of the registration. Only in this way can a copyright owner complete the customs action application in a manner that is satisfactory to the customs authorities and provide them with the level of legal security that enables them to carry out intellectual property rights enforcement at the border.

MAPiNET — Movimento Cívico Anti Pirataria na Internet

In General

Enforcing copyright through the Portuguese courts is a process that takes several months at best and requires many legal formalities. Meanwhile, with the growth of the Internet, copyright infringement has increased exponentially and can be committed very rapidly by hundreds of thousands of persons, leaving many content owners with a feeling of total helplessness and frustration.

With a view to easing the copyright infringement problem in Portugal, some of the major copyright protection stakeholders in Portugal drafted a plan on how to more effectively enforce copyright. This led to a memorandum signed on 30 July 2015 by eighteen entities,[30] with the patronage of the Secretary of State for Culture. This self-regulatory solution has been hailed as a revolution in terms of copyright enforcement and a case study throughout the world.

MAPiNET Procedures

The result of this multi-lateral cooperation effort has been a platform called MAPiNET that is managed by a civic movement with the same name (*MAPiNET, Movimento Cívico Anti Pirataria na Internet*). The manner in which the MAPiNET system operates is as follows:

(1) Upon becoming aware of copyright infringing content (e.g., a motion picture or a song that is made available online without the necessary authorization), the copyright owner denounces the situation to MAPiNET.

---

30 Inspeção Geral das Atividades Culturais (IGAC); Direção Geral do Consumidor (DGC); Associação dos Operadores de Telecomunicações (APRITEL); Associação Portuguesa das Agências de Publicidade, Comunicação e Marketing (APAP); Associação Portuguesa das Agências de Meios (APAME); Associação Portuguesa de Anunciantes (APAN); Associação (DNS.PT); Movimento Cívico Anti Pirataria na Internet (MAPINET) em representação dos seus associados: AFP – Associação Fonográfica Portuguesa; APEL – Associação Portuguesa de Editores e Livreiros; API – Associação Portuguesa de Imprensa; AUDIOGEST – Associação para a Gestão e Distribuição de Direitos; ASSOFT – Associação Portuguesa de Software; FEVIP – Associação Portuguesa de Defesa de Obras Audiovisuais; GDA – Cooperativa de Gestão dos Direitos dos Artistas, Intérpretes ou Executantes, CRL; GEDIPE – Associação para a Gestão de Direitos de Autor, Produtores e Editores; VISAPRESS – Gestão de Conteúdos dos Media, CRL.

(2) MAPiNET attempts to contact the site and informs them that they have been denounced and that they have the opportunity to reply and justify the use of the copyright-protected content. MAPiNET does its own research to see if the site merits enforcement. The criteria that is used by MAPiNET is whether the site contains at least 500 illegal works or if two-thirds of the site's content is pirated.
(3) If there is no response or the users of the content are unable to show that they have the necessary authorization, a complaint is made to IGAC. In accordance with the agreement, MAPiNET expects to send to IGAC two blocks of 50 piracy sites per month.
(4) IGAC notifies the Internet Service Providers (ISPs) and DNS (the entity in Portugal that manages the .pt domain names) and orders them to block the websites that have been denounced.
(5) The ISPs and DNS have assumed the commitment of complying with IGAC's order within 15 days and placing on the offending sites the notices "site unavailable" or "site not found".

The MAPiNET solution is seen by copyright owners as a welcome revolution in Portugal given that it is fast, inexpensive, and does not rely on any judicial intervention. Naturally, there are those on the other side of the barricade that criticize and complain of the lack of due process and judicial control that leads to situations of abuse and illegality. At present, the MAPiNET solution is highly recommended for copyright owners that wish to prevent or halt illegal streaming and placing of content on the Internet.

Copyright Infringement Criminal Proceedings

Criminal Proceedings Related to Copyright Infringement

With the exception of the infringement of an author's moral rights, all other crimes cited in the Copyright and Related Rights Code are considered public crimes and, therefore, do not require a complaint to initiate the proceedings.

In other words, the police and the Public Prosecutor's Office have not only the ability, but also the obligation, to open an enquiry when they suspect a copyright infringement crime has been committed. It is common for police authorities to raid fairs, markets, and office buildings in search of copyright infringing goods such as fake music CDs, DVDs, and software. In these raids, the police authorities often seize hundreds or thousands of infringing goods.

During the enquiry stage, the Public Prosecutor's Office collects evidence (or instructs the police authorities to collect it on their behalf) as to whether a crime has been committed. The person suspected of having committed the crime and placed under investigation is given the status of *arguido*, which provides that person with certain rights and obligations.

During the investigation stage, the criminal court can apply certain measures to prevent the continuance of the crime and destruction of evidence, prevent the flight of the suspected party, and ensure the security of other third parties. In exceptionally serious cases, it is possible to detain and imprison someone preventatively for a certain period.

If, based on the evidence collected, the Public Prosecutor's Office is convinced that a crime has been committed and it would be able to secure a conviction, it must press criminal charges against the infringer. The person charged with the criminal charges often has the opportunity to request that a court judge confirm that the requisites for a criminal case are present and that the case should go to trial (*abertura de instrução*).

If the case goes to trial, the Public Prosecutor's Office must try to support the accusation by providing evidence and the *arguido* will try to defend himself. Portugal guarantees all the same legal principles that can be found in other European jurisdictions, such as the presumption of innocence, *in dubio pro reo*, the right to not self-incriminate, and *non bis in idem*.

Portuguese criminal law further provides many guarantees and safeguards to those accused of crimes, and there are generally multiple opportunities to appeal decisions, acceptance of evidence, and convictions. It also is possible for third parties (the injured parties or other interested parties) to request to join the proceedings as assistants (*assistentes*) of the Public Prosecutor's Office. Although provided in the law, imprisonment for copyright infringement is rare. The majority of those convicted of copyright infringement are ordered to pay fines or otherwise have jail sentences suspended.

Proceedings Related to Crime of Infringement of Moral Rights

As mentioned above, the only situation in which a complaint is mandatory to initiate criminal proceedings is when an author's moral rights have been infringed. The complaint must be filed within six months of obtaining knowledge of the offense. After the complaint is filed, the proceedings follow essentially the same steps as those described above.

In criminal cases related to the infringement of moral rights, it is possible for the author to request to the court that instead of the destruction of the infringing copies, they should be handed over to the author for him to rectify them if possible, namely, placing the proper identification of the author or making the changes that are necessary for the integrity of the work to be respected.

Costs

The cost of copyright litigation in Portugal varies tremendously from case to case due to the complexity, time needed, size of the litigation team, and so forth. Court fees for prosecuting a copyright-related case also will fluctuate depending on the complexity of the proceedings and how they develop.

Nevertheless, it is possible to make the general statement that litigating in Portugal is generally far less expensive than in other countries, where hourly rates tend to be higher than those found in Portugal and can involve extensive discovery of documents. As a rule, the losing party pays the winner's court fees and a contribution towards attorneys' fees. In those cases where there is no loser in the declaratory action, it will be the person who benefited from the action who will bear the court costs. If there are various losing parties, costs will be divided among them.

Whereas legal fees were traditionally not considered in the compensation granted to the winning party, Article 211(2) of the Copyright and Related Rights Code implicitly provides the recovery of legal fees related to the investigation and enforcement actions. However, as mentioned above, there is still no firm case law on this, and the winning party tends to be unable to recover all legal fees.

Conclusion

Portugal is a long-standing member of the EU and has joined most of the major copyright-related international treaties. It is not surprising, therefore, that one finds the same or similar substantive legal rules in Portugal that can be found in other EU Member-States that have a similar legal tradition. However, the interpretation of those substantive legal provisions by the Portuguese courts sometimes strays from settled case law elsewhere, which can lead to some surprising decisions.[31]

Where the more significant differences arise is in the procedural aspects. Portuguese procedural law is a complex system, particularly for copyright infringement in which the copyright owner must make a choice between following the civil liability path or the criminal liability one. The way a copyright infringement case is litigated in Portugal, the evidence that must be produced, the deadlines, and the legal presumptions are different from what one finds in other jurisdictions and, therefore, it is advisable that these type of cases be handled by attorneys and law firms that are experienced in copyright infringement litigation.

Above all, the speed with which technology is changing the manner in which people consume and share copyright-protected works requires lawmakers, not only in Portugal but also on the international scene, to reflect deeply about how copyright law should be reformed and dispute resolution mechanisms improved.

---

[31] The Supreme Court decision published in the *Official Bulletin* of 16 December 2013, dealing with the difference between broadcasting and communication to the public, was controversial for apparently having conflicted with settled European Court of Justice case law.

Russia

Taras Derkatsch
Beiten Burkhardt
Moscow, Russia

Introduction

The regulation of copyright in Russia has seen significant changes since 2008, when Part 4 of the Civil Code entered into force. Part 4 governs all items of intellectual property, from inventions, utility models, and industrial prototypes to trade marks and copyrighted material.

In 2013, due to the need to provide rights holders with additional, more effective protection of their online rights, amendments were made to the Federal Law on Information, Information Technology, and the Protection of Information. These amendments gave rights holders the ability to block websites containing unlicensed content. Current practice in the application of this law has proved fairly positive for rights holders. However, the illegal posting of content such as music, audiovisual works (films), and literature online is not the only way that copyright is infringed. Copyright violations such as the illegal distribution of computer software and illegal implementation of design or architectural solutions also are common.

Russian Intellectual Property Law

Russian intellectual property law is entirely codified in the Civil Code and is contained in Part 4 of the Code, which entered into force on 1 January 2008. Part 4 of the Civil Code has a pandect structure typical of many continental legal systems divided into a general section and a special section.

The general section provides an exhaustive list of items of intellectual property, describes the content of the exclusive rights and powers of the rights holder, establishes the effective term of exclusive rights and provisions on the state registration of separate items of intellectual property (e.g., inventions), and regulates contracts on the alienation of exclusive rights and licensing agreements.

The special section of Part 4 of the Civil Code is dedicated to governing specific items of intellectual property, grouped based on their common legal and actual natures and similarity of legal regulation. Part 4 contains chapters on patent law (which governs inventions, utility models, and industrial prototypes), copyright (which governs copyright and software), and rights to means of identification (which contains detailed provisions on trade marks, trade mark registration procedures, and powers of the rights holders).

However, Part 4 does not constitute the entire body of legal regulation of intellectual property. Russia is signatory to numerous international treaties and conventions relating to intellectual property. These include the 1883 Paris Convention for the Protection of Intellectual Property, the 1886 Berne Convention for the Protection of Literary and Artistic Works, the Madrid trade mark agreements, and other international treaties related to intellectual property. Russia is a member of the World Trade Organization (WTO) and the Agreement on Trade-Related Aspects of Intellectual Property Rights (TRIPS).

Copyright

In General

In accordance with Article 1259 of the Civil Code, copyrighted items include works of science, art, and literature, regardless of the work's merits and purpose and regardless of the means of its expression (e.g., literary works, musical works with or without text, audiovisual works, geographical maps and other maps, and works of architecture and design).

Items of copyright also include computer programs that are protected as literary works, and databases, protected as composite works. In addition to traditional copyrighted materials (works of literature, art, and science), copyright in Russia also protects more specific items, some of which will be considered below.

Pursuant to Clause 6 of Article 1259 of the Civil Code, items of copyright do not include official documents of the state authorities (e.g., laws and court decisions), state symbols and emblems (e.g., banknotes), works of folk art without specific authors, and reports of events and facts that are purely informational in nature (e.g., bus schedules and television listings). Nor does copyright extend to ideas, concepts, principles, methods, processes, systems, tools, solutions to technical, organizational or other problems, discoveries, facts, programming languages, and geological information on the subsoil.

From both a theoretical and a practical standpoint, the most disputed issue is the criteria to deteremine if works are protectable. Article 1257 of the Civil Code states that the author of a work is recognized as the person through whose creative labor the work was made. In other words, the Civil Code recognizes that the main criterion for the protectability of a work is the creative nature of the labor of its author. Russian legislation does not contain a definition of the term "creative labor" or "creativity" as a whole. The Supreme Court interprets this standard as follows:

> "When analysing the issue as to whether a specific result is an item of copyright, courts should take into consideration the fact that in the sense of Articles 1228, 1257, and 1259 of the Civil Code of Russia with reference to each other, only a result made through creative labour is such a thing. At the same time, it should be kept in mind that unless proven otherwise, intellectual property is assumed to have been made through creative labour.
>
> "It also must be remembered that in and of itself the absence of novelty, uniqueness, and/or originality of intellectual property is not evidence that this intellectual property was made not through creative labour, and consequently is not an item of copyright.[1]"

In one case,[2] a television station showed a video clip of a volcanic eruption, taken by an individual on the Kamchatka Peninsula in northeast Russia. The individual filed a claim in court against the station for the payment of compensation; however, both the Court of First Instance and the Court of Appeals dismissed the claim, citing the fact that the individual had not planned the subject in advance, had not created a scenario, and had not employed a creative means of recording the image.

In other words, the events recorded in the video were not created through the creative labor of the claimant. In addition, the uniqueness was not in the video recorded by the claimant *per se*, but in the unique natural phenomenon — the volcanic eruption. Thus, by itself, the video file reflecting the ongoing events did not meet the criteria of novelty, uniqueness, or originality and, consequently, was not subject to copyright. However, the Court of Cassation overturned the decisions of the

---

[1] Judgment Number 5 of the Plenum of the Supreme Court of the Russian Federation and Judgment Number 29 of the Plenum of the Supreme Commercial Court of the Russian Federation of 26 March 2009, Clause 28.
[2] Decision of the Commercial Court of Kamchatka Region of 30 July 2013, Case Number A24-1669/2013.

lower courts. The Court proceeded on the assumption that the process of creating any photograph or video recording is creative activity. A cameraman selects the exposure, sites the object of the recording in space, selects a position from which to record, and adapts the location to available light. Thus, the cameraman's copyright was recognized and compensation from the broadcaster was awarded.

Thus, an item is considered protectable from the standpoint of copyright unless proven otherwise, even if such an item is not new, unique, or original. Previously, before the entry into force of Part 4 of the Civil Code, courts did proceed on the assumption that, if a work was not new, unique, or original, the work could not be recognized as an item of copyright.[3]

Such blurred boundaries for the protectability of works are only possible under conditions of their protection by virtue of the very fact of their creation. Therefore, no special registration of copyright is required in Russia. Copyright arises for the author by virtue of the fact of creation of the work. In this situation, many parties may assume that they hold copyright over specific items that, in essence, are not works. However, it has been noted in legal literature that this lowering of requirements on items of copyright is indicative of a general trend in this area occurring all over the world.

In the event of a dispute, the courts will draw the final conclusion regarding the protectability of such items. In this regard, in certain cases, Russian courts reject claims of copyright infringement, citing the fact that the protected work is not an item of copyright. Thus, reports on events and facts that are exclusively informational in nature (e.g., reports of the news of the day, television listings, and transport schedules) are not items of copyright. In one case, a newspaper article contained information on cities, indicating their populations, major production and economic facilities, and other statistical data. The editorial board of another publication copied this information and published it on their website. The court concluded that in this case the newspaper article was not an item of copyright, since it constituted a report on facts that were exclusively informational in nature.[4]

Court practice on geographical maps as items of copyright also is interesting. The Russian Supreme Court has noted that the creation of

---

[3] North-Caucasus District Federal Commercial Court Judgment Number F08-5998/2007 of 17 September 2007, Case Number A53-13387/2006-S4-38.
[4] Moscow District Federal Commercial Court Judgment Number KG-A40/8665-11 of 17 August 2011, Case Number A40-30624/10-51-226; Intellectual Property Court Judgment Number S01-305/2015 of 24 April 2015, Case Number A46-10011/2014.

maps may be technical and production-related in nature, and may be the result of scientific activity, i.e., may be creative in nature.[5] Accordingly, in certain cases, geographical maps will be items of copyright and may be protected in court.

Thus, in one case, the claimant was a company that compiled a map of a Russian city. The respondent had used an illustration in its advertising materials showing its location and how to get there. The court recognized the claimant's map as an item of copyright, but did not find the actions of the respondent to constitute infringement, since the graphic used in the respondent's advertising materials was based on generally known facts that were informational in nature. The similarity between the claimant's map and the simplified graphic used by the respondent followed from the uniformity of the information and facts underlying both representations.[6]

Today, companies frequently use maps in the "contacts" section of their websites to show where the company is located. In this case, if the company that uses a map fragment has not concluded the relevant agreement with the rights holder to the map, the court will recognize an infringement of the mapmaker's copyright.[7] For this reason, a number of companies have decided not to use maps from Google or Yandex in their "Contacts" section, preferring to create their own schematic maps.

In connection with copyright protectability, copyright protects not only a work as a whole but also any part thereof. By virtue of Clause 7 of Article 1259 of the Civil Code, copying extends to the name of the work and the characters of the work, if by their nature they can be considered the independent result of the author's creative labor.

Court practice recognizes as independent protectable subjects of copyright such characters as Fröken Bock[8] (a character from the Soviet cartoon "Karlsson Returns"), Matroskin the Cat[9] (a character from the series of Soviet cartoons about the village of Prostokvashino), Masha[10]

---

5 Ruling Number 306-ES14-5432 of the Judicial College on Economic Disputes of the Supreme Court of the Russian Federation of 8 April 2015.
6 Judgment Number 2096/07 of the Presidium of the Supreme Commercial Court of the Russian Federation of 26 June 2007.
7 Judgment of the Volgo-Vyatsky District Federal Commercial Court, Case Number A43-26685/2008-39-714 of 5 November 2009.
8 Intellectual Property Court Judgment Number S01-787/2016 of 21 October 2016, Case Number A40-83318/2015.
9 Intellectual Property Court Judgment Number S01-811/2017 of 5 October 2017, Case Number SIP-150/2017.
10 Intellectual Property Court Judgment Number S01-414/2017 of 9 June 2017, Case Number A82-7654/2016.

(a character from the modern Russian cartoon "Masha and the Bear"), and many others. At the same time, the Supreme Court noted that, in order to receive protection, a character in the work must possess a group of characteristics that make it original, recognizable, and distinct from other protagonists of the work by virtue of external appearance, movement, voice, expressions, and other qualities intended for visual and audio perception.[11]

In this regard, Article 1259 of the Civil Code understands part of the work to mean not only its name and characters, but also excerpts of the literary work (e.g., phrases and word combinations) and individual frames or excerpts of an audiovisual work, including audio (e.g., without images). However, they can be recognized as parts of the corresponding work, eligible for independent legal authorial protection, if they show sufficient originality arising as the result of the creative labor of the author.

The effective term of exclusive rights to a work is established by Article 1281 of the Civil Code as seventy years from 1 January of the year following the year of death of the author. If the work is created in co-authorship, the exclusive right to such work is in effect throughout the entire life of the last surviving author plus seventy years, reckoned from 1 January of the year following their death.[12]

On the expiration of the valid term of exclusive rights, the work passes into the public domain.[13] This means that this work may be freely used by anyone without requiring consent or permission and without paying royalties. The following rights belong to the author of a work:

(1) Exclusive rights to the work;
(2) Right of authorship;
(3) Right of the author to a name;
(4) Right to the inviolability of the work; and
(5) Right to the release of the work.

Other than the exclusive right to the work, all of the other listed rights are moral rights. If such rights are infringed, Russian legislation provides the possibility of compensation for moral damages.[14]

---

11 Award of the Supreme Court of the Russian Federation of 11 June 2015; in violation of copyright, the burden of proof for the resulting circumstances lies with the claimant, Case Number 309-ES14-7875.
12 Civil Code, Article 1281, Clause 1, Paragraph 2.
13 Civil Code, Article 1282, Clause 1.
14 Civil Code, Article 151.

Computer Software

One of the items of copyright in Russia that is most relevant to business is computer software (programs). At the same time, it should be noted that Russian statutory regulation of computer programs does not always keep pace with rapid technical progress.

Under Russian legislation, computer programs are protected as literary works. There is no special, detailed legal regulation of computer programs, and the corresponding disputes do not become the subject of judicial proceedings all that often. The Civil Code understands a computer program to mean the objectively presented aggregate of data and commands intended for the functioning of a computer and other computing devices for the purposes of obtaining a specific result.[15] The preparatory materials obtained during the development of the computer program and the audiovisual imagery produced by it are included in the concept of a computer program and are protected accordingly.

In this regard, effective practice has yet to be formed in Russia regarding the protection of merely the audiovisual imagery of a computer program. Only a few decisions are known. Specifically, in one case, the court denied protection of software rights because only the program's interface was provided for expert evaluation and, as the experts indicated, it is not acceptable to compare programs by their interfaces alone. This is due to the fact that the images sent to the screen by the program may be created using a virtually unlimited number of algorithms (i.e., externally identical programs may work differently).[16] Thus, the mere fact of a coincidence of interfaces may be insufficient to prove infringement of a computer program.

Like other literary works, computer programs are not subject to registration and are protected by virtue of their creation. The Russian patent agency keeps a state register of computer programs, in which each author may register his authorship of a computer program. The register is entirely voluntary. It does not establish rights but aims only to make it easier to prove authorship to a program in the event of a dispute, since it establishes the need for the other party to prove the contrary.

Gaps in statutory regulation of computer programs are especially evident in the example of the acceptability of revisions to the program. Russian legislation understands a revision (modification) of a computer program to mean any changes to it, including translation from one

---

15 Civil Code, Article 1261.
16 Appeals Ruling of Moscow Municipal Court of 20 February 2014, Case Number 33-3436/2014.

language to another, other than adaptation, i.e., amendments made exclusively for the purpose of having the program function on the user's specific technical devices or under the administration of the user's specific programs.[17] For example, revisions of a computer program include its translation from one language to another, the creation of a derivative program that substantially borrows the source code of the initial program, or one that adds new functions to the initial program.

As a general rule, revision of a program is permitted only with the consent of the rights holder. If no particular legal issues arise with the translation of a program from one language to another (even though here, too, there is an ongoing discussion as to whether the law's drafters had in mind the translation of the interface from one human language to another or a translation from one programming language to another), the issue of how substantial the revision of the source code must be to result in the creation of a derivative work (new program) is not so obvious.

In court practice, one can find positions that argue that the creation of a derivative program means the borrowing of a large part of the source code of the program being revised.[18] As the same time, revision as a type of creative activity should lead to a change in the source code of the program being revised.[19] The courts usually determine the percentage of borrowing of source code of the program being revised by ordering the corresponding expert evaluation.[20]

Web Pages

The online segment of business activity in Russia is on a significant upswing. Virtually every business seeks to make sure that it has an Internet presence. One of the traditional means of doing business using the Internet is the creation of a company website (usually with an eponymous domain name), where advertising and other materials related to the company's operations are published.

The creation of a website (its content) may be protected as a special type of work, i.e., as an item of copyright. The principles for determining the protectability of such a non-traditional item of copyright are

---

[17] Civil Code, Article 1270, Clause 2, Sub-Clause 9.
[18] Intellectual Property Court Judgment Number S01-328/2016 of 21 November 2016, Case Number A56-21040/2015.
[19] Intellectual Property Court Judgment Number S01-1269/2016 of 21 March 2017, Case Number A40-154016/2014.
[20] Judgment Number 17AP-13101/2012-GK of the Seventeenth Commercial Appeal Court of 27 March 2013, Case Number A60-27815/2012.

becoming clear from recent court practice.[21] In a court order, the Supreme Court described the content of a website as the aggregate of "materials specially selected and arranged in a particular way (text, drawings, and photographs), which may be used with the help of a computer program (computer code) that is an element of the site".

The Court also explicitly indicated that the content of the website is a composite work in the sense of Articles 1259 and 1260 of the Civil Code. Accordingly, the composite work may not be used by third parties without the consent of the author (normally, the owner of the site). Exclusive rights to the content of the website may be freely licensed and alienated to any parties at the discretion of the rights holder.

Theatrical Shows and Audiovisual Works

The example of theatrical shows and audiovisual works (e.g., films and clips) can illustrate the differing approach of Russian legislation to the regulation of complex items of copyright that consist of a multitude of independent works (e.g., screenplay, music, and video footage).

According to Clause 1 of Article 1240 of the Civil Code, the party that organizes the creation of a complex item that includes several protectable intellectual properties (e.g., film, other audiovisual production, theatrical presentation, multimedia product, and database) acquires the right to use the given results on the basis of agreements on the alienation of exclusive rights or licensing agreements concluded by such party with the holders of exclusive rights to the corresponding intellectual properties.

By virtue of the explicit indication of Clause 4 of Article 1263 of the Civil Code, as a general rule, the exclusive right to an audiovisual work as a whole belongs to the producer, i.e., the party that organized the creation of the work. In other words, Russian legislation regards the audiovisual work as a unified item of copyright, the right to dispose of which belongs by force of law to a single subject (the producer). This approach substantially simplifies the practice of the public rental of an audiovisual work and the collection of the corresponding remuneration. All potential users interact only with a single, easily identifiable party that holds exclusive rights to the audiovisual work.

However, Russian legislators did not make a similar stipulation with respect to a theatrical production and, as a result, establishing the rights

---

21 Judgment of the Supreme Court of the Russian Federation of 13 September 2016 in Cases Number 305-ES16-7224 and Number A40-26249/2015.

holder for a theatrical production is a somewhat more complicated task. Proceeding from the positions reflected in court practice, a theatrical production does not have a single rights holder, and it is not an independent item of copyright.[22] The party that organized the creation of the theatrical production (usually, the theatrical studio or producer's center) "holds" the bundle of exclusive rights on the basis of contracts concluded thereby with the authors of the individual components of the show (e.g., script and music).

In practice, this situation creates certain difficulties, since the contractual documentation for public shows of a theatrical production requires a more detailed and considered approach. For example, if the creator "holds" exclusive rights on the basis of licenses, when organizing a public performance of the theatrical production it will conclude sublicensing agreements with the relevant venue.

Items of Design and Architectural Works

Of separate interest are such protectable items of copyright as items of design (e.g., furniture) and architectural works. As a general rule,[23] the practical application of the provisions constituting the content of the work, including provisions making up the technical, economic, organizational, or other solution, does not constitute the use of the work. One exception has been made to this rule. Practical implementation is use of such copyrighted material as an architectural draft, design, and urban-planning or landscape projects.

Pursuant to Sub-Clause 10 of Clause 2 of Article 1270 of the Civil Code, the practical implementation of architectural draft, designs, and urban-planning or landscape projects is considered to be use of the work, regardless of whether the actions are taken for the purpose of generating a profit or without such purpose. Moreover, in respect of works of architecture, the Civil Code prohibits their use in the form of reproduction (practical implementation) even for personal use, if such practical implementation is made without the consent of the rights holder.

The content of the concept of an architectural work has received detailed interpretation in court practice. The Presidium of the Supreme

---

[22] Intellectual Property Court Judgment Number S01-113/2013 of 10 August 2015, Case Number A76-13283/2012.
[23] Civil Code, Article 1270, Clause 3.

Commercial Court of the Russian Federation has made the following conclusions regarding the boundaries of protectability of an architectural work:

"Taking into account the specifics of architectural activity consisting of a two-stage procedure for the manifestation of an architectural solution, the legislators stipulated two forms of its objectification: either in the form of a work of architecture, town planning and landscape design, and in the form of designs, drawings, images and mock-ups, protected by copyright.

"For this reason, for the purposes of establishing the presence (absence) of the unlawful use of an architectural work, it is essential to identify in the disputed item the idea, the conception (architectural solution), and compare it with the architectural solution embodied in the protected item, regardless of the objective form (architectural design or architectural object) of the solutions being compared.

"Identification of infringement of copyright to a work of architecture is possible when comparing a design with a design, a design with an object, or an object with an object. Each of these means of proof may confirm the infringement of copyright to a work of architecture. The means of proof of copyright infringement is chosen by the claimant."[24]

Of interest are the provisions of Russian copyright law in respect of items of design. According to Clause 1 of Article 1259 of the Civil Code, works of design are items independent of copyright. Under the general rule, as copyrighted material, works of design are not subject to state registration. However, if this item of design can simultaneously be registered as an industrial prototype, the rights holder is entitled to carry out such registration (and receive the relevant patent). However, the rights holder also is entitled not to register the work of design as an industrial prototype and to protect it only as a copyrighted work.

If the rights holder can demonstrate the existence of rights to the work of design, and the fact of the practical implementation of the work of design by the infringer, the rights holder is entitled to demand that the

---

24 Judgment Number 7697/12 of the Presidium of the Supreme Commercial Court of the Russian Federation of 6 November 2012, Case Number A60-10618/2011.

violation cease and that losses or compensation be paid and to exercise other rights to protect its work of design. The question that arises in this regard relates to cases where the infringer does not produce an exact copy of the design but merely an item strongly similar to it. As the Intellectual Property Court notes,[25] copyright does not rely on the terms "similarity to the point of confusion" or "identity" (which are characteristic of trade marks). Other categories are inherent in copyright:
(1) "Reproduction of a work", which means exact reproduction of the copyrighted material; and
(2) "Derivative work", which means a conversion of the work.

In other words, if the rights holder has created a work of design and its competitor reproduces not exactly the same work of design, but something similar, the rights holder must prove that the infringer converted its initial design. It should be taken into consideration that Judgment Number 2995/10 of the Presidium of the Supreme Commercial Court of the Russian Federation of 20 July 2010 contains a legal position under which the use of a work in the form of an illegal conversion and its distribution are two distinct cases of generating profit from the unjust use of a work, which form independent *corpora delicti* and serve as the grounds for collecting compensation for each of such cases.

Management of Copyright on Collective Basis

For the rights holder of a specific work, especially if the work is popular (e.g., hit songs), it is extremely difficult, whether independently or with the help of their promoters or producers, to monitor the lawfulness of the use of these songs, even in a single country, to say nothing of the entire world.

Instead of authors, in many countries (including Russia), special non-profit organizations have been founded for the collective management of copyright. The authors provide these organizations with the right to collect compensation from parties that use the authors' works. In so doing, authors themselves determine the list of works for the use of which they would like to receive compensation. After receiving compensation from users of works, the organization transfers it to the authors, withholding a small amount to support its operations. For example,

---

25 Intellectual Property Court Judgment of 30 March 2016, Case Number A76-12136/2014.

the largest Russian organization on collective copyright management, the Russian Authors' Society, retains five per cent of collected compensation.

Together with the system described above for collecting authors' compensation enshrined in Articles 1242 and 1243 of the Civil Code, which follows directly from the principle of freedom of contract, Russia also has "accredited organizations on collective copyright management" (which includes the Russian Authors' Society).

By virtue of Clause 3 of Article 1244 of the Civil Code, such an accredited organization has the right, together with the management of rights of rights holders with whom it has concluded contracts pursuant to the procedure described above, to manage rights and collect compensation for rights holders with whom it has not concluded contracts. State accreditation to perform activity in each of the areas of collective management (collecting compensation for specific means of using specific types of works) may be received by only one organization. In other words, proceeding from the law, virtually any public performance in Russia of music, for example, must be preceded by the conclusion of the corresponding contract by the user of the work with the corresponding accredited organization.

It also must be taken into consideration that, in parallel with the activity of the accredited organizations, there may be "classical" voluntary organizations on collective copyright management. Indeed, there is no prohibition on authors themselves collecting compensation for the use of their works. As a result, a situation arises where users of works (potentially all individuals and legal entities in Russia) are in an onerous position. On the one hand, users of works in good faith understand that they need to pay for the use of works. On the other hand, they sometimes cannot determine whom they should pay so that the author or accredited organization does not demand repeat payment.

Clause 4 of Article 1244 of the Civil Code, under which authors have the right at any time to decline the accredited organization's management of their rights in whole or in part by sending a written notice, does not help ease the situation since the majority of authors (e.g., virtually all foreign authors) do not suspect the existence of such accredited organizations in Russia and provide the right to use their works to users in Russia directly, receiving from them the appropriate compensation. The absurdity of this situation is best illustrated by an example from recent Russian court practice.

In May 2012, a world-famous musical group performed a concert in Moscow. The production company that organized the event concluded a contract with the group's producers. Since the group was performing songs that they themselves had composed, everyone justifiably assumed that no one other than the authors themselves had the right to receive the compensation that the production company should pay from the amount collected from the sale of concert tickets. However, two days before the concert, the production company concluded a contract with the Russian Authors' Society for the public performance of the songs of the group.

As a result, the Russian Authors' Society filed a claim for the payment of royalties with the production company, while the latter filed a claim with the Moscow Commercial Court to have the contract with the Russian Authors' Society declared void due to the absence of the subject of the contract as stated by the parties. The respondent (Russian Authors' Society) asserted that all of the compensation received would be transferred to the authors (the musical group) through the relevant foreign organization (i.e., the musicians should pay themselves and five per cent of this for the operation of the Russian Authors' Society).

Courts of three instances declared the agreement void, after which the Supreme Commercial Court as a supervisory instance overturned all of the lower courts' decisions and returned the case for a new hearing.[26] In so doing, the Court indicated that the production company's contract with the Russian Authors' Society, although not void, might be invalid by virtue of Clause 2 of Article 1243 of the Civil Code. According to Clause 2, if the licensing agreement with the user is concluded directly by the author, the collective rights management organization may only collect compensation for the use of this author's work if this is explicitly stipulated by the agreement in question. None of the courts of any instance had examined the contract of the production company with the group; therefore, the case was returned for a new hearing to the Moscow Commercial Court where, on 16 April 2013, the Court confirmed dismissal of the claim of the claimant (production company).[27]

Thus, the victor in this long court proceeding was the Russian Authors' Society, which received the right to collect compensation for the public performance of songs by the songs' own authors. This is not the only case of this kind; the Russian Authors' Society has pursued an active campaign to collect compensation for the public performance of musical works (including by their authors).

---

[26] Judgment Number 11277/12 of the Presidium of the Supreme Commercial Court of the Russian Federation of 4 December 2012, Case Number A40-74258/11-51-639.
[27] Moscow Commercial Court Judgment of 16 April 2013, Case Number A40-74258/11.

All of the foregoing is aimed at ensuring that foreign authors who organize concerts in Russia keep in mind the curious opportunity to pay for the right to sing their own songs and take the appropriate steps. To avoid this situation, in their contracts with Russian users, authors may explicitly indicate that the Russian Authors' Society and other Russian-accredited organizations for collective copyright management do not have the right to collect compensation for the use of licensed works by these users. An extreme measure would be the author's complete refusal of the collection by Russian-accredited organizations of compensation for the use of some or all of the author's works. This refusal would take the form of a written notice to each Russian-accredited organization, attaching a list of the author's works, or without a list (if the notice constitutes a blanket refusal).

Lawful Use of Works without Author's Consent

In General

As noted above, as a general rule, any use of another party's copyrighted material is only permitted with the prior consent of the rights holder. However, Russian legislation does contain a number of exceptions, instances of the so-called free use of a work, which is covered by Articles 1273–1279 of the Civil Code.

These cases can be divided into two groups. The first relates to situations where the use of a work is permitted without the consent of the author and without the payment of compensation. The second relates to cases of the use of works without the author's consent but with the payment of compensation.

Use of Works without Author's Consent and without Compensation

This group includes cases of truly free use of works, which in essence excludes the possibility of defending exclusive rights to the work. Article 1273 of the Civil Code allows citizens, when necessary, to use lawfully released works exclusively for their personal purposes. In this regard, in its Judgment of the Plenum, Number 5 of 26 March 2009, the Supreme Court noted that use exclusively for personal purposes means non-commercial use to meet the individual's needs or the needs of the normal family of the individual. Following this position of the Supreme Court, the placement of copyrighted works (e.g., photographs) on the Internet, such that a large number of people have access to them, cannot be considered use for personal purposes.

At the same time, Article 1245 provides a number of exceptions to this type of free use. For example, it does not include cases of the reproduction of computer software or databases. By virtue of Article 1245 of the Civil Code, the reproduction of sound recordings and audiovisual works (including for personal purposes) requires the payment of compensation to their authors, makers, and performers.

Pursuant to Article 1274 of the Civil Code, the following are permitted without the consent of the author or other rights holders and without the payment of compensation, but with the mandatory indication of the name of the author whose work is being used, and the source of the borrowing:

(1) Citation in the original and in translation for research, polemical, critical, informational, and educational purposes, for the purposes of disclosing the creative motive of the author of lawfully released works to the extent justified by the purpose of citation, including the reproduction of excerpts from newspaper and magazine articles in the form of press reviews;

(2) Use of lawfully released works and excerpts from them as illustrations in teaching materials, to an extent justified by the stated purpose;

(3) Use of political speeches, addresses, reports, and similar works to an extent justified by the informational purpose;

(4) Recording of the abstracts of dissertations on an electronic medium, including recording in computer memory, and their dissemination to the public; and

(5) Certain other situations.

These possibilities of free use of a work allow bad-faith actors committing infringement of authors' rights to cite this article in their defense. For example, a person may post a video to YouTube that contains negative information on a company's product. The video contains photographs of the product, and the rights holder of the photographs is the company rather than the person posting the video. In this case, if the company wishes to block the video citing the violation of its exclusive rights as an author, the company must show that the person posting the video is violating its copyright and that the use of the copyrighted works is not covered by free use.

At the same time, the infringer may assert that it is using the photographs in the video as a citation and that the citation is being used for polemical or critical purposes. In this case, the rights holder's position will be complicated from a legal standpoint since, pursuant to the position of the Supreme Court expressed in Ruling Number 305-ES16-18302 of 25 April 2017, photographs also may be cited (however, the citation must be accompanied with an indication of the name of the author whose work is being used and the source of the borrowing). Accordingly, the person posting the video and using the copyrighted photos may assert their citation for critical or polemical purposes. Another example of the free use of a work would be its use during law enforcement, at official ceremonies, or at funerals.

Use of Works Without Author's Consent but with Payment

As noted, cases of the use of a work without the author's consent but with the payment of compensation include cases of free reproduction of sound recordings and audiovisual works exclusively for personal purposes.[28]

Funds for the payment of such compensation are collected by accredited organizations for collective copyright management.[29] By virtue of Clause 1 of Article 1242 of the Civil Code, rights holders also are entitled to delegate their powers on the collection of compensation to ordinary (unaccredited) organizations for collective copyright management. In so doing, compensation is distributed among rights holders in the following proportions:

(1) Forty per cent to authors;
(2) Thirty per cent to performers; and
(3) Thirty per cent to the makers of the sound recording or audio-visual works.[30]

This compensation is paid to the rights holders from the funds that are payable to the manufacturers and importers of equipment and physical media used for the free reproduction of works for personal use. The procedure for collecting funds for the payment of compensation is regulated in detail by the Russian government.[31] Importers of the aforementioned equipment must pay a Russian-accredited organization (the Russian Rights Holders Union) remittances of one per cent of the value of equipment imported into Russia.

---

28 Civil Code, Article 1245, Clause 1.
29 Civil Code, Article 1244.
30 Resolution Number 829 of 14 October 2010 on Compensation for the Free Reproduction of Sound Recordings and Audiovisual Works for Personal Purposes.
31 Resolution Number 829 of 14 October 2010 on Compensation for the Free Reproduction of Sound Recordings and Audiovisual Work for Personal Use.

In practice, importers conclude agreements with the Russian Rights Holders Union that specify the amounts for imported equipment, which may be used for the free reproduction of works for personal use, and the amount of the corresponding remittance to the Russian Rights Holder Union. At the same time, the Russian courts usually stand on the side of the Russian Rights Holder Union, sometimes collecting payments from importers even for corporate technology that could not theoretically be used by individuals for personal use (e.g., the case of the Russian Rights Holder Union against Dell).[32]

Liability for Violation of Intellectual Rights to Copyrighted Material

Provisions on Liability

In Russian law, civil legal liability is traditionally divided into contractual and non-contractual liability. Non-contractual liability may have at its base either a tort or an unjustified enrichment. In this regard, Russian legislation contains a special feature in the area of liability arising from a contract on the use of intellectual property (specifically copyrighted material).

Under the general rule, if the rights holder has permitted the licensee to use intellectual property within a certain restricted scope, the licensee's use of the intellectual property beyond the scope is a breach of contractual obligations. For example, if the rights holder to a literary work has permitted a publishing house to publish an article in a certain number of copies, but the publisher exceeds the agreed print run, the publisher has breached the contract and, under the general rule, will be subject to liability in the form of reimbursement of losses or a contractual penalty.

The Supreme Court has held that, when such a contractual violation is committed, the first penalties to be applied should be those stipulated in the Civil Code for the violation of exclusive rights to intellectual property (as if the subject were a breach of a delictual obligation and not a contractual obligation), and contractual liability (e.g., a contractual penalty) is merely supplemental. The fact that the parties established a

---

[32] Judgment Number 305-ES16-17051 of the Supreme Court of 9 August 2017, Case Number A40-97879/2015.

contractual penalty for a violation of the license will be taken into consideration when determining the amount of monetary compensation.

However, it is rare to find contractual liability in the field of copyright. For the most part, talk of liability for copyright violations implies non-contractual liability when a third party uses copyrighted material without permission. Liability for the violation of intellectual rights (including copyright) can be considered to be a separate type of non-contractual civil liability that cannot be reduced to contractual liability, delictual liability, or liability for unjust enrichment.

The general provisions on liability for violation of intellectual rights are given in Articles 1250–1252 of the Civil Code. Remedies will depend on the type of intellectual right to be defended, i.e., personal non-property rights or exclusive (property) rights. Article 1251 of the Civil Code stipulates the following remedies for an author's personal non-property rights:

(1) Recognition of rights;
(2) Restoration of the situation prevailing prior to the violation (*restitutio ad integrum*);
(3) Suppression of actions violating rights or threatening to do so;
(4) Compensation for pain and suffering (moral damages); and
(5) Publication of a court decision on the violation committed.

Article 1252 of the Civil Code permits rights holders to make the following claims against those infringing their exclusive rights for:

(1) The recognition of a right, against a party that denies or otherwise does not recognize the right, thereby violating the interests of the rights holder;
(2) The suppression of actions violating the right or threatening to do so, against a party that performs such actions or creates the necessary preparations for them, and against other parties that may suppress such actions;
(3) The reimbursement of losses, against a party that unlawfully uses intellectual property without concluding an agreement with the rights holder or which otherwise violates its exclusive rights and causes it harm;
(4) The payment of compensation (in lieu of reimbursement of losses), against a party that unlawfully uses intellectual property without concluding an agreement with the rights holder or which otherwise violates its exclusive rights;
(5) The seizure of physical media, against the manufacturer, importer, warehouser, carrier, vendor, or other distributor or bad-faith purchaser of such media; and

(6) The publication of a court decision on the violation committed, indicating the actual rights holder — against an infringer of exclusive rights.

Civil Liability

As noted above, the author of a work has both personal non-property rights and exclusive (property) rights to their work. For their violation, Russian legislation stipulates civil liability (the relevant norms are contained in the Civil Code), administrative liability (the relevant norms are contained in the Code of Administrative Offences), and criminal liability (the relevant norms are contained in the Criminal Code).

When considering the issue of civil liability for copyright violations, it is important to consider the specifics of copyright and, specifically, the fact that authors can exercise their rights in various forms. For example, an author may permit the reproduction of a work, distribute copies of it, publicly exhibit it, and exercise other powers. In this regard, the same work can be violated by numerous means.

In a court case, a literary work (a poem) was published on a website in the form of text and in the form of an audio recording, and visitors to the site were given the ability to download the work to a mobile phone. In this regard, the Intellectual Property Court noted that the copyrighted material was violated in three different forms: publication on the site as text, publication as an audio file, and provision of the opportunity to download, i.e., release to the general public.[33] Pursuant to the Civil Code, the grounds for liability in the form of reimbursement of losses are:

(1) Wrongful act;
(2) Losses, including their amount;
(3) Causal link between them; and
(4) Culpability of the offender.

In this connection, the rights holder must prove in court that all of the aforementioned grounds are present. However, if the respondent is a party engaged in business activity (any for-profit legal entity or individual entrepreneur), the claimant is released from having to prove culpability, as this is presumed. Thus, in the commercial arena, a rights holder needs only to prove the first three grounds. However, even this

---

[33] Intellectual Property Court Judgment of 11 October 2013, Case Number A27-20650/2012.

can frequently be problematic. Certain problems can arise in proving losses. Under Russian law, losses may be expressed either as real damages (expenses that the party whose rights were violated incurred or will incur to restore their violated rights, the loss of or damage to their property) or lost profits (income that the party would have received in the normal course of business if their rights had not been violated).

As can be seen from the definitions given above, when copyright is violated, it is unlikely that losses in the form of real damages will arise for the rights holder. At the same time, losses in the form of lost profits may arise. However, Russian courts have traditionally taken a formal approach to establishing lost profits and their amounts. This is facilitated by Article 393 of the Civil Code that establishes that, when determining lost profits, it is essential to take into account measures taken by the creditor to obtain them and preparations made to this end.

As a rule, to prove losses, the rights holder uses the method of analogous licenses whereby, to prove lost profits in court, a licensing agreement is submitted that indicates the amount of licensing payments for the use of the work. Accordingly, the court proceeds on the assumption that, if the infringer concluded a licensing agreement with the rights holder, the rights holder would have received a benefit in an amount not less than in the licensing agreement submitted to the court.[34]

In this regard, Russian law offers rights holders whose copyright has been violated the opportunity to file a claim for the payment of monetary compensation instead of reimbursement of losses. In so doing, to file a claim for the payment of monetary compensation against an infringer, it is sufficient for the rights holder to prove only the fact of the offence. This significantly eases the ability of rights holders to defend their rights, since the grounds that must be proven in court are substantially reduced compared to those that must be proven for a claim for reimbursement of losses. Compensation for copyright violation is calculated as follows:

(1) RUB 10,000 to RUB 5-million, to be determined at the discretion of the court proceeding from the nature of the violation;
(2) Two times the value of the counterfeit copies of the works; and
(3) Two times the value of the right of use of the work, determined proceeding from the price normally collected under similar circumstances for the lawful use of the work by the means used by the infringer.

---

[34] Intellectual Property Court Judgment of 6 October 2017, Case Number A55-18816/2015.

The specific means of calculation of compensation is selected by the rights holder.

Protection of Copyright on Internet

In the event of a violation of copyright on the Internet, Russian legislation provides the possibility of blocking the website in question for Russia. The blocking is carried out by Roskomnadzor, the government authority responsible for oversight in the fields of information, mass communications, and information technology. To block the site, Roskomnadzor contacts hosting providers and, if they do not carry out Roskomnadzor's instructions, it has the right to contact communications operators to block the site.

Blocking is carried out exclusively on the basis of a court act that has entered into force. The act may be a court judgment on selecting a preliminary injunction or a court decision in a case that has entered into force. Thus, if the rights holder of the copyrighted material believes that its rights have been violated by a particular website, it has the right to file a claim in court to defend its rights. This applies both to websites administered within the ".ru" domain and in foreign domains (e.g., ".com", ".net", and ".de"). Of course, if a foreign website is blocked, it is blocked only for Russia, i.e., for users with a Russian Internet protocol address. The procedure indicated above for blocking a website is only available if a subject of copyright other than photographs is violated.

Before filing a claim, the rights holder is entitled to file a petition to the Moscow Municipal Court for the pre-court blocking of the website that, in the rights holder's opinion, is violating its rights. The petition may be sent in electronic form and signed with a digital signature. Several websites may be indicated in a single petition simultaneously. When considering a petition for a provisional injunction, the court focuses on two circumstances:

(1) Has the petitioner provided documents that confirm their exclusive right to the copyrighted material; and
(2) Has the petitioner provided evidence confirming the use of the given material on the websites?

As a rule, a notarized record of viewing the website would serve as such a document. The choice of a preliminary injunction also is possible if the website does not use the copyrighted material itself but merely contains information on how to obtain the material. For example, the website may contain a link to download audiovisual works (films). In this case, the website does not contain the protected copyrighted material itself but contains information on how to obtain the material. Accordingly, a petition for a preliminary injunction also can be filed against this website in the Moscow Municipal Court.

If the court grants the petition, the petitioner can contact Roskomnadzor to request blocking of the domain (as described above). The petitioner must submit a statement of claim with the Moscow Municipal Court within 15 calendar days; failing this, the court will revoke the injunction blocking the website.

Conclusion

There can be no doubt that the legal regulation of measures against copyright infringement in Russia is currently in need of improvement. This applies not only to copyright legislation itself, but also to the associated procedural legislation that allows rights holders to defend their rights in court. In this respect, many foreign companies assert the need to reduce procedural requirements, such as the provision in court of documents confirming the certificate of state registration of a legal entity.

Certain peculiarities of Russian copyright legislation are certainly related to the fact that the corresponding economic relations have not yet reached the necessary level and, as a result, there is no legal regulation of such legal relations. For example, a number of legal lacunae remain in Russian law on certain issues in the field of the protection of software. From the position of Russian law, it is not entirely clear whether software bots intended to automate computer games are a violation of the copyright of the game's rights holder.

Among other things, there are problems with traditional institutions of copyright such as the collective management of copyright, which is manifested in the lack of transparency of collective rights management. However, it must be admitted that, on the whole over the past several years, Russian law has been augmented not only with legislative innovations that allow rights holders to more effectively defend their rights, but also with the corresponding court practice, which has provided answers to many questions that arise in the defense of copyright.

Turkey

Yegân Liaje and Elçin Karatay
Pekin & Pekin
Istanbul, Turkey

Introduction

Recognition of the copyrights and the protection of rights on intellectual and artistic works began in the middle of the nineteenth century with bilateral treaties. Accordingly, the need for a uniform system led to the adoption of the Berne Convention for the Protection of Literary and Artistic Works (the "Berne Convention") of 1886.[1] Turkey became party to the Berne Convention in 1951 and accepted the amended text of the Berne Convention of Paris of 1979 on 12 July 1995.

Following the adoption of the Berne Convention, Turkey enacted the Law on Intellectual and Artistic Works, Law Number 5846, published in the *Official Gazette* of 31 December 1951, (the "Intellectual Property Law") to regulate the general rules and protection procedures regarding copyright infringement in Turkey. To reflect the changes in the legislative environment in both Turkey and the European Union (EU), the Intellectual Property Law[2] has been amended several times.

In addition to the copyright protection provisions provided under the Intellectual Property Law, if a copyright infringement constitutes unfair competition, the Commercial Code, Law Number 6102,[3] provides protection in order to sustain fair competition. If a work also constitutes an industrial property, such as a trade mark, design, patent, or geographical sign, the Law on Industrial Properties, Law Number 6769,[4] prohibits the infringement of rights on such industrial property and provides a binary protection mechanism for such works.

---

1 World Intellectual Property Organization, *WIPO Intellectual Property Handbook*, 2004, at Paragraph 5.165.
2 The law in this article is stated as of 1 September 2017 and includes the latest changes on the Intellectual Property Law, published in the *Official Gazette* of 12 December 2014.
3 *Official Gazette* of 14 February 2011.
4 *Official Gazette* of 10 January 2017.

Turkey is also a party to the Agreement on Trade Related Aspects of Intellectual Property Rights (the "TRIPS Agreement"), an international agreement administered by the World Trade Organization (WTO), as well as the Rome Convention for the Protection of Performers, Producers of Phonograms, and Broadcasting Organizations.

Works, Authorship, and Copyright under Turkish Intellectual Property Law

Works

Copyright is a right granted to protect a definite group of original works.[5] The works which are subject to protection under the Intellectual Property Law are defined as intellectual or artistic products which are deemed scientific, literary, musical work, work of fine arts, or cinematographic work, which are externalizing the characteristic of their author.[6] Accordingly, in order to be protected by the Intellectual Property Law, a work:

(1) Must bear the characteristic of its author which is the originality aspect of the work; and
(2) Must be deemed as one of the categories of work that are scientific and literary works, musical works, works of fine arts or artistic works, or cinematographic works.[7]

In addition to moral and economic rights regarding the works, the Intellectual Property Law protects the compilation of works. Under Turkish law, industrial properties, mainly trade marks, designs, patents, and geographical signs, are regulated and protected under the Law on Industrial Properties. Works that are protected under the Intellectual Property Law also can be protected under the Law on Industrial Properties, if such works are deemed as industrial property under the Law on Industrial Properties.

---

[5] Yilmaz, *Copyright in the European Union with Special Reference to Turkey* (1998), at p. 28.
[6] Intellectual Property Law, Article 1/B (a).
[7] Intellectual Property Law, Articles 2, 3, 4, and 5.

Copyright and Authorship

The works defined under the Intellectual Property Law are protected with regards to two main categories of rights which are moral rights and economic rights.[8] In principle, the moral and economic rights are subject to the ownership of the author of the work.[9]

As in most of the legal systems,[10] the Turkish law copyright system is developed on the assumption that the creator is a real person. However, the legal persons who employ or appoint civil servants, employees, and workers can exercise and exploit economic rights created by such persons during the execution of their duties[11] unless it is agreed otherwise in a contract or the nature of the work implies the contrary.

Under Turkish law, if a work is created jointly by more than one person and such work is indivisible, the creators will become joint owners of the work.[12] If the work can be divided into parts, each person will be deemed the owner of such part.[13]

The establishment of moral and economic rights is not subject to a registration procedure, and they are established following the creation of the work. However, in order to prevent violation of rights, and prove the holder of the economic and moral rights, as well as determine the person to exercise the economic rights, film producers that make the first fixation of films and phonogram producers who make the first fixation of sounds must record and register their productions containing cinematographic and musical works.[14]

Protected Rights

In General

A work defined under the Intellectual Property Law is protected with regards to two main categories of rights, which are moral rights and economic rights.[15]

---

8 Intellectual Property Law, Article 13; Berne Convention, Article 6.
9 Surmeli, *The Enforcement of Intellectual Property Rights (IPR) in Turkey in the EU Accession Process: A Perception Analysis of the Police Officers Dealing with IPR Crimes* (2011), at p. 18. Intellectual Property Law, Article 8.
10 Karnow, *Data Morphing: Ownership, Copyright and Creation* (1994), Volume 27, Number 2, at pp. 117–122.
11 Intellectual Property Law, Article 18, Paragraph 2.
12 Intellectual Property Law, Article 10, Paragraph 1.
13 Intellectual Property Law, Article 9, Paragraph 1.
14 Intellectual Property Law, Article 13, Paragraph 3.
15 Intellectual Property Law, Article 13; Berne Convention, Article 6.

Economic Rights

Turkish law provides a limited list of economic rights.[16] These are:
(1) The right of adaptation and translation;
(2) The right of reproduction;
(3) The right of distribution;
(4) The right of public performance;
(5) The right of broadcasting of the performance and making it available to the public; and
(6) The right to payment of a share on the resale of specific copies.

Unlike moral rights, economic rights can be subject to several legal transactions, such as assignment, right of lien, and right of retention. These economic rights can be used and exploited as to third parties independently from each other.[17] However, the authorship title and the work itself cannot be assigned to third parties in full.

Contracts and disposals concerning economic rights, such as assignment of economic rights, must be in writing, and the rights that are subject to such contracts or disposal must be individually specified and referred to in order for the contract or disposal to be valid.[18]

Economic rights are protected during the lifetime of the author and for seventy years after his death.[19] If there is more than one author, this period will end upon the expiry of seventy years after the death of the last remaining author. The term of protection of the derivative works, such as adaptations, are not connected to the original work and designated for the author of such derivate work.[20] Although the general time limit is seventy years after the death of the author, there are different limits on protection times for several works, such as databases, which are protected for fifteen years after disclosure to the public.[21]

Right of Adaption and Translation

The exploitation right of a work by adaptations and translations exclusively belongs to the author[22] apart from several exceptions provided by

---

[16] Intellectual Property Law, Article 20, Paragraph 1.
[17] Intellectual Property Law, Article 20, Paragraph 1.
[18] Intellectual Property Law, Article 52.
[19] Intellectual Property Law, Article 27, Paragraph 1.
[20] Yilmaz, Copyright in the European Union with Special Reference to Turkey (1998), at p. 445.
[21] Intellectual Property Law, additional Article 8, Paragraph 2.
[22] Intellectual Property Law, Article 21.

the Intellectual Property Law. Translations and adaptations are themselves works protected by copyright and the author of an adaptation or translation may exercise his economic rights to the extent permitted by the author of the original work.[23]

Right of Reproduction

The right to reproduce the work or copies of a work, in whole or in part, belongs exclusively to the author regardless of the method or form used to reproduce such works.[24]

Reproduction of a work is interpreted in a broad sense and includes the making of a second copy of the original, as well as recording the work on all types of current devices and devices to be developed in the future that enable transmission or repetition of signs, sounds, and images, which are deemed as reproductions,[25] which means that digital copies are under the protection provided by the Intellectual Property Law.

Right of Distribution

The right to lease, lend, sale, or distribute the original copies of a work belongs to the author of such work exclusively.[26] In addition, it is explicitly stated under the Intellectual Property Law that importing the copies of a work that have been reproduced abroad is an exclusive right of the author.[27]

The right of distribution provided under Turkish law recognizes the first-sale doctrine that subjects the right of distribution to exhaustion upon first sale or other transfer of ownership of a particular copy.[28] Accordingly, when the author or the owner of the right of distribution of a work has sold or transferred ownership of a particular copy of such work, the owner of the copy may use or dispose such copy without obtaining permission of the copyright owner.[29] However, under Turkish

---

23 Intellectual Property Law, Article 20, Paragraph 4.
24 Intellectual Property Law, Article 22, Paragraph 1.
25 Intellectual Property Law, Article 22, Paragraph 2.
26 Intellectual Property Law, Article 23, Paragraph 1.
27 Intellectual Property Law, Article 23, Paragraph 2.
28 World Intellectual Property Organization, *WIPO Intellectual Property Handbook*, 2004, Paragraph 2.184.
29 Intellectual Property Law, Article 23, Paragraph 2.

law, although the lawful owner of the copy may resell such copy, it is not permitted for the owner to rent or lend such copy to the public.[30]

Right of Public Performance

The right to use a work by performing belongs exclusively to the author.[31] Such performance includes reciting, acting, or displaying in public directly or by devices.

The right of performance cannot be exercised without the written permission of the author and, if the author is a member of a collecting society, the right will be administered and exercised by the organization under the specific regulations and the permission shall be obtained from such collecting society.[32]

Right of Broadcasting of Performance and Making It Available to Public

The right to communicate the work to the public by institutions making wire or wireless broadcasting with means such as radio-television, satellite, and cable, or by using other means available for diffusion of signs, sounds, or images, including the digital transmission of works, belongs to the author exclusively.[33] In addition, authors will have the exclusive right of authorizing any sale, distribution in any form, or communication to the public of their works.[34]

Right to Payment of Share on Resale of Specific Copies

For several works defined under the Intellectual Property Law[35] and except for architectural works, such as signed copies of a work that is copied in a limited number, Turkish law provides that, if such works are resold within the protection period by sale at an exhibition or auction or

---

30 Intellectual Property Law, Article 23, Paragraph 2.
31 Intellectual Property Law, Article 24, Paragraph 1.
32 Intellectual Property Law, Article 24, Paragraph 3.
33 Intellectual Property Law, Article 25, Paragraph 1.
34 Intellectual Property Law, Article 25, Paragraph 2.
35 Included are works of fine arts, mentioned in Article 4 of the Intellectual Property Law, or copies that are deemed to be original works as they were produced by the author in limited numbers or under the supervision of the author and with his permission and were signed by the author or marked by him, and the originals of works listed in Paragraph 1 of Article 2 and Article 3 of the Intellectual Property Law that are handwritten by authors and composers. Intellectual Property Law, Article 45.

similar ways and provided that there is a material disparity between such sale price and the first sale price, the author of the work or the heirs will have a right to obtain an appropriate share of the sale price.

Moral Rights

Moral rights have arisen in consequence of the relationship between an author and his work. Moral rights are the rights to be identified as author and the right to prevent unapproved changes to the works.[36] Turkish law provides a limited list of moral rights, which are:

(1) The right to disclose the work to the public;
(2) The right of attribution;
(3) The right to the integrity of the work; and
(4) The right of the author against persons who own or possess a work.

The listed moral rights are inalienable rights in principle and strictly belong to an author's personality.[37] Even when an author has transferred his economic rights, moral rights remain with the author. In addition, in principle, under Turkish law, transfer, restriction, or waiver of moral rights is not possible; only right of usage of moral rights can be transferred, which means that an author can empower third parties to exercise his moral rights. Unlike economic rights, in principle and except for minor exceptions, the protection of moral rights is not limited in time.

Right to Disclose Work to Public

The disclosure of a work to the public can be performed by several ways, such as publishing, exhibiting, or disclosure on the Internet. The author has exclusive right to determine the disclosure of his work to the public, as well as the time and form of such disclosure to the public.[38]

It is possible for the author to assign to third parties the authority to exercise the right to disclose the work to the public.[39] The agreement is not required to be in writing to be valid. However, even if the author has given written approval to third parties regarding publishing and disclosing the work to public, he may prohibit such

---

36 Sterk, "Rhetoric and Reality in Copyright Law", *Michigan Law Review* (1996), Volume 94, Number 5, at pp. 1197–1249.
37 Berne Convention, Article 6 *bis*, Paragraph (i).
38 Intellectual Property Law, Article 14, Paragraph 1.
39 Intellectual Property Law, Article 14, Paragraph 3.

disclosure if disclosure of the work to the public will damage the honor and reputation of the author.[40]

A waiver by the author on such prohibition of disclosure will be null and void.[41] However, it is argued by Turkish scholars that, if the authority to exercise the right to disclose a work to the public is assigned to a third person and the author has prohibited disclosure based on the assumption that disclosure of the work to the public will damage his honor and reputation, such third person's right to compensation is reserved.

Under the majority view of Turkish doctrine, for works created by civil servants, employees, and workers during the execution of their duties, the right of use of disclosure of the work to the public is deemed to be exercised by the persons who employ or appoint them.[42] After disclosure to the public, the right regarding disclosure of the work to the public is deemed as used, and cannot further be infringed.[43]

Right of Attribution

An author has exclusive right to determine the disclosure of his work to the public with his name, with his pseudonym, or anonymously.[44] The right of attribution also includes the right of the author of the work to express in public that he is the author of such work.

It is required for the name or mark of the original author to be reflected on the copies of a work of fine arts created by reproduction, as well as on the original and copies of an adaption,[45] as agreed upon by the parties or as it is customary. In addition, it is required for the copy or adoption to be clearly expressed as a copy or adoption.[46] The right of attribution cannot be assigned to third parties.

However, the author who is obliged to not disclose that he is the author of a work can be required to pay compensation if such obligation is violated by the author. If it is disputed who created a work, or a person who did not create the work claims to be the author of the work,

---

40 Intellectual Property Law, Article 14, Paragraph 3.
41 Intellectual Property Law, Article 14, Paragraph 3.
42 By analogy, Intellectual Property Law, Article 18, Paragraph 2.
43 Decision of the 11th Civil Chamber of Court of Appeals of 22 December 2005; Decision Number 14950/12769.
44 Intellectual Property Law, Article 15, Paragraph 1.
45 Intellectual Property Law, Article 15, Paragraph 2.
46 Intellectual Property Law, Article 15, Paragraph 2.

the real creator, or owner of the work, can ask the court to determine the holder of the rights and accordingly the author of the work.[47]

Right to Integrity of Work

Without consent of the author, no one may make modifications, additions, or abbreviations to the work or the name of its author.[48] A person who adapts, discloses to the public, reproduces, performs, or distributes a work pursuant to law or an agreement with the author may make mandatory modifications for such activities, without obtaining further approval of the author.[49]

However, even if the author has given written and unconditional consent, the author may prohibit all modifications that damage his honor and reputation or damage the nature and characteristics of the work.[50] For example, the author can prohibit the use of its works on mediums that damage the nature and characteristic of the work even if the work itself is not modified. The right to integrity of the work also includes the right of destruction of the work. The work could not be destroyed without the consent of the author.[51] The rule regarding the destruction of the work is not applicable for the reproduced copies of the work.[52]

The right for the exercise of modification of the work or destruction of the work can be given to third parties with an agreement. The agreement is deemed valid only if such authority would not damage the author's honor and reputation or damage the nature and characteristics of the work. Although there are different opinions on the form requirement of the agreement regarding the limitation of the right to the integrity of the work or the assignment of the right to exercise modification and destruction of the work, the Court of Appeals decided that the agreement shall be made in writing in order for it to be valid.[53]

---

[47] Intellectual Property Law, Article 15, Paragraph 3.
[48] Intellectual Property Law, Article 16, Paragraph 1.
[49] Intellectual Property Law, Article 16, Paragraph 2.
[50] Intellectual Property Law, Article 16, Paragraph 3.
[51] Decision of the 11th Civil Chamber of Court of Appeals of 13 June 1991; Decision Number 2679/3979; Decision of the 11th Civil Chamber of Court of Appeals of 29 March 2001; Decision Number 143/2548.
[52] Decision of the 11th Civil Chamber of Court of Appeals of 14 October 2004; Decision Number 9774/9844.
[53] Decision of the 11th Civil Chamber of Court of Appeals of 29 November 1999; Decision Number 10031/250.

Rights of Author against Persons Who Own or Possess Work

The author may demand his work from the owner or possessor of the work in necessary conditions provided by the Intellectual Property Law in order to benefit from such work.[54] The right can only be exercised for several works such as oil paintings or water colors, drawings, patterns, works drawn or fixed on other mediums by engraving, carving, or similar methods, sculptures, and reliefs, and the original handwritten works and computer programs and all kinds of technical and scientific photographic works, maps, and architectural and industrial models.[55]

In addition, it is explicitly stipulated under the Intellectual Property Law that, if the work has only one original copy, the author may request his work from the owner or possessor to use it in exhibitions covering all of his work, provided that the author will protect such work and return the work to the owner or possessor.[56] An author cannot waive and assign the right of beneficial use or use for exhibitions.

Related (Derivative) Rights

Similar to the international approach,[57] Turkish law protects related rights.[58] The rights of performers, phonogram producers, radio and television broadcasting organizations, and film producers have several rights under the Intellectual Property Law, such as right to the fixation of performances and the reproduction and lease of such fixations.[59]

Infringement of Economic and Moral Rights

Direct Infringement

In order to apply for civil or criminal remedies, the economic or moral rights of an author or a holder of the relevant rights must be infringed or there must be a threat of infringement. An infringement is deemed as an act that violates the rights vested to the author or right holder of the work.

---

[54] Intellectual Property Law, Article 17, Paragraph 1.
[55] The works listed under Intellectual Property Law, Article 2, Paragraphs 1 and 3; Intellectual Property Law, Article 4, Paragraphs 1 and 2.
[56] Intellectual Property Law, Article 17, Paragraph 3.
[57] TRIPS Agreement, Article 14; Rome Convention.
[58] Intellectual Property Law, Articles 80–82.
[59] Intellectual Property Law, Articles 80, Paragraph 2.

Indirect Infringement

Indirect infringement that includes contributory infringement or vicarious liability for infringement by another person is not separately regulated by the Intellectual Property Law.

However, according to the general principles of the law of obligations and criminal law, a person who knows or should have known that he is assisting, inducing, or contributing to infringement of a copyright, or a person who has a financial benefit and has the authority and ability to control another person who infringes any copyright, can be subject to civil and criminal outcomes similar to the person who is directly infringing the relevant copyright.

Infringement Proceedings

Turkey has a number of specialized criminal and civil intellectual property courts and special prosecutors for infringements of intellectual property rights. In addition, customs authorities can enforce several protective remedies through customs applications that can be filed for intellectual and artistic works.

Although the duration of the infringement proceedings change due to the complexity of the case and involvement of the parties, civil procedures regarding infringement of economic or moral rights take approximately two years at the first instance court.

Remedies

In General

In the case of an infringement of moral or economic rights, there are several remedies provided by the Intellectual Property Law, such as civil and criminal remedies, as well as special remedies for prevention of piracy.

Civil Remedies

The Intellectual Property Law provides several civil remedies if moral or economic rights are infringed, such as:
(1) Determination of the owner of the work;
(2) Prohibition of the infringement;
(3) Prevention of the infringement; and
(4) Compensation for damages and acting without authority (*negotiorum gestio*).

In general, the author of the work, the owner of economic rights, and exclusive licensees are entitled to claim civil remedies. Furthermore, if an author has not determined a person who will exercise the right to disclose the work to the public or the right of attribution, after the author's death, the rights may be exercised by the testamentary executor and, if no executor is appointed, successively by the surviving spouse, children, heirs, parents, and siblings.[60]

The Intellectual Property Law provides this opportunity for multiple inheritors as, in principle, moral rights are not assigned to inheritors of the author. Accordingly, except from the infringement of the right to disclose the work to the public or the right of attribution, the inheritors cannot benefit from remedies available to the author regarding the infringement of the moral rights. However, inheritors can claim compensation for non-pecuniary damages if they, as inheritors themselves, face non-pecuniary damages.[61]

Determination of Owner of Work

If there is a dispute regarding the owner of the work, determination of the owner of the work can be requested by the court. The subject of this lawsuit is to determine which of the multiple persons claiming the work is the actual author of the work.[62]

Prohibition of Infringement

Action regarding the prohibition of infringement can be brought regarding an existing and ongoing infringement of economic or moral rights.[63] The author or the relevant holders of rights can bring action even if the person in violation of moral or economic rights is not at fault.[64]

The court will take necessary precautions to eliminate the infringement, including issuing preliminary injunctions. In addition to the preliminary injunctions set forth under the Code of Civil Procedures,[65] the Intellectual Property Law provides specific provisions for preliminary

---

[60] Intellectual Property Law, Article 19, Paragraph 1.
[61] Decision of the Assembly of Civil Chambers of the Court of Appeals, of 18 December 1981; Decision Number 1/2.
[62] Intellectual Property Law, Article 15, Paragraph 2.
[63] A lawsuit, in which an unpublished work is released without the consent of the author, can be brought only if the disclosure to the public has been conducted by the publication of reproductions of the work.
[64] Intellectual Property Law, Article 66, Paragraph 1.
[65] Code of Civil Procedures, Law Number 6100, *Official Gazette* of 4 February 2011.

injunctions. Accordingly, when a person whose rights are infringed requests a preliminary injunction, the court can order several measures, including seizure of the works, before or during the legal proceedings.

If the name of the author is not placed on the works or is affixed in a manner to cause ambiguity, the author may request the removal of further infringement in addition to the determination proceeding explained above. In such case, the court may order the infringing party to affix the name of the author on the copies.[66] Similarly, if the author does not want his name to be included on the works, the court may order removal of the name from the work and copies.

As for artistic works, if an alteration on the work is made without the consent of the author or the holder of rights, the author of the work may demand several remedies from the court, such as reinstatement of the work if it is possible, or removal of his name from the work and reproduced copies.[67] In addition to the remedies provided above, the author or holder of the rights whose rights are infringed may claim from the court for the infringing party to pay:

(1) Compensation up to three times of the amount that would have been paid if the right were granted under a contract; or
(2) Compensation up to three times of current value, which will be determined according to Turkish law.

If the reproduced copies have not been offered for sale to the public, copies and devices enabling reproduction may be ordered to be destroyed or seized in return for an equitable remuneration not exceeding the production cost.[68] Unlike the general rules of the law of obligations, the author or the holder of the rights can claim such remedies even if the party in infringement is not at fault.

In principle, for related rights, the same civil enforcement procedures are applicable. However, as to names,[69] signs, pictures, sounds,[70] and letters,[71] the enforcement mechanisms provided under the Intellectual Property Law are not applicable but may be implemented under the Commercial Code, the Turkish Code of Obligations,[72] and the Civil Code.[73]

---

66 Intellectual Property Law, Article 67, Paragraph 2.
67 Intellectual Property Law, Article 67.
68 Intellectual Property Law, Article 68, Paragraph 2.
69 Regulated under Intellectual Property Law, Article 83.
70 Regulated under Intellectual Property Law, Article 84.
71 Regulated under Intellectual Property Law, Article 85.
72 Code of Obligations, Law Number 6098, *Official Gazette* of 4 February 2011.
73 Civil Code, Law Number 4721, *Official Gazette* of 8 December 2001.

Prevention of Infringement

The owner of the work subjected to the threat of infringement of economic or moral rights may bring an action for the prevention of the possible infringement.[74] The same provision applies to the cases where the continuation or repetition of a realized infringement is highly possible.

Compensation for Damages and Acting without Authority

A person whose moral rights have been infringed can bring an action for non-pecuniary damages.[75] In addition, the court may order other remedies for the damages suffered as per the infringement of moral rights, such as public apology.[76] A person whose moral rights have been infringed also may claim compensation regarding pecuniary damages under the general principles of the Code of Obligations.

A person whose economic rights have been infringed may claim compensation within the framework of the provisions concerning tortious acts pursuant to the Code of Obligations, if the person who is infringing such rights has fault regarding the relevant infringing actions.[77] In addition, a person whose moral or economic rights are infringed may claim the profits gained by the infringing party.[78]

Statute of Limitations for Civil Remedies

For civil remedies, the Intellectual Property Law does not provide specific provisions on a statute of limitations. Accordingly, the general time statute of limitation provisions of the Code of Obligations should be applicable. If the copyright infringement claim is based on a contractual relationship, the statute of limitations will be ten years.

If the copyright infringement claim is based on tort, the statute of limitations will be two years from the date on which the injured party became aware of the loss and the person liable for such loss, and in any event ten years as of the date on which the infringement has occurred. However, if the action causing such loss is an offence under the criminal law, the statute of limitations provided for such criminal remedy shall be applicable to the civil law claim. In addition, the statute of limitations will not commence if the infringement is enduring.

---

74 Intellectual Property Law, Article 69, Paragraph 1.
75 Intellectual Property Law, Article 70, Paragraph 1.
76 Intellectual Property Law, Article 70, Paragraph 1.
77 Intellectual Property Law, Article 70, Paragraph 2.
78 Intellectual Property Law, Article 70, Paragraph 3.

Criminal Remedies

The Intellectual Property Law mainly regulates the criminal liability for the infringement of moral and economic rights deriving from the ownership of a work and related rights. However, specific criminal liability provisions are regulated under the Intellectual Property Law, such as banderole protection and criminal liability for persons who produce, offer to sell, sell, or possess, for any purpose other than private use, software or technical hardware that would circumvent the protective additional programs developed to prevent illegal reproduction of computer programs.[79]

The criminal actions provided by the Intellectual Property Law and relevant legislation regarding the infringement of moral and economic rights regulate remedies that include imprisonment, heavy fines, restraining orders (i.e., prohibition of commerce), seizure, and destruction. The acts of infringement are specifically defined under the Intellectual Property Law and relevant legal penalties are foreseen.

The general penalties for infringement of moral or economic rights vary between three months to five years of imprisonment and/or judicial fines.[80] For example, a person exploiting the economic rights of an author or holder of the economic rights without the consent of such person may be sentenced to imprisonment from one year to five years or a judicial fine.[81] Similarly, a person who uses a different name on another person's work as his own may be sentenced to imprisonment from six months to two years or a judicial fine and, where such act is committed by distributing or publishing, such person may be sentenced to imprisonment for up to five years.[82]

In addition, citing from a work without making reference to the source is subject to imprisonment from six months to two years or a judicial fine,[83] and referring to a work in an incorrect or incomplete manner is subject to imprisonment for up to six months.[84] Furthermore, a person who declares a work to the public that has not been

---

[79] Intellectual Property Law, Articles 71 and 72. Persons who produce, offer to sell, sell, or possess, for any purpose other than private use, software or technical hardware that would circumvent the protective additional programs developed to prevent illegal reproduction of computer programs may be sentenced to imprisonment from six months to two years.
[80] Intellectual Property Law, Article 71.
[81] Intellectual Property Law, Article 71, Sub-Paragraph 1.
[82] Intellectual Property Law, Article 70, Sub-Paragraph 2.
[83] Intellectual Property Law, Article 70, Sub-Paragraph 3.
[84] Intellectual Property Law, Article 70, Sub-Paragraph 5.

made public without permission of the right holder may be sentenced to imprisonment for up to six months.[85]

A person who reproduces, distributes, publishes, or broadcasts a work or related works by virtue of a well-known person may be sentenced to imprisonment from three months to one year or a judicial fine.[86] In addition, the court may order the confiscation and destruction of counterfeit products, along with machinery and other equipment used to produce the counterfeits.

Remedies regarding Prevention of Piracy

In addition to the remedies provided for the infringement of copyrights, the Intellectual Property Law provides special provisions to prevent piracy and for the civil and criminal remedies to be applied to piracy. Under Turkish law, for musical and cinematographic works and non-periodical publications, it is compulsory to affix banderoles on the reproduced copies.

The banderoles are provided by the Ministry of Culture and Tourism or the agencies of the collecting societies. For other works that can be easily reproduced, upon the request of the author or right holder, it is compulsory to affix banderoles.[87] The Ministry of Culture and Tourism and the local representatives of the central government are authorized to inspect the affixation of banderoles in any time *ex officio* or upon request.[88]

Where a copyright infringement is determined during the inspections, further remedies provided under the Intellectual Property Law will be carried out by the authorities. In addition, even if the works bear the required banderoles, it is prohibited under the Intellectual Property Law to sell such works on roads, squares, open markets, sidewalks, bridges, or similar places.[89]

A person who reproduces a work without the required banderole and offers to sell, sells, distributes, or with commercial purpose, buys or accepts banderoles may be sentenced to imprisonment from one year to five years and fined up to 5,000-day penalty.[90] A person who offers to

---

[85] Intellectual Property Law, Article 70, Sub-Paragraph 4.
[86] Intellectual Property Law, Article 70, Sub-Paragraph 6.
[87] Intellectual Property Law, Article 81, Paragraph 1.
[88] Intellectual Property Law, Article 81, Paragraph 5.
[89] Intellectual Property Law, Article 81, Paragraph 7.
[90] Intellectual Property Law, Article 81, Paragraph 4. The fine for one day varies between TL 20 and TL 100.

sell, sells, distributes, buys, or accepts counterfeit banderoles may be sentenced to imprisonment from three years to seven years and fined up to 5,000-day penalty.[91]

A person who uses duly obtained banderoles on another work may be sentenced to imprisonment from one year to five years and fined up to 1,500-day penalty.[92] In addition, a person who obtains banderoles without authority and with collusive behavior or provides banderoles to persons without authority may be sentenced to imprisonment from one year to five years and fined up to 5,000-day penalty.[93] If such actions are conducted under a legal personality, such as a company, the legal person may face security measures such as prohibition of commerce.

Exemptions to Infringement of Copyright

In General

There are several exemptions provided under the Intellectual Property Law where certain acts are not deemed as infringements on economic or moral rights of the author or the right holder.

Public Order

Works can be used as evidence before the judicial authorities or when they are the subject matter of criminal proceedings without infringement of moral or economic rights.[94] Accordingly, a work that is used for these reasons will not be deemed as violating moral or economic rights on a work.

Public Interest

There are several exemptions provided under the Intellectual Property Law in line with the Berne Convention for:
(1) Legislation and court decisions;
(2) Speeches;

---

[91] Intellectual Property Law, Article 81, Paragraph 10. The fine for one day varies between TL 20 and TL 100.
[92] Intellectual Property Law, Article 81, Paragraph 11. The fine for one day varies between TL 20 and TL 100.
[93] Intellectual Property Law, Article 81, Paragraphs 12 and 13. The fine for one day varies between TL 20 and TL 100.
[94] Intellectual Property Law, Article 30, Paragraph 1.

(3) Performance of published works in educational institutions for educational purposes;
(4) Creation of selected or collected works for educational and instructional purposes;
(5) Quotations provided under certain conditions;
(6) Content of newspapers; and
(7) News that does not exceed the limits of giving information.[95]

In addition, the Intellectual Property Law provides exemptions for the benefit of disabled persons that permit the reproduction or lending of a work in an alternative format in order to make it more accessible for disabled persons, provided that such copies are not used for commercial purposes.[96]

Interests of Individuals

In General. Exemptions regarding personal use are limited to personal use, reproduction and exhibition, and use of works in public premises.

Personal Use. As long as it is for personal use, and provided that the user does not pursue profit and it does not prejudice the legitimate interest of the holders of economic rights, it is permitted to reproduce all works.[97] As to computer programs, in the absence of explicit contractual terms, the lawful user of a computer program is permitted to reproduce or adapt the computer program for legitimate purposes, including error correction.

Furthermore, it is prohibited by the Intellectual Property Law to waive the rights on loading, running, and error correction of a computer program by a person who has lawfully acquired such program.[98] Computer programs also may be tested, observed, or explored for the purpose of comprehending principles and ideas underlying any element of the program.[99]

---

[95] Intellectual Property Law, Articles 30–37.
[96] Intellectual Property Law, Article 11.
[97] Intellectual Property Law, Article 38, Paragraph 1.
[98] Intellectual Property Law, Article 38, Paragraphs 3 and 4.
[99] Intellectual Property Law, Article 38, Paragraph 5.

Reproduction and Exhibition. Works of art that are placed on streets, avenues, or squares permanently are allowed to be reproduced by drawings, photographs, and similar mediums and to be broadcast.[100]

Use of Works in Public Premises. Regardless of the existence of an entrance fee, public premises must execute agreements regarding the assignment of rights with holders of the relevant rights or collecting societies in order to obtain permission for the use and communication of such works.[101]

Legal representatives of such premises must make payments for economic rights under these contracts. As provided by the Intellectual Property Law, the collecting societies set tariffs for fees arising from the use and communications of works.[102]

Conclusion

Turkish law, like many continental systems, provides useful and applicable remedies for infringement of both moral and economic rights of authors and holders of such rights. Especially with the recent developments regarding specialization of first instance and appeal courts and prosecutors' offices on intellectual property law, for both civil and criminal proceedings, a uniform and effective application of the law is procured.

In addition, the Ministry of Culture and Tourism and the Directorate General for Copyrights, as well as the collective societies are working together for the improvement of legislation and amendment of the Intellectual Property Law, which was expected to be reflected in a draft bill in the near future.

---

[100] Intellectual Property Law, Article 40, Paragraph 1.
[101] Intellectual Property Law, Article 41, Paragraph 1.
[102] Intellectual Property Law, Article 41, Paragraph 3.

United Kingdom

Gareth Dickson
Taylor Vinters LLP
Cambridge, United Kingdom

Introduction

Copyright is, alongside patents, one of the best known of the intellectual property rights.[1] That is not to say that it is necessarily popular in a country with a strong record of accomplishment in innovation and entrepreneurship. As technological innovation enables more content to be created than ever before, and enables those creations to be disseminated to and accessed from more locations than ever before, the potential for a dispute between two or more parties, who each believes they are entitled to exclusivity in a work, increases.

Strictly speaking, however, copyright does not regulate whether two or more creations may be similar. Instead, it operates to allow the owner of the copyright in a work to prevent a third party from performing certain acts in relation to that work without permission. These "restricted acts" include reproducing the work, either by itself or by incorporating it into another work (which itself may benefit from its own copyright protection), or performing or disseminating it. Copyright will not restrain the exploitation of a later work that is similar to an earlier work but was created independently of that earlier work.

Of course, similarity between two works will often lead to an inference that the later work has been copied from the earlier work and was not created independently of it. The strength of the inference will depend upon a number of factors, including the relationship between the parties responsible for each work, the degree of similarity, and the complexity of the earlier work.

Provisions exist in legislation and in Common Law to regulate a third party's involvement in a primary infringer's activity. Secondary liability addresses the conduct of those who deal in infringing copies of a work or who otherwise enable or facilitate that infringement, subject to what they

---

[1] The author acknowledges with thanks the assistance of William Haig, Associate at Taylor Vinters LLP, in finalizing this chapter.

knew or had reasonable grounds to know. The concept of joint tortfeasorship enables a right holder to obtain a remedy against a party who is so involved in a primary infringer's activity that he has in effect made the primary infringing act his own.

Proceedings for copyright infringement in the United Kingdom are normally commenced in the Chancery Division of the High Court (or the Court of Session in Scotland). There also is, however, a specialist intellectual property court in England and Wales called the Intellectual Property Enterprise Court. The Intellectual Property Enterprise Court has most of the powers of the High Court, including the ability to make preliminary references on the interpretation of European Union law to the Court of Justice of the European Union. What distinguishes the Intellectual Property Enterprise Court is that, in its efforts to make it easier for smaller companies to obtain access to justice, it only deals with claims of lower value (up to £500,000 in damages), trials usually last no more than two days, and there are restrictions on the level of costs which can be recovered (£50,000 in total).

Regardless of the venue for infringement proceedings, a claimant in a successful action for copyright infringement must show that it is the owner of copyright in the work, that the defendant has performed a restricted act within the term of the copyright and without the owner's authorization, and that no defense applies. The proceedings also must be commenced within the relevant limitation period. Remedies available to a successful claimant include an award of damages or an account of profits, an injunction, dissemination of the outcome of the proceedings and, potentially, an award of costs.

Copyright is an intricate and pervasive part of modern life. Its reach extends into the minutiae of creation and collaboration, and so too do exceptions and defenses to a claim of infringement. The Copyright, Designs and Patents Act 1988 is the primary source of United Kingdom copyright law, supplemented as it is by regulations of the European Union and decisions on the interpretation of European Union (EU) law by the Court of Justice of the European Union. It extends to thousands of provisions and definitions that cannot all be discussed here. Instead, this chapter will offer an overview of each of the most common areas of copyright law that are litigated in civil courts in the United Kingdom. An overview of available remedies also is provided.

Subsistence

In General

In the United Kingdom, copyright arises automatically and without the need for registration.[2] It is common practice for a party asserting copyright in a work to add a notice to the work in the following format "© [year] [name]", but this is not a precondition to the subsistence or enforcement of copyright in any work.

Instead, the first requirement for a claimant in copyright proceedings is to show that the work at issue in the proceedings is protected by copyright. On the face of it, this ought to be a relatively straightforward task but, in reality, it can present complex issues that, in some cases, have no clear answer. The starting point is Section 1(1) of the Copyright, Designs and Patents Act, which provides that copyright subsists in the following descriptions of work:

(1) Original literary, dramatic, musical, or artistic works;
(2) Sound recordings, films, or broadcasts; and
(3) The typographical arrangement of published editions.

Section 1(1) of the Copyright, Designs and Patents Act, therefore, sets out an exhaustive list of the descriptions of works that are capable of being protected by copyright under the Copyright, Designs and Patents Act. Yet, the Court of Justice of the European Union, in *Infopaq I*,[3] determined that copyright protects "the expression of the author's own intellectual creation".

This is problematic since not every expression of an author's own intellectual creation will necessarily fall neatly within one of these descriptions of work. This raises the prospect that such expressions may not be protected in the United Kingdom. This issue is acute in the case of original artistic works, as will be seen below. While courts in the United Kingdom will endeavor to interpret United Kingdom laws in

---

2 Section 153 of the Copyright, Designs and Patents Act provides that various "qualification requirements" must be satisfied with regard to the author of a work or the country in which the work was first published or from which a relevant broadcast was made, but these are usually satisfied and rarely litigated.
3 Court of Justice of the European Union, Case C-5/08, *Infopaq International A/S vs. Danske Dagblades Forening* [2009] ECR I-6569. Under the rule in *Infopaq I*, a Tweet could be protected as a literary work.

accordance with EU law,⁴ their obligation to do so does not permit them to rewrite legislation passed in Parliament.

In other words, if a provision of United Kingdom law simply cannot be read in a way that gives protection to a work that is the expression of its author's own intellectual creation, the work in question is likely to fall outside of the protection afforded by the Copyright, Designs and Patents Act even if that means that the United Kingdom is in breach of its obligations under EU law.

Difficulty also arises where more than one type of work is incorporated into a single product. Computer games, for example, are likely to incorporate literary and artistic works as well as sound recordings and potentially dramatic works. Yet different rules apply to each of these descriptions of work. Each category of work is described in detail in the Copyright, Designs and Patents Act, as follows.

Original Literary, Dramatic, Musical, or Artistic Works

In General

The Copyright, Designs and Patents Act defines a musical work as "a work consisting of music, exclusive of any words or action intended to be sung, spoken or performed with the music" and provides that a dramatic work "includes" a work of dance or mime. Recent case law suggests that television formats can be protected as dramatic works depending on their distinguishing features and the presence of a sufficiently coherent framework to enable reproduction in a recognizable form.⁵

A literary work means any work, other than a dramatic or musical work, which is written, spoken, or sung. The Copyright, Designs and Patents Act expressly provides that tables, compilations, computer programs,⁶ preparatory design material for computer programs, and databases⁷ can all be protected as literary works. A computer program's functionality, language, and data formats are generally considered not to be protected by copyright, although there is insufficient clarity in the

---

4 Court of Justice of the European Union, Case C-106/89, *Marleasing SA* vs. *La Commercial Internacional de Alimtacion SA*.
5 *Banner Universal Motion Pictures Limited* vs. *Endemol Shine Group Limited & Others* [2017] EWHC 2600 (Ch).
6 A narrow definition of "computer program" has been applied by the Court of Justice of the European Union, beginning with Case C-393/09, *Bezpečnostní softwarová asociace*, suggesting that a multimedia video game may not be a "computer program".
7 Databases also can be protected by the *sui generis* database right under the Copyright and Rights in Databases Regulations 1997.

authorities to state this definitively.[8] A work can only be protected as an artistic work if it falls within the following exhaustive list of artistic works:

(1) A graphic work, photograph, sculpture, or collage, irrespective of artistic quality;
(2) A work of architecture being a building or a model for a building; or
(3) A work of artistic craftsmanship.

Requirement of Originality

The Copyright, Designs and Patents Act requires that, to be protected by copyright, literary, dramatic, musical, and artistic works must be "original". Except in the case of a literary work consisting of a database, the Copyright, Designs and Patents Act does not set out how originality is to be assessed in this context. As a minimum, however, a claimant must show that the work is the expression of the author's own intellectual creation, in that it originated with the author as opposed to having been copied from another work.

Requirement of Recording

Copyright does not subsist in a literary, dramatic, or musical work unless and until it is recorded, in writing or otherwise. No such requirement exists for artistic works or for any of the other descriptions of works set out in the Copyright, Designs and Patents Act.

Unclear Status of "Design Classics"

There is considerable disagreement currently as to what amounts to a "work of artistic craftsmanship", since the Copyright, Designs and Patents Act does not define it, and the United Kingdom's leading decisions on these works[9] have potentially been overtaken by the Court of Justice of the European Union decision in *Infopaq I*.[10]

---

8 *SAS Institute Inc.* vs. *World Programming Ltd*, Case C-406/10.
9 *Hensher* vs. *Restawile* [1976] AC 64, a 1976 decision of the House of Lords (the United Kingdom's highest appellate body until it was replaced by the United Kingdom Supreme Court), and *Lucasfilm Limited & Others* vs. *Ainsworth & Another* [2008] EWHC 1878 (Ch), a 2008 decision of the High Court.
10 Court of Justice of the European Union, Case C-5/08, *Infopaq International A/S* vs. *Danske Dagblades Forening* [2009] ECR I-6569.

Although there is no express bar on an item being both functional and a work of artistic craftsmanship, the United Kingdom's House of Lords held, in 1976, that certain pieces of furniture were not works of artistic craftsmanship despite their aesthetic appeal[11] and, in 2008, the High Court held that Stormtrooper helmets from the Star Wars movies were also not works of artistic craftsmanship.[12]

Since these decisions, however, the Court of Justice of the European Union has ruled in *Infopaq I* that, as a matter of EU law, copyright protects the "expression of an author's own intellectual creation", and there appears to be little disagreement that the classic furniture pieces that inhabit museums and high-value office blocks, so-called "design classics", are indeed the "expression of their author's own intellectual creation". In that regard, they appear to meet the test for copyright protection set out by the Court of Justice of the European Union, but they may not meet the tests that exist under United Kingdom law.

Sound Recordings, Films, and Broadcasts

Copyright law in the United Kingdom protects sound recordings, films, and broadcasts. Sound recordings are defined as either "a recording of sounds, from which the sounds may be reproduced", or "a recording of the whole or any part of a literary, dramatic or musical work, from which sounds reproducing the work or part may be produced, regardless of the medium on which the recording is made or the method by which the sounds are reproduced or produced".

Films are defined as "a recording on any medium from which a moving image may by any means be produced", and the sound track accompanying a film is treated as part of the film, notwithstanding that copyright also can subsist in a film sound track as a sound recording.

Under the Copyright, Designs and Patents Act, a broadcast means an electronic transmission of visual images, sounds, or other information which is transmitted for simultaneous reception by members of the public and is capable of being lawfully received by them, or is transmitted at a time determined solely by the person making the transmission for presentation to members of the public. Certain Internet

---

11 *Hensher* vs. *Restawile* [1976] AC 64.
12 *Lucasfilm Limited & Others* vs. *Ainsworth & Another* [2008] EWHC 1878 (Ch). The United Kingdom Supreme Court also held in this case that the helmets were not sculptures: *Lucasfilm Limited & Others* vs. *Ainsworth & Another* [2011] UKSC 39.

transmissions are excluded from that definition. Unlike other categories of works, which can attract copyright in their own right even if they incorporate material that infringes a third party's copyright, copyright does not subsist in a broadcast to the extent that it infringes the copyright in another broadcast.

Typographical Arrangement of Published Editions

Copyright law also protects the typographical arrangement of published editions. The Copyright, Designs and Patents Act defines a "published edition" in this context as a published edition of the whole or any part of one or more literary, dramatic, or musical works.

No copyright subsists, however, in the typographical arrangement of a published edition that reproduces the typographical arrangement of a previous edition.

Combined Works

Many articles will embody several descriptions of work within a single article. A computer game is a prime example, since it is not necessarily simply a "computer program" as defined and interpreted by the Court of Justice of the European Union.[13] Instead, what is delivered on a disk or is downloaded from the Internet will be an inseparable combination of computer code, graphical elements, audio files, plots, and databases.

An overly strict reading of the applicable legislation would lead to the conclusion that each of these works should be dealt with separately, with potentially different durations of copyright and with only some of the incorporated works being protected against acts of secondary infringement (as to which, see further below). Such a conclusion would be unworkable. Instead, the Court of Justice of the European Union has suggested that, where multiple works are incorporated in a single item, the greatest protection available to any element of that work should apply to that whole work, thereby securing for rights holders a high level of protection as intended by the legislation.[14]

---

13 Court of Justice of the European Union, Case C-393/09, *Bezpečnostní softwarová asociace*.
14 Court of Justice of the European Union, Case C-355/12, *Nintendo Co. Ltd. and Others* vs. *PC Box Srl and 9Net Srl*.

Duration

In General

As part of its obligation to prove that copyright subsists in a work, a claimant in infringement proceedings also must show that the act complained of took place during the relevant term of copyright. Separate provisions apply for Crown and parliamentary copyright, and to copyright with certain international aspects, but the general rules are set out below.

Literary, Dramatic, Musical, and Artistic Works

Copyright in a literary, dramatic, musical, or artistic work lasts for the life of the author plus seventy years, such seventy-year period beginning to run from 1 January on the year immediately following the death of the author. A book written by an author who died on 1 January 2017 will, therefore, enter the public domain on the same day as an artistic work created by an author who died on 31 December 2017 (i.e., 1 January 2078). An exception to this is computer code, whose copyright expires at the end of the period of fifty years from the end of the calendar year in which the work was made.

Where there is more than one known author of a work, the term of copyright in that work is calculated according to the death of the last known author. Copyright in works of unknown authorship will expire at the end of the period of seventy years from the end of the calendar year in which the work was made, unless the work has been made available to the public within that period, in which case it expires at the end of the period of seventy years from the end of the calendar year in which it is first so made available.

Sound Recordings

Copyright in sound recordings normally expires at the end of the period of fifty years from the end of the calendar year in which the recording is made. However, if the recording is published or if it is made available to the public by being played or communicated to the public within that fifty-year period, copyright expires seventy years from the end of the calendar year in which it is first so published or so made available.

Owners of sound recordings are therefore incentivized to publish or make available their recordings as close to the end of the fifty-year period as possible, thereby making it difficult to predict when some recordings will enter the public domain and therefore when they can be exploited without authorization.

Films

Copyright in films expires at the end of the period of seventy years from the end of the calendar year in which the death occurs of the last to die of the following persons whose identity is known or becomes known:
(1) The principal director;
(2) The author of the screenplay;
(3) The author of the dialogue; and
(4) The composer of music especially created for and used in the film.

If the identity of any of these people remains unknown following reasonable enquiry, copyright expires at the end of the period of seventy years from the end of the calendar year in which the film was made, or first made available to the public (if that act of making available occurred within the initial seventy-year period). If the film does not have a principal director, an author of screenplay or dialogue, or a composer of music, copyright expires at the end of the period of fifty years from the end of the calendar year in which the film was made.

Broadcasts

Copyright in a broadcast generally expires at the end of the period of fifty years from the end of the calendar year in which the broadcast was made.

Typographical Arrangement of Published Editions

Copyright in the typographical arrangement of a published edition expires at the end of the period of twenty-five years from the end of the calendar year in which the edition was first published.

Authorship and Ownership

In General

Since copyright is a property right, it can be bought and sold, licensed, mortgaged, and transmitted on death. Each of the acts reserved for the owner of copyright (see text, below) is capable of being dealt with separately. For commercial or administrative reasons, copyright might not be owned by the person exploiting it. Therefore, care must be taken when commencing proceedings to ensure that the correct entity is the claimant and that the lawyers are taking instructions from the correct entity.

The general rule is that the author of a work, i.e., the person who created it, is the first owner of any copyright in it. That general rule is supplemented by a number of presumptions discussed below, as well as a number of exceptions. One of the most important exceptions is where a literary, dramatic, musical, or artistic work or a film is made by an employee in the course of their employment.

In such a case, the employer is the first owner in the work, subject to any agreement to the contrary. It is normal practice, however, for employment contracts to put the matter beyond doubt by including a provision that any copyright arising out of the performance by the employee of obligations under their contract of employment is to be owned by the employer, and that the employee will take whatever steps are necessary to ensure that the employer is or becomes the owner of such copyright. Similar provisions may be included in consultancy agreements.

The author of a literary, dramatic, musical, or artistic work which is computer generated is subject to special provisions whereby the author of such a work is taken to be the person by whom the arrangements necessary for the creation of the work are undertaken. A work also may be a work of joint authorship (in which case all the authors own the copyright) where it was produced by the collaboration of two or more authors in which the contribution of each author is not distinct from that of the other author or authors.[15]

Presumptions Relevant to Literary, Dramatic, Musical, and Artistic Works

In proceedings for infringement of copyright in a literary, dramatic, musical, or artistic work, it is presumed that a name purporting to be the author's name and appearing on a copy of a work as published (or on the work when it was made) is the name of the author and the work is presumed to have been made otherwise than in the course of that person's employment.

---

15 The contribution of minor plot suggestions to and helpful criticism of drafts of a work generally will not make the contributor a joint author of the final work: *Martin* vs. *Kogan* [2017] EWHC 2927 (IPEC).

A party seeking to rebut that presumption must prove that the author is not the person whose name appears on the work as that of the author, and/or that the work was made in the course of employment. If no name appears on the copy as published or on the work when it was made, but a name purporting to be the publisher's name appears on the work as first published, then, depending on where the work was first published, that person is presumed to have owned the copyright as at the date of publication. Again, this is a rebuttable presumption, and a party seeking to displace it must prove the contrary.

Where litigation is commenced over a work whose author is dead or whose identity cannot be ascertained by reasonable inquiry, it will be presumed (although not until the contrary is proved, but merely until there is evidence to the contrary) that the work at issue in the proceedings is an original work, and that the claimant's allegations as to what and where was the first publication of the work are correct.

If there appears on printed copies of the work a statement of the year in which a literary, dramatic, or musical work in which Crown copyright subsists was first published commercially, that statement would be presumed to be correct in the absence of evidence to the contrary.[16]

Presumptions Relevant to Sound Recordings and Films

Where proceedings are commenced in relation to a sound recording, it is presumed that a statement on copies of the recording as issued to the public that a named person was the owner of copyright in the recording at the date of issue, or that the recording was first published in a particular country or year, is correct. The presumption is rebuttable by proving the contrary.

When proceedings concern copyright in a film, a statement on copies issued to the public that a person was the director or the producer of the film, the principal director, the author of the screenplay or of the dialogue, or the composer of music specifically created for and used in the film, or the owner of copyright in the film at the date of issue of the copies, is presumed to be correct until the contrary is proved. A statement on such copies that the film was first published in a particular country or year also is presumed to be correct until the contrary is proved.

---

16 Copyright, Designs and Patents Act 1988, Section 106.

Presumptions Relevant to Computer Programs

A statement on copies of a computer program issued to the public in electronic form that a person owned the copyright in the program when those copies were issued to the public, or specifying the country of the first publication of the program or the year they were first issued to the public in electronic form, is presumed to be correct until the contrary is proved.

Presumptions Relevant to Films

Various presumptions also exist in relation to a film shown in public or communicated to the public. When such a film bears a statement that a person was the director or producer of the film, the author of the screenplay or the dialogue, or the composer of music specifically created for and used in the film, or was the owner of copyright in the film immediately after it was made, that statement is presumed to be correct until the contrary is proved.

Infringement

In General

Copyright is infringed when a restricted act is carried out within the relevant term of copyright protection, without the consent of the copyright owner, and in the absence of a defense. The Copyright, Designs and Patents Act divides infringements into two categories, namely:

(1) Primary infringement; and
(2) Secondary infringement.

The Common Law concept of joint tortfeasorship also has been asserted in a number of copyright cases, particularly where online platforms are involved. As will be seen, however, the threshold for establishing joint tortfeasorship is quite high, and relatively few cases have been successful.

Primary Infringement

In General

Under the Copyright, Designs and Patents Act,[17] the owner of copyright in a work is granted various exclusive rights in relation to the exploitation

---

[17] Copyright, Designs and Patents Act 1988, Sections 16–21.

of that right, and the EU legislation on which parts of United Kingdom copyright law are based repeats often the requirement that intellectual property in general and copyright in particular be granted a "high level of protection".[18]

Those rights entitle the copyright owner to prevent a third party not having his permission from carrying out (or from authorizing another to carry out) in the United Kingdom any of the "restricted acts" set out in the statute. For each of the restricted acts, the right covers acts carried out directly or indirectly, and applies to the whole or to a substantial part of the protected work.

A claimant (and thereafter a potential defendant and eventually the court) will therefore be able to assess the original work in order to determine whether the allegedly infringing act involves the whole or a substantial part of the original work.

This can present a difficulty for a claimant whose original work is confidential, for example, because it is unpublished or because it is software code hosted in the cloud that also contains trade secrets. In such circumstances, the parties may enter into a confidentiality club to restrict access to the original or copies of a work, or they may agree to determination being carried out by an independent expert.

The Copyright, Designs and Patents Act provides for six restricted acts in respect of a protected work, namely the acts of:

(1) Copying the work;
(2) Issuing copies of the work to the public;
(3) Renting or lending the work to the public;
(4) Performing, showing, or playing the work in public;
(5) Communicating the work to the public; and
(6) Making an adaptation of the work or doing any of the above in relation to an adaptation of the work.

Infringement of Copyright by Copying

The restriction against copying a work applies to every description of copyright work. In relation to a literary, dramatic, musical, or artistic work, copying means reproducing the work in any material form, including by storing the work in any medium by electronic means.

---

[18] Recitals 4 and 9 of Directive 2001/29/EC of the European Parliament and of the Council of 22 May 2001 on the harmonization of certain aspects of copyright and related rights in the information society; Recitals 10 and 11 of Council Directive 93/98/EEC of 29 October 1993, harmonizing the term of protection of copyright and certain related rights.

Copying an artistic work includes making a three-dimensional copy of a two-dimensional work, as well as the making of a two-dimensional copy of a three-dimensional work.

Copyright in a literary work can be infringed by the copying of a central theme or a substantial part of the plot.[19] Films and broadcasts can be copied by making a photograph of the whole or any substantial part of any image forming part of the film or broadcast and, in relation to the typographical arrangement of a published edition, copying means making a facsimile copy of that arrangement.

Emulating the functionality of a computer program is not necessarily an infringement of the literary copyright in the underlying code and it will be difficult for a claimant to prove such an infringement if he cannot prove that the defendant had access to that code. Reproducing the graphical user interface or the "look and feel" of a computer program, however, is likely to infringe any artistic copyright that subsists in the original work.[20]

A copy of a work does not need to be a permanent copy in order to infringe the reproduction right: copies which are transient or incidental to some other use of the work also are covered. Importantly, however, not all temporary copies infringe copyright. As will be seen, one of the exceptions to the reproduction right is the exemption for temporary copies.

Infringement by Issue of Copies to Public

The Copyright, Designs and Patents Act regulates the issue of copies (in every description of work) to the public both within and outside the European Economic Area (EEA). Principally, the right is infringed where copies of a work not previously put into circulation in the EEA by or with the consent of the copyright owner are then put into circulation in the EEA.

Copies of a work that have not been put into circulation outside the EEA "or elsewhere" cannot be put into circulation outside the EEA without the consent of the copyright owner. Once a copy of a work has been put into circulation in the EEA by or with the consent of the right

---

19 *Baigent & Leigh* vs. *The Random House Group Limited* [2007] EWCA Civ 247.
20 *SAS Institute Inc.* vs. *World Programming Ltd* [2013] EWCA Civ 1482; *Navitaire Inc.* vs. *EasyJet Airline Company & Anor* [2004] EWHC 1725 (Ch).

holder, that copy can be recirculated without the need to obtain the consent of the right holder to that further circulation.[21]

To avoid liability under this head, any "copies" put into circulation by a defendant must be the very same physical copies that the right holder allowed to be put on the market. An example will illustrate the point. A right holder has two identical copies of a book in which he owns the literary copyright. Each book is made with his consent. He authorizes a distributor to put one of those books into circulation in the EEA, but he withholds the other.

It is obviously not an infringement of copyright for the distributor to put the first book into circulation, but it would be an infringement of copyright for him to put the second book into circulation, since that copy has not already been put into circulation in the EEA by the right holder or with his consent.

In some cases, there are good reasons for territories to be divided up in this way. Where regulations are not harmonized across a border, a right holder may want copies of his work to be made available to the public in one territory only because they only comply with regulations in the first territory but not the second. In other cases, goods are simply priced differently in different territories. In other cases, the right holder will consent to his goods being put into circulation anywhere in the world, so that the fact that a particular copy of his work is first available in one particular territory is mere happenstance and not indicative of any restriction on the further circulation of that copy.

The fact that the same act could be infringing or non-infringing depending on whether or not the right holder has given consent to goods being put into circulation presents a challenge for resellers. Absent a communication from the right holder confirming the limits of his consent, resellers have no sure way of knowing whether their attempt to resell goods will infringe copyright. Some works may be marked with language such as "Only for circulation within the EEA", but where this is not the case, there is a significant infringement risk for resellers.

In such cases, the reseller may take some comfort from a warranty or an indemnity in their contract of purchase from the seller of the works to be resold. Such an indemnity will not absolve the reseller from liability

---

21 The potentially far-reaching consequences of the decision of the Court of Justice of the European Union in case C-128/11 *UsedSoft GmbH* vs. *Oracle International Corp.* that a personal, non-transferable license to download a copy of a computer program should be treated as a "sale" of a copy of that program in certain circumstances has been mitigated by the software industry's move away from the licensing of downloads of software towards cloud-based subscription services.

but may, provided the seller is solvent and traceable, provide some mitigation in the event that the reseller suffers loss as a result of a claim by a third-party right holder in respect of the unauthorized issuing of copies of a work to the public.

Infringement by Rental or Lending Work to Public

The copyright owner's permission is required before a party can engage in the rental or lending of a literary, dramatic, or musical work, certain artistic works, a film, or a sound recording.

Infringement by Performance, Showing, or Playing Work in Public

A public "performance" can only infringe copyright in a literary, dramatic, or musical work, although the performers in an infringing performance are not responsible for the infringement. The performance can be by way of a lecture, address, speech, or sermon, and is likely to cover any mode of visual or acoustic presentation. The presentation of a literary, dramatic, or musical work via a sound recording, a film, or a broadcast of a work is therefore likely to infringe copyright under this head.

Copyright in a sound recording, a film, or a broadcast itself may be infringed if the work is either played or shown in public without the right holder's consent. However, in none of these cases, whether by performance, playing, or showing in public, is a person by whom images or sounds are sent by electronic means to effect the performance, play, or show, responsible for the infringement.

Infringement by Communication to Public

Infringement by the unauthorized communication of a work to the public has perhaps been the most litigated, and almost certainly the most controversial, aspect of copyright infringement proceedings in the last several years. It applies broadly, covering literary, dramatic, musical, or artistic works, sound recordings, films, and broadcasts.

The restricted act requires communication to the public by electronic transmission, whether by broadcast, by the making available of a work to the public so that members of the public can access the work from a place and at a time individually chosen by them (i.e., on demand), or otherwise.

The right has been litigated extensively in the context of new media services that deliver content over the Internet. Some of the services found to amount to a communication to the public include services converting television signals to digital transmissions and permitting users to watch "terrestrial" television programs in (near) real-time,[22] enabling users to watch illicit streams online, thereby avoiding the need for the user to obtain a subscription to receive the content,[23] and enabling users to consume on demand or to download popular movies, television programs, or music for free, using torrent or peer-to-peer technology.[24]

The posting of hyperlinks to unlawful online material also can be an act of communication of that material to the public.[25] The Court of Justice of the European Union has drawn a distinction in these cases so that linking to or making available works which are already freely available to the public with the right holder's consent is not a communication to the public, whereas such dealing with works not already freely available to the public with the right holder's consent could be a communication to the public, but only if the alleged infringer knows or ought to have known that the works had been unlawfully published.[26]

Infringement by Making Adaptation or Act Done in Relation to Adaptation

There are two ways in which an adaptation might infringe copyright. The first is where an adaptation is made (i.e., is recorded in writing or otherwise) of a literary, dramatic, or musical work, without the permission of the right holder.

The second is where the defendant deals in an adaptation of a literary, dramatic, or musical work, whether or not that adaptation has been recorded. In this instance, the copying, issuing to the public, renting or lending to the public, or performing, showing, or playing in public of an adaptation or communicating it to the public is an infringement of the

---

[22] *British Telecommunications Plc & Others* vs. *TV Catchup Limited* [2011] EWHC 1874 (Pat); Court of Justice of the European Union, Case C-607/11, *ITV Broadcasting Ltd & 6 Ors* vs. *TV Catchup* (TV Catchup).
[23] Court of Justice of the European Union, Case C-279/13 C, *More Entertainment AB* and Case C-527/15, *Stichting Brein*.
[24] *Twentieth Century Fox Film Corporation & Others* vs. *British Telecommunications Plc* [2011] EWHC 1981 (Ch) (aka "Newzbin2").
[25] Court of Justice of the European Union, Case C-466/12, *Svensson and Others* vs. *Retriever Sverige AB*.
[26] Court of Justice of the European Union, Case C-160/15, *GS Media BV* and Case C-527/15, *Stichting Brein* (aka Filmspeler).

original work. Similarly, copyright in a literary, dramatic, or musical work can be infringed by the making of an adaptation *of an adaptation* of that work.

What constitutes an adaptation under United Kingdom law depends on the underlying work. Literary works other than computer programs and databases are adapted by being translated. Dramatic works are adapted in the same way, and may be adapted by their conversion into a non-dramatic work. It also is an adaptation to convert a non-dramatic work into a dramatic work, and to convey the story or action of a work in picture form. A musical work can be adapted by being arranged or transcribed. An arrangement, altered version, or translation of a computer program or a database also is an adaptation of that work. A computer program is translated by compiling or decompiling it, or by converting it to a different computer language.

Secondary Infringement

In General

Unlike primary infringement[27] of copyright, which has a strict liability standard and therefore can be made out regardless of the defendant's state of mind, each act of secondary infringement requires a defendant to have a certain level of knowledge or reason to believe that there is dealing in an infringement.

Proving a defendant's knowledge of an infringement will rarely be an easy task, but demonstrating an awareness of pertinent facts that would be perceived as relevant by an objective person may suffice to raise a rebuttable inference that the defendant had reason to believe that he was dealing in an infringing copy or an infringing performance.

The Copyright, Designs and Patents Act does not define an infringing performance, but an "infringing copy" of a work is generally taken to mean a copy whose making constituted an infringement of the original work. An article that has been or is proposed to be imported into the United Kingdom also can be an infringing copy if its making in the United Kingdom would have infringed copyright in the underlying work or would have amounted to a breach of an exclusive license in relation to that work. An article that is a copy of a work in which copyright has ever subsisted is presumed to have been made when copyright subsisted in the work, until the contrary is proved.

---

27 Copyright, Designs and Patents Act 1988, Sections 22–27.

Dealings with Infringing Copy

Unless it is for private and domestic use, anyone who imports an infringing copy of a work into the United Kingdom, in the knowledge or with reason to believe that it is an infringing copy, infringes the copyright in that work.

A person who possesses, distributes, or publicly exhibits an infringing copy of a work in the course of business, who offers it for sale or for hire, or who otherwise distributes it to an extent that is prejudicial to the copyright owner, with knowledge or reason to believe that that copy is an infringing copy, also is liable for infringement of copyright.

Providing Means for Making Infringing Copies

Certain dealings in articles specifically designed or adapted for making copies of a work can infringe copyright where, again, the defendant has knowledge or reason to believe that the article will be used to make infringing copies.

The transmission of a work via a telecommunications system that does not amount to a communication to the public infringes copyright where the person responsible for the transmission knows or has reason to believe that infringing copies of the work will be made by means of the reception of the transmission in the United Kingdom or elsewhere.

As will be seen below, the temporary reproduction of a work in memory of a computer or set top box may qualify for the temporary copies exemption: where that is the case, the reception of a work will not result in the creation of an "infringing copy", so the transmitter will not be liable as a secondary infringer (at least not on that basis).

Permitting Use of Premises for Infringing Performance

Merely giving permission for a literary, dramatic, or musical work to be performed in a place of public entertainment can render a person liable for an infringement caused by that performance. Liability will not arise if that person believed on reasonable grounds when giving permission that the performance would not infringe copyright.

It is anticipated that since this cause of action is limited to performances in "places of public entertainment", most potential defendants will be aware of the need to consider issues of copyright licensing and public performance rights (and may even require performers as a matter of course to give a warranty in their hire agreement that they have all the necessary rights to perform the work), but this may not always be the case.

Provision of Apparatus for Infringing Performance

An infringement occasioned by a public performance of a work or by the playing or showing of it in public using apparatus for playing sound recordings, showing films, or receiving visual images or sounds conveyed by electronic means, can result in liability for those involved in what might normally be considered to be the background or support role of merely providing that apparatus.

Depending on their knowledge and belief, these secondary infringers can include the person who supplied the apparatus used for the infringement, the occupier of the premises in which the apparatus was situated when the primary infringement took place, and the person who supplied the copy of the sound recording or film used in the infringement.

Intermediaries and Joint Tortfeasorship

The challenge facing right holders in the increasingly digitally connected world is acute. Not only are there increasing numbers of infringements (and infringers) for right holders to challenge, but infringers can resume their illicit activities almost as and when they please: taking action against such infringers is neither proportionate nor cost-effective.

Therefore, in many actions for copyright infringement, a claimant will seek to add other parties to their claim even though those potential defendants themselves have not carried out one of the primary or secondary acts of infringement found in Sections 16–27 of the Copyright, Designs and Patents Act, as discussed above. In most cases, the claimant will seek to join the new defendant as a joint tortfeasor under the Common Law.

Joint tortfeasorship operates to hold a party liable for infringements carried out by another. The essence of it is that the third party has acted so closely with the infringer as to make the infringing act his own. Since liability depends on the extent of cooperation and direction between the parties, the test for establishing liability has not been affected by technological development in the same way as, for example, the development of the communication to the public right.

The bar for establishing joint tortfeasorship remains relatively high. That is not to say that claimants have not asked the courts for a declaration of joint tortfeasorship each time a service provider's technological development has improved the speed, accuracy, or profitability of infringers, from the advent of twin deck cassette recorders, to Internet service providers to online auction platforms.

In most cases, the court has, when applying the established principles of joint tortfeasorship, found that the mere facilitation or even knowledge of infringing activity is insufficient to establish liability as a joint tortfeasor.[28] For example, in *CBS Songs Ltd* vs. *Amstrad Consumer Electronics plc*,[29] which concerned the sale of twin deck cassette recorders that were being used to copy protected sound recordings, the Court of Appeal held that joint tortfeasorship required two or more persons acting in concert with one another in the furtherance of a common design in the infringement.

The Court rejected the idea that "facilitating the doing of an act" is the same as "procuring the doing of an act" and found that, as a rule, "inducement, incitement or persuasion to infringe must be by a defendant to an individual infringer" and that it must "identifiably procure a particular infringement". A supplier's knowledge that its equipment would be used to infringe copyright was held to be an insufficient basis for liability as a joint tortfeasor in *Amstrad Consumer Electronics plc* vs. *The British Phonographic Industry Ltd*.[30]

The extent of the agreement required between the infringer and the joint tortfeasor has also been explored in several cases. In *Unilever plc* vs. *Gillette (United Kingdom) Ltd.*,[31] the court held that the infringer and the alleged joint tortfeasor did not explicitly need to intend to infringe: a "tacit agreement" to combine to perform the acts complained of will suffice. Knowing assistance also is insufficient: the alleged joint tortfeasor must have "conspired with the primary party or procured or induced his commission of the tort . . . ; or he must have joined in the common design pursuant to which the tort was committed".[32] These cases were summed up in *SABAF SpA* vs. *Meneghetti SpA*[33] by the Court of Appeal:

> "The underlying concept for joint tortfeasance must be that the joint tortfeasor has been so involved in the commission of the tort as to make himself liable for the tort. Unless he has made the

---

28 Information society service providers are exempt from liability under certain conditions by virtue of the safe harbors found in the Electronic Commerce (EC Directive) Regulations 2002 (see text, below).
29 *CBS Songs Ltd* vs. *Amstrad Consumer Electronics plc* [1988] AC 1013.
30 *Amstrad Consumer Electronics plc* vs. *The British Phonographic Industry Ltd* [1986] FSR 159.
31 *Unilever plc* vs. *Gillette (United Kingdom) Ltd.* [1989] RPC 583.
32 *Credit Lyonnais Bank Nederland NV* vs. *Export Credit Guarantee Department* [1998] 1 Lloyds Rep 19.
33 *SABAF SpA* vs. *Meneghetti SpA* [2002] EWCA Civ 976.

infringing act his own, he has not himself committed the tort. That notion seems to us what underlies all the decisions to which we were referred. If there is a common design or concerted action or otherwise a combination to secure the doing of the infringing acts, each of the combiners has made the act his own and will be liable."

The court went on to find in that case that merely supplying goods to a purchaser who was then free to do with those goods what he wanted was not a sufficient basis for a finding of joint tortfeasorship. None of this is to say that the judiciary in the United Kingdom does not understand or have any sympathy with the right holders. In *L'Oréal SA & Others* vs. *eBay International AG and Others*,[34] a case concerning trade marks but to which the principles of joint tortfeasorship apply *mutatis mutandis*, Arnold J. said that, eBay having created via their platform the increased risk of infringement and having profited from it, there was much to be said for the view that "the consequences of that increased risk should fall upon eBay rather than upon the owners of the intellectual property rights that are infringed".

That view was insufficient, however, to found an action for joint tortfeasorship. It also was insufficient that the defendant platform facilitated the infringements, knew that such infringements occurred (and indeed were likely to occur), and profited from them: "these factors are not enough to make eBay Europe liable as joint tortfeasors".

The response from right holders has been, in part, to look for assistance from the intermediaries whose services are being used for infringements (e.g., through eBay's VeRO system or more generic "notice and takedown" style arrangements). Typically, this cooperation involves the right holder filing a complaint through the intermediary's chosen channels, providing it with the information it requires (such as evidence of the complainant's rights in the content and the reason why the objectionable content is believed to infringe those rights), so that the intermediary can enforce the terms of their user agreement and remove the allegedly infringing content.

In many cases, this cooperation is purely for efficacy. The intermediary is given the information it requires to satisfy itself that it should not permit the content to be hosted or made available through its services; and the right holder secures the removal of content. Both parties avoid

---

[34] *L'Oréal SA & Others* vs. *eBay International AG & Others* [2009] EWHC 1094 (Ch).

the time, expense, delay, and uncertainty of court proceedings. In other instances, right holders have moved from seeking to apportion liability on intermediaries to simply obtaining orders against them to force them to block access to infringing content, as discussed below.

Defenses

In General

A party accused of copyright infringement can defend itself in a number of ways. Some of these defenses will be the result of the alleged infringer's early appreciation of the infringement risk and their having taken measures to ensure that their acts remain within the applicable statutory defenses. Others will depend upon the claimant not making out their case or bringing their case within the relevant limitation period.

Procedural Defenses

A defendant can avoid liability in copyright infringement proceedings if the acts complained of took place more than six years before proceedings were commenced (by the issue of a claim form) and therefore are outside the relevant limitation period.

Given the sometimes complex matrix of employer-employee relationships and possibly joint authorship, a defendant may even argue that the wrong party is bringing the claim (although, except in cases where the defendant is the rightful owner of the copyright, this is a deficiency which can usually be fixed by an assignment of the copyright to the claimant or, at worst, by new proceedings being commenced by a new claimant).

Defenses of laches, acquiescence, and estoppel will turn on their own facts but, at least where claims brought to establish ownership of a work are concerned, they may be more difficult to establish following the decision in *Fisher* vs. *Brooker*,[35] where the claimant's claim of joint authorship of the track *Whiter Shade of Pale* was allowed to proceed despite his delay of 38 years in bringing his claim.

---

35 *Fisher* vs. *Brooker* [2009] UKHL 41.

Defenses on Burden of Proof

In the United Kingdom, it is the claimant's burden to prove his case and to do so on the balance of probabilities. If a claimant cannot prove all the elements of his claim on the balance of probabilities, the claim should fail.

A defendant will therefore usually argue that the act in respect of which proceedings have been brought is not a "restricted act", either because they are not dealing in the whole or a substantial part of the protected work or because their work has been created independently and without any copying of the protected work. They also may argue that the act complained of took place after the expiry of the relevant copyright term, or that the copyright owner had in fact authorized the act.

Statutory Defenses

In General

The Copyright, Designs and Patents Act sets out a large number of defenses to copyright infringement in Sections 28–76A inclusive. The most significant of these provisions are set out in more detail below.

Miscellaneous Defenses

The remaining provisions are grouped as follows:
(1) Making accessible copies for persons with disabilities (Sections 31A–F);
(2) Illustrations for instruction, anthologies for educational use, and various acts by educational establishments education (Sections 32–36A);
(3) Acts carried out by libraries, archives, educational establishments, librarians, and archivists (Sections 37–44A);
(4) Permitted uses of orphan works and use for public administration, including in Parliamentary and judicial proceedings, Royal Commissions, and statutory inquiries (Sections 44B–50 and Section 76A);
(5) Typefaces (Sections 54 and 55);
(6) Transfers of copies of works in electronic form (Section 56); and
(7) Miscellaneous acts in relation to literary, dramatic, musical, and artistic works (Sections 57–65), lending of works and playing of sound recordings (Sections 66), films and sound recordings (Sections 66A and 67), broadcasts (Sections 68–75), and adaptations (Section 76).

Making Temporary Copies

The objectives of this defense (Section 28A) are to "allow and ensure the development and operation of new technologies" and to "safeguard a fair balance between the rights and interests of right holders, on the one hand, and of users of protected works who wish to avail themselves of those new technologies, on the other".[36] The temporary copies exception (Section 28A) provides that temporary acts of reproduction do not infringe the reproduction right when the act:

(1) Is temporary;
(2) Is transient or incidental;
(3) Is an integral and essential part of a technological process;
(4) Has as its sole purpose the enabling of a transmission in a network between third parties by an intermediary or a lawful use of a work or protected subject matter; and
(5) Has no independent economic significance.

The Supreme Court has held that copies of works appearing on a computer screen are exempted from the reproduction right by virtue of the temporary copies exception, as are those that are stored temporarily in a web browser's cache.[37] The court noted that such copies were necessary for the user to be able to consume the underlying works, and that they were deleted automatically, after a short period of time and without requiring the intervention of the user of the computer making the copies.

Personal Copies for Private Use

Although this defense (Section 28B) remains on the statute books, it only applies, at best, to copies made before July 2015, which is the date on which a legal challenge against the defense succeeded.[38]

---

[36] Court of Justice of the European Union, Joined Cases C-403/08 and C-429/08, *Football Association Premier League Ltd.*, discussing Article 5 of Directive 2001/29/EC of the European Parliament and of the Council of 22 May 2001 on the harmonization of certain aspects of copyright and related rights in the information society (the "Copyright Directive"), from which Section 28A of the Copyright, Designs and Patents Act is derived.

[37] *Public Relations Consultants Association Limited* vs. *The Newspaper Licensing Agency Limited and Others* [2013] UKSC 18.

[38] *British Academy of Songwriters, Composers and Authors & Others* vs. *Secretary of State for Business, Innovation and Skills* [2015] EWHC 2041 (Admin).

The Judge refused to rule on whether the defense should be quashed retrospectively. If it can apply at all, it will provide an individual with a defense to his reproduction (before July 2015) of a work (other than a computer program) acquired by him on a permanent basis for his own private and non-commercial use.

Research and Private Study

Fair dealing with a work for private study does not infringe copyright in that work (Section 29). Fair dealing with a work for non-commercial research purposes does not infringe copyright if it is accompanied by a sufficient acknowledgement (if possible).

What is fair dealing is not defined in the Copyright, Designs and Patents Act, but acts that prejudice the rights of the right holder while enriching the defendant are less likely to amount to fair dealing.

Copies for Text and Data Analysis for Non-Commercial Research

A person with lawful access to a work can make a copy of that work without infringing copyright if the copy is made to enable him to carry out a computational analysis of anything recorded in the work (Section 29A). The sole purpose of the analysis must be non-commercial research for a non-commercial purpose, and the copy must be accompanied by a sufficient acknowledgement (if possible).

Criticism, Review, Quotation, and News Reporting

Copyright in a work made available to the public is not infringed by fair dealing with that work for criticism or review, if it is accompanied by a sufficient acknowledgement (Section 30), if possible. A quotation from a work made available to the public can be used without infringing copyright if the quotation is fair dealing, is no more than is required by the purpose for which it is used, and is accompanied by an acknowledgement, if possible. A contractual term seeking to restrict or prevent such a quotation is unenforceable.

Fair dealing with a work other than a photograph to report current events does not infringe copyright. The fair dealing must be accompanied by a sufficient acknowledgement. This requirement is only excused in relation to reporting by means of a sound recording, film, or broadcast, and only where it would be impossible.

Caricature, Parody, or Pastiche

Copyright in a work is not infringed by fair dealing for the purposes of caricature, parody, or pastiche, and a contractual term seeking to restrict or prevent such dealing is unenforceable (Section 30A). The Court of Justice of the European Union has ruled[39] that "parody" in this context is an autonomous concept of EU law and that the characteristics of parody are to:
   (1)   Evoke, but to be noticeably different from, an existing work; and
   (2)   Constitute an expression of humor or mockery.

Beyond that, the parody does not need to display an original character of its own; nor must it relate to the original work or mention its source.

Incidental Inclusion of Copyright Material

A party who incidentally includes a work in an artistic work, sound recording, film, or broadcast does not infringe copyright in that work and that later work can be issued to the public, or played, shown, or communicated to the public without infringing copyright in the earlier work. However, several works relating to music are not to be regarded as having been "incidentally" included in another work if they are deliberately included.

Dealings with Computer Programs and Databases

A lawful user of a copy of a computer program is permitted to undertake a number of acts in relation to the computer program and any contractual term seeking to restrict or prohibit this right is void. A "lawful user" is defined simply as a person who has a right to use the program (Sections 50A–D).

A lawful user can make a back-up copy of a computer program if it is necessary for him to have it for the purposes of his lawful use (Section 50A). Similarly, a lawful user can decompile a copy of a computer program if it is necessary to obtain the information necessary to create an independent program, provided that the information gained from the decompiling is not used for any other purpose (Section 50B).

A lawful user also may observe, study, or test the functioning of a program while loading, displaying, running, transmitting, or storing the

---

[39] Court of Justice of the European Union, Case C-201/13, *Deckmyn*.

program, in order to determine the ideas and principles that underlie the program. Otherwise, copying or adapting a computer program by a lawful user is only permitted to the extent necessary for his lawful use of the program and only if such copying or adapting is not prohibited by any agreement giving him the right to use the program (Section 50C).

A person having a right to use any part of a database can do anything in the exercise of that right which is necessary for the purposes of accessing and using that part of the database without infringing copyright in it. Any contractual term seeking to restrict or prohibit this right is void (Section 50D).

Designs

The overlap of copyright and protection for designs is a complex area with a detailed history. The Copyright, Designs and Patents Act seeks to simplify this relationship in two areas in particular (Sections 51 and 53). First, it states that making an article to a design (or copying an article made to a design) is not an infringement of copyright in the design document (or model recording or embodying a design), if the design is for something other than an artistic work or a typeface.

As has been seen above, it is not always clear whether or not an item is an artistic work, but if a defendant can argue that it is not an artistic work, then Section 51 may afford a defense to any claim of copyright infringement and the dispute may fall to be determined under the rules for designs (which attract much shorter terms). The Copyright, Designs and Patents Act also states that copyright is not infringed by anything done pursuant to an assignment or license of a registered design, in certain circumstances.

Representation of Certain Artistic Works on Public Display

Unlike some other countries, the United Kingdom expressly permits the representation of buildings in graphic works, photographs, films, and broadcasts (Section 62). If a sculpture, a model for a building, or a work of artistic craftsmanship is permanently situated in a public place or in premises open to the public, those same representations are permitted as a matter of law.

Intermediary Safe Harbors

The Electronic Commerce (EC Directive) Regulations 2002 implement provisions of the E-Commerce Directive[40] insofar as they apply to the safe harbors from liability under Section IV of that Directive for Information Society Service Providers in certain circumstances.

An information society service is defined as "any service normally provided for remuneration, at a distance, by electronic means and at the individual request of a recipient of services". There is no requirement of a direct, causal connection between the "service" and the "remuneration". Services supported by advertising revenue rather than subscriptions are therefore probably still eligible to qualify as an information society service provider.

In essence, the Regulations provide that an information society service provider may not be liable for damages or a pecuniary remedy or for a criminal sanction as a result of information transmitted, cached, or hosted by it under certain conditions. It can, however, still be the subject of an injunction and right holders in the United Kingdom have succeeded in obtaining injunctions against Internet service providers that force them to block access to infringing content.

The Court of Justice of the European Union also has held that the hosting exemption is only available where the service provider is "neutral, in the sense that [its] conduct is merely technical, automatic and passive, pointing to a lack of knowledge or control of the data which it stores". That safe harbor may be lost where the host "has provided assistance which entails, in particular, optimizing the presentation of the [infringing content] in question or promoting [that content]", or where it is "aware of facts or circumstances on the basis of which a diligent economic operator should have identified the illegality in question" and does not expeditiously remove the material or disable access to it.[41]

Criminal Liability

Actions in respect of the infringement of copyright in the United Kingdom are not limited to claims of civil infringement. Certain infringing

---

40 Directive 2000/31/EC of the European Parliament and of the Council of 8 June 2000 on certain legal aspects of information society services, in particular electronic commerce, in the Internal Market.
41 Court of Justice of the European Union, Joined Cases C-236/08 to C-268/08, *Google France*; Case C-324/09, *L'Oréal* vs. *eBay*.

acts also can attract criminal liability. These acts are enforceable by local weights and measures authorities (or the Department of Economic Development in Northern Ireland) and are punishable by a fine and/or imprisonment.

The criminal court also has power to make orders for delivery up, forfeiture, or destruction of certain goods in the course of proceedings, and can issue a warrant authorizing a constable to enter and search premises, using such reasonable force as is necessary and, when there, to seize an article if he has a reasonable belief that it is evidence that certain offences have been or are about to be committed. The owner of copyright in a variety of works also can request that Customs and Excise (now the department of HM Revenue and Customs) treat infringing copies of various works as prohibited goods.

Criminal liability can attach to the making of or dealing with an article that is, and which the defendant knows or has reason to believe is, an infringing copy of a copyright work and to the making or possessing of an article specifically designed or adapted for making copies of a particular copyright work, when he knows or has reason to believe that it is to be used to make infringing copies for sale, for hire, or for use in the course of business. Directors and officers of a body corporate also can be liable with their company for an offence committed with their consent or connivance.

Notwithstanding the harsher deterrent effect on potential infringers, criminal proceedings in relation to copyright infringement are relatively rare and typically revolve around infringement in a commercial context where the alleged offender knows or has reason to believe that he is dealing with an infringement. Furthermore, right holders do not always want to be involved in criminal proceedings since, unlike in civil proceedings, their prospects of recovering their costs are remote, nor are they able to retain control of proceedings.

Remedies

In General

Remedies for infringement of copyright[42] are available to the copyright owner or, as the case may be, the licensee (although only certain remedies

---

42 Copyright, Designs and Patents Act 1988, Chapter IV.

are available to a non-exclusive licensee, as addressed in more detail below). Broadly speaking, the remedies are:
(1) Damages;
(2) Account of profits;
(3) Injunction;
(4) Order for delivery up of infringing articles;
(5) Seizure by the copyright owner or a person authorized by him; and
(6) Costs.

Once it has proved that its copyright has been infringed, the various remedies are generally available at the election of the copyright owner. However, the court will only order a remedy if it considers that it is in the interests of justice, and injunctions in particular have requirements that are more stringent.

Damages

The purpose of an order for damages in a copyright infringement action is to compensate the copyright owner for the damage he has suffered. When assessing the quantum of damages, the court will take into account all the circumstances of the claim and, in particular, the flagrancy of the infringement (which may result in an award of additional damages under Section 97), and the benefits to the infringing party.

The court may order damages in addition to other remedies except an account of profits. It is a defense to a claim for damages for the infringing party to show that they did not know and had no reason to believe that the work they copied was protected by copyright. In practice, merely pleading ignorance will be insufficient. Even if a defendant avails himself of this defense, the other remedies are available to the copyright owner.

Account of Profits

An award for an account of profits allows a successful claimant to reach into the profits the infringer has made as a result of his infringing activity and to recover those profits for himself.

In effect, the copyright owner says that the profits were generated from his copyright and therefore belong to him. A claimant may elect to recover either damages or an account of profits: he cannot recover both. He may wait to make that election until he has sufficient information to understand the value of each one.

Injunction

An injunction may be available under Section 97A of the Copyright, Designs and Patents Act against a service provider who has actual knowledge that another person is using their services to infringe another person's copyright. The copyright owner would be well advised to formally put the intermediary on notice of the infringement before commencing proceedings for an injunction, by a notice specifying the right holder's name and address, the claim to copyright in the infringed work, and details of the infringement.

Several such injunctions have been awarded against Internet service providers in the High Court[43] and their availability is now well established. In practice, therefore, many service providers will, on receipt of a notice, stop the infringement without the need for the copyright owner to seek the injunction. The principles relevant to the granting of an interim injunction, that is, one pending trial of the substance of the matter, are as set out in *American Cyanamid Co* vs. *Ethicom Ltd.*,[44] namely:

(1) Whether there is a serious issue to be tried;
(2) Whether the balance of convenience between the parties favors the granting of the injunction;
(3) Whether damages would be an adequate remedy in respect of the infringing act; and
(4) Whether there are any special factors.

An applicant for an interim injunction also will be required to give a cross-undertaking in damages, meaning that it must undertake to make the defendant whole for losses caused by the injunction if it is later determined that the injunction should not have been granted.

Order for Delivery Up of Infringing Articles

This remedy is only available where the defendant in the course of business has possession, custody, or control of an infringing copy, or if they (regardless of whether or not it is in the course of business) have an article designed or adapted to make copies of a particular copyright work.

In the latter case, the copyright owner must show that the defendant had knowledge or reason to believe that the article had been or was

---

43 *Twentieth Century Fox Film Corporation & Others* vs. *British Telecommunications Plc* [2011] EWHC 1981 (Ch).
44 *American Cyanamid Co* vs. *Ethicom Ltd* [1975] AC 396.

going to be used to make infringing copies of a copyright work. The copyright owner should also seek an order for the copy or article in question to be disposed of or forfeited to them. This remedy is usually only available for six years after the article or infringing copy was made.

Seizure of Infringing Articles

A copyright owner (or person authorized by them) may seize and detain any items that would be subject to an order for delivery up if they are "found exposed or otherwise immediately available for sale or hire".

There are certain restrictions to this remedy, and in particular the copyright owner must first notify the local police station of the time and place at which they propose to carry out the seizure, and they may only carry out a seizure in a place to which the public have access and is not the permanent or regular place of business of the person who has possession, custody, or control of the infringing items. They also must leave a notice with a prescribed form of wording setting out the person conducting the seizure (or who authorized it) and the grounds on which the seizure was made.

Action by Licensee

The rights and remedies of an exclusive licensee in relation to infringement of the licensed rights will run concurrently with the copyright owner.

Therefore, in order to seek a remedy (other than an injunction) in the courts, the general position is that both owner and licensee must be joined as a party to the action. The court has discretion to make an exception and, if a party is joined but chooses to play no active role in the proceedings, they will not have any liability for the other parties' costs.

Action by Non-Exclusive Licensee

In order for a non-exclusive licensee to bring an action for the infringement of the rights licensed to it, the infringement must be directly connected to an act taken by the licensee under the license (for example, producing copies of an article previously produced by the licensee which incorporated the licensed work).

However, this only applies where the license is in writing, signed by or on behalf of the owner, and expressly grants the licensee a right of action under Section 101A of the Copyright, Designs and Patents Act. In practice, this is uncommon and a non-exclusive licensee who wishes to enforce their rights against infringers should insist that the license includes either an express grant of a right of action or an obligation on the copyright owner to take action in the case of infringement of the licensed rights. As with an exclusive licensee, any rights and remedies available to a non-exclusive licensee are concurrent with those of the copyright owner.

Brexit

Although much of the copyright law that applies in the United Kingdom is based on domestic legislation, some of it is derived from directives and regulations of the EU. Courts interpret the laws of the United Kingdom, so far as possible, in a way that is consistent with the law of the EU and frequently refer questions about how a provision of the EU law should be interpreted in the domestic context to the Court of Justice of the European Union.

There are both legal and commercial reasons for these efforts to pursue consistency, if not harmonization and, when interpreting a domestic provision of EU law, courts will often look not just to the jurisprudence of the Court of Justice of the European Union but also to decisions of the domestic courts of Member States who have interpreted the same provision.

Brexit, whereby the United Kingdom ceases to be a Member State of the EU, could have a significant impact on the United Kingdom's copyright law. It is not currently possible, however, to put the position any more definitively than that it "could" have a significant impact, since as at the date of writing there are no guarantees as to what the post-Brexit legal landscape might look like.

Bearing in mind that much of copyright law is based on treaty obligations under the Berne Convention, the impact might be limited in terms of how judges will approach the concept of copyright protection and copyright infringement in a Common Law jurisdiction.

Three areas where divergence between the EU and United Kingdom could be pronounced, however, are in the exhaustion of the right to prevent a third party from putting into circulation copies of works which have first been put onto the market in the EEA (in the event that the United Kingdom ceases to be a member of the EEA), the determination of whether copyright subsists in a work, and in the concept of the right to prevent others from communicating a work to the public. It is to be expected that the movement of copies of protected works across borders will fall to be determined by a bilateral agreement between the United Kingdom and the EU, and that such an agreement will not leave judges with much room for judicial discretion.

As has been noted above, the Court of Justice of the European Union has determined that works are "original" where they are the expression of the author's own intellectual creation. That fluid test appears to be at odds with the set categories of works in which copyright can subsist under the Copyright, Designs and Patents Act, and it is possible to envisage a work that would qualify for protection under the Court of Justice of the European Union's "intellectual creation" test while remaining outside the descriptions of works set out in the Copyright, Designs and Patents Act.

Similarly, it is not clear whether United Kingdom courts would have adopted the Court of Justice of the European Union's interpretation of the communication to the public right if it was not obliged to do so. If it should cease to be so obliged in the future, it could continue to apply it anyway, modify it, or disregard it.

In reality, the United Kingdom's judges are respected around the world, not just for the quality of their decision-making but also for their appreciation of commercial reality, meaning that even if they are no longer bound by decisions of the Court of Justice of the European Union, they will in all likelihood continue to refer to them in the same way that they currently refer to decisions of other jurisdictions when it is helpful to do so. Whether the courts of other Member States, or even the Court of Justice of the European Union itself, will consider the United Kingdom's judgments in the same way remains to be seen.

Conclusion

Copyright is a complex and intricate area of law in which technological developments have a profound impact on public discourse around its scope and duration, particularly in fast-moving areas such as software and online services. As has been seen in this chapter, however, United Kingdom courts eschew rigidity and favor a more nuanced approach towards the balance between the ability of the copyright owner to exploit their rights and the advancement of the common good through permitted reuse and redistribution of existing content.

Nonetheless, courts in the United Kingdom value certainty in the rule of law and have resisted the urge to upset decades of jurisprudence in response to the increasingly influential role of intermediaries in general and information society service providers in particular. The courts also recognize that works protected by copyright are exploited and misused on an increasingly global scale: an awareness of, and even some alignment to, international norms can be a good thing in such circumstances, even where it is not legally required.

The possibility that the United Kingdom may not be bound to new laws of the European Union after Brexit raises many interesting questions, particularly in the questions of copyright subsistence and the exhaustion of rights in works first put into circulation in the EEA.

Procedural innovations such as the Intellectual Property Enterprise Court permit smaller companies to obtain access to justice and protection for their creations, with judgments delivered by well-respected judges. With all matters taken together, the United Kingdom provides a forum for meeting the challenges facing litigants in copyright infringement proceedings in a predictable yet commercially sensible way.

United States

Jonathan I. Feil
Simburg, Ketter, Sheppard & Purdy, LLP
Seattle, Washington, United States

Introduction

Under United States copyright law,[1] copyright infringement consists of "violat[ing] any of the exclusive rights of the copyright owner", importing unauthorized copies of copyrighted works into the United States, or exporting them from the United States.[2]

The United States is generally regarded as providing strict protection of the rights of intellectual property owners. On the other hand, no United States agency has a general mandate to bring enforcement actions for copyrights.[3] Copyright enforcement is primarily left for copyright holders to pursue in court through a civil action. However, "criminal copyright infringement, including infringement without monetary gain, is investigated by the [Federal Bureau of Investigation] and is punishable by fines and federal imprisonment" in a prosecution brought by the United States Justice Department.[4]

In recent years, United States courts have grappled with significant issues in copyright law, including copyrightability of useful articles, fair use, contracts and licensing, the meaning of "substantial similarity",

---

[1] In this article, "copyright law" refers to the general body of United States law governing copyright. "Copyright Act" refers to the Copyright Act of 1976 and its amendments, codified in Title 17 of the United States Code. See Copyright Law of the United States and Related Laws Contained in Title 17 of the United States Code (December 2016), United States Copyright Office Circular Number 92, see https://www.copyright.gov/title17/title17.pdf.

[2] 17 United States Code, Section 501(a). As a formal matter, the statute distinguishes between "copies" and "phonorecords" (17 United States Code, Section 101) in defining material objects in which works eligible for copyright may be fixed, perceived, reproduced, or otherwise communicated. In this article, the term "copies" will be used to refer to either or both.

[3] Furchtgott-Roth, *The Asymmetric Enforcement of Federal Copyright Laws* (2014), see https://www.hudson.org/research/10301-the-asymmetric-enforcement-of-federal-copyright-laws.

[4] Department of Justice Federal Property Management Regulations, 41 Code of Federal Regulations, Section 128-1.5009(e)(2); 17 United States Code, Section 506.

contributory liability, and how works become public domain. New technologies for creating and distributing content and international commerce have been prime influences in shaping United States copyright law.

Legal Basis for Copyright Protection in the United States

Federal Copyright Legislation

Copyright law in the United States is entirely a matter of national (federal) law and administration. The power to enact copyright legislation was expressly granted to Congress in the United States Constitution: "Congress shall have Power . . . To promote the Progress of Science and useful Arts, by securing for limited Times to Authors and Inventors the exclusive Right to their respective Writings and Discoveries".[5]

The Copyright Act of 1976 (the "1976 Act"),[6] which took effect on 1 January 1978, provides the basic framework for the current copyright law, and expressly preempts all state laws that grant the same or "equivalent" rights as the federal law, whether or not those state laws conflict with federal law.[7] There have been 70 amendments since its enactment on 19 October 1976. The most important amendments have involved new technologies and international harmonization:

(1) Computer Software Copyright Act of 1980, providing the framework for protection of computer programs;[8]

---

[5] United States Constitution, Article I, Section 8.
[6] Pub. L. Number 94-553, 90 Stat. 2541.
[7] 17 United States Code, Section 301(a); Myers, Principles of Intellectual Property Law (3d Ed., 2017), at pp. 154 and 155. *Maloney* vs. *T3Media Inc.*, 853 F.3d 1004 (9th Cir., 2017) (athletes' state law right of publicity claim against licensing of photographs for non-commercial art use preempted by Copyright Law).
[8] Pub. L. Number 96-517, 94 Stat. 3015. Unable to agree on the proper scope or application of copyright law to computer programs in the 1976 Act, Congress created a National Commission on New Technological Uses of Copyrighted Works (CONTU) to study the issues and report. The 1980 amendments incorporate most of the recommendations of the CONTU Final Report, specifically (i) defining "computer program" as a "set of statements or instructions to be used directly or indirectly in a computer in order to bring about a certain result" and (ii) providing that it is not an infringement for the owner of a copy of a computer program to make copies or adaptations needed in utilizing the program on a machine or copies for archival purposes.

(2) Semiconductor Chip Protection Act of 1984, providing design protection for semiconductor chips;[9]
(3) Berne Convention Implementation Act of 1988, implementing United States accession to the Berne Convention for the Protection of Literary and Artistic Works;[10]
(4) Visual Artists Rights Act of 1990 (Visual Artists Rights Act), protecting, consistent with Article 6 *bis* of the Berne Convention, the "moral rights" of attribution and integrity to paintings, drawings, prints, sculptures, and still photographic images produced for exhibition only and existing in single copies or limited editions;[11]
(5) Architectural Works Copyright Protection Act (1990), providing explicit copyright protection for original designs of architecture in virtually any form, including plans, drawings, and buildings themselves;[12]
(6) Uruguay Round Agreements Act (1994), restoring United States copyright to certain foreign works that were in the public domain in the United States but protected by copyright in their countries of origin;[13]
(7) No Electronic Theft (NET) Act (1997), removing from criminal copyright infringement the requirement that the infringement was for the purpose of "commercial advantage or private financial gain";[14]
(8) Sonny Bono Copyright Term Extension Act (1998), extending the term of copyright protection for most works to life plus 70 years;[15]
(9) Digital Millennium Copyright Act (1998), exempting from copyright infringement liability Internet and other online service providers that follow prescribed "safe harbor" guidelines, criminalizing the circumvention of copy-prevention, digital rights management, and access control systems, and heightening the penalties for copyright infringement on the Internet;[16]

---

[9] Pub. L. Number 98-620, Title III, 98 Stat. 3335, at p. 3347 (adding 17 United States Code Chapter 9).
[10] Pub. L. Number 100-568, 102 Stat. 2853.
[11] Pub. L. Number 101-650, 104 Stat. 5089, at p. 5128.
[12] Title VII of the Judicial Improvements Act of 1990, Pub. L. Number 101-650, 104 Stat. 5089, at p. 5133.
[13] Pub. L. Number 103-465, 108 Stat. 4809, at p. 4973.
[14] Pub. L. Number 105-147, 111 Stat. 2678.
[15] Title I of Pub. L. Number 105-298, 112 Stat. 2827.
[16] Pub. L. Number 105-304, 112 Stat. 2860.

(10) Fraudulent Online Identity Sanctions Act (2004), criminalizing the knowing provision of false contact information for domain names used in connection with copyright infringement;[17] and
(11) Artists' Rights and Theft Prevention Act (2005) authorizing criminal penalties for unauthorized recording of motion pictures.[18]

United States Copyright Office

The United States Copyright Office, a department within the Library of Congress (not part of the Executive Branch), is responsible for administering the registration of copyrights, recordation of title and licenses, a number of statutory licensing provisions, and other aspects of the United States copyright law.

The Register of Copyrights also is the principal advisor to Congress on national and international copyright matters.[19] The Copyright Office does not, however, have authority to take action directly against copyright infringement.

Protection of Foreign Works

The United States offers considerable protection to foreign works under international copyright treaties and conventions. It is a member of the two principal international copyright conventions, the Berne Convention for the Protection of Literary and Artistic Works (Berne Convention)[20] and the Universal Copyright Convention.[21] Works that are not subject to these conventions may be protected under bilateral agreements between

---

[17] Pub. L. Number 108-482, 118 Stat. 3912 and 3916.
[18] Pub. L. Number 109-9, 119 Stat. 218.
[19] Overview of the Copyright Office, https://www.copyright.gov/about/.
[20] Berne Convention Implementation Act of 1988, Pub. L. Number 100-568, 102 Stat. 2853, full text on the United States Copyright Office website, see https://copyright.gov/title17/92appk.pdf. Berne Convention full text on the official WIPO website, see http://www.wipo.int/treaties/en/text.jsp?file_id=283698. Under United States copyright law, no right or interest in a work eligible for copyright protection may be claimed specifically under the Berne Convention, but only by the implementing provisions in the Copyright Act. 17 United States Code, Section 104(c).
[21] 17 United States Code, Section 104(b)(2); Universal Copyright Convention as revised at Paris on 24 July 1971, with Appendix Declaration relating to Article XVII and Resolution concerning Article XI 1971, full text on UNESCO website, see http://portal.unesco.org/en/ev.php-URL_ID=15241&URL_DO=DO_TOPIC&URL_SECTION=201.html.

the United States and other countries, and may be protected in other countries under specific provisions of the country's national laws.[22]

Since almost all countries are either members or aspiring members of the World Trade Organization (WTO) and are thus conforming to the Agreement on Trade-Related Aspects of Intellectual Property Rights (TRIPS),[23] the Universal Copyright Convention has lost significance. TRIPS sets down minimum standards for the regulation by national governments of many forms of intellectual property as applied to nationals of other WTO member nations.

Elements of Copyright Infringement

Two basic elements must be proven to establish copyright infringement:
(1) Ownership of a valid copyright; and
(2) Activity by the defendant that violates any of the copyright owner's exclusive rights respecting the work.[24]

Most copyright claims are asserted against the direct infringer — the writer or composer who copies portions of another's work, the unlicensed publisher of a copyrighted work, the YouTube channel that uploads a copyrighted movie. To establish the defendant's liability for direct infringement, the plaintiff must show that the defendant was the cause of the infringement.[25]

A limited liability entity will not protect the individual tortfeasor who commits direct infringement as an officer, employee, or agent from liability, even without piercing the corporate veil or alleging alter ego liability. Direct copyright infringement is generally a strict liability tort.

---

[22] United States Copyright Office, Circular Number 38A, see https://www.copyright.gov/circs/circ38a.pdf.
[23] TRIPS Agreement, as amended on 23 January 2017, full text on WIPO website, see https://www.wto.org/english/docs_e/legal_e/31bis_trips_01_e.htm.
[24] *Feist Publications* vs. *Rural Telephone Service Co.*, 499 U.S. 340, at p. 361 (1991). The word "copying" is "shorthand" for the various activities that may infringe a copyright owner's exclusive rights. *Range Rd. Music, Inc.* vs. *E. Coast Foods, Inc.*, 668 F.3d 1148, at pp. 1153 and 1154 (9th Cir., 2012).
[25] *Perfect 10, Inc.* vs. *Giganews, Inc.*, 847 F.3d 657, at p. 666 (9th Cir.) cert. denied, 138 S. Ct. 504 (2017) ("where it is clear that infringement has occurred, courts must determine who is close enough to the [infringing] event to be considered the most important cause").

There is no requirement on the plaintiff to show how the defendant behaved intentionally, recklessly, or even negligently.[26]

A defendant also may be secondarily liable for acts that lead to copyright infringement by another. Copyright law allows imposition of vicarious liability "when the defendant profits directly from the infringement and has a right and ability to supervise the direct infringer, even if the defendant initially lacks knowledge of the infringement".[27] A defendant may be liable for contributory infringement engaged in by another based on knowledge or reason to know of the infringing activity and intentionally inducing or materially contributing to that infringing activity.[28]

Sale of a device, product, or service that has the potential to infringe may constitute contributory infringement — even if the device is capable of substantial non-infringing use — if the defendant's intent to induce the infringing activity is shown by clear expression of that intent or other affirmative steps to encourage.[29]

Whether breach of a copyright license is actionable as copyright infringement turns on whether the provision breached is a condition of the license or a mere covenant. The licensor will have a breach of contract claim, not a copyright infringement claim, for breach of a mere covenant but, if the nature of the licensee's violation consists of failure to satisfy a condition to the license grant, rights dependent upon satisfaction of such condition have not been effectively licensed and, therefore, use by the licensee is without authority and may constitute infringement of copyright.[30]

---

26 Goldstein, *Goldstein On Copyright*, Volume 2, Section 8.1, Note 1 (3rd ed., 2014); Goold, "Is Copyright Infringement a Strict Liability Tort?", 30 *Berkeley Tech. L.J.* 305 (2015), see http://scholarship.law.berkeley.edu/btlj/ol30/iss1/7.

27 *Metro-Goldwyn-Mayer Studios Inc.* vs. *Grokster, Ltd.*, 545 U.S. 913, 930 n.9 (2005); *Ellison* vs. *Robertson*, 357 F.3d 1072, at p. 1076 (9th Cir., 2004) ("A defendant is vicariously liable for copyright infringement if he enjoys a direct financial benefit from another's infringing activity and has the right and ability to supervise the infringing activity.").

28 *Perfect 10, Inc.* vs. *Giganews, Inc.*, 847 F.3d 657, at pp. 671 and 672 (9th Cir.); *cert. denied*, 138 S. Ct. 504 (2017); *MDY Indus., LLC* vs. *Blizzard Entm't, Inc.*, 629 F.3d 928, at pp. 937 and 938 (9th Cir., 2010), amended and superseded on denial of reh'g, 2011 WL 538748 (9th Cir., 17 February 2011).

29 Compare *Metro-Goldwyn-Mayer Studios Inc.* vs. *Grokster, Ltd.*, 545 U.S. 913, at p. 939 (2005) with *Sony Corp. of Am.* vs. *Universal City Studios, Inc.*, 464 U.S. 417, at p. 442 (1984).

30 *Jacobsen* vs. *Katzer*, 535 F.3d 1373, at p. 1380 (Fed. Cir., 2008) (applying doctrine to open course software licensing); *Sun Microsystems, Inc.*, vs. *Microsoft Corp.*, 188 F.3d 1115, at p. 1121 (9th Cir., 1999).

Rights Covered by Copyright in the United States

Exclusive Rights of Owner of Copyrighted Work

The copyright owner of a work protected by United States copyright law possesses the exclusive right, personally or through licensees, to:
(1) Reproduce the work;
(2) Prepare derivative works based on the work;
(3) Distribute copies of the work to the public;
(4) Perform the work publicly; and
(5) Display the copyrighted work publicly.[31]

The right to reproduce copies of the work is often the most important right to the copyright owner. Indeed, it is the oldest right under British copyright law.[32] No one other than the copyright owner may make or authorize copies of the work. It is not necessary that the entire original work be copied for an infringement of the reproduction right to occur. All that is necessary is that the copying be substantial and material[33] and not trivial or *de minimis*.[34] This can be a highly subjective question and depend on the nature of the work.

"Not all copying constitutes infringement, however . . . [T]he substantial similarity analysis must focus on similarity of expression, i.e., material susceptible of copyright protection . . . . [I]n an action for infringement, it must be determined both whether the similarities between the works are substantial from the point of view of the lay observer and whether those similarities involve copyrightable material."[35]

The right to prepare derivative works overlaps somewhat with the reproduction right. Under copyright law, a derivative work is "a work based upon one or more preexisting works" and includes translations, musical arrangements, dramatizations, motion pictures, art reproductions,

---

[31] 17 United States Code, Section 106.
[32] Act for the Encouragement of Learning, by Vesting the Copies of Printed Books in the Authors or Purchasers of Such Copies, during the Times therein mentioned (Statute of Anne or Copyright Act of 1710), 8 Ann., c. 21.
[33] *Harper & Row Publishers Inc.* vs. *Nation Enterprises*, 471 U.S. 539 (1985) (300 words of verbatim quotes from unpublished memoir).
[34] *Newton* vs. *Diamond*, 388 F.3d 1189, at pp. 1192 and 1193 (9th Cir., 2004) (use is considered *de minimis* "if it is so meager and fragmentary that the average audience would not recognize the appropriation").
[35] *Oravec* vs. *Sunny Isles Luxury Ventures, L.C.*, 527 F.3d 1218, at p. 1224 (11th Cir., 2008).

and abridgments — any "form in which a work may be recast, transformed, or adapted".[36] Like the reproduction right, a substantial and material, rather than a trivial or *de minimis*, portion of the copyright-protected content must be used, and the purpose and amount of transformation may determine whether the derivative work constitutes an infringement.[37]

The distribution right grants to the copyright holder the exclusive right to make the work available to the public by sale, rental, lease, or lending. In addition to entitling the copyright holder to prevent the distribution of unauthorized copies, it allows the copyright holder to control the first publication and distribution of the work. The exclusive distribution right extends to importing or exporting copies "without the authority of the owner of copyright".[38] The distribution right is limited, however, by the "first sale doctrine" (see text, below).

Under United States copyright law, the public performance right applies only to literary, musical, dramatic, audiovisual, choreographic works, pantomimes, and motion pictures.[39] A performance is considered "public" when the work is performed in a "place open to the public or at a place where a substantial number of persons outside of a normal circle of a family and its social acquaintances is gathered", or if it is transmitted to multiple locations, such as through television, radio, or digital audio transmission (notably, Internet streaming).[40] Since computer programs are considered literary and also many audiovisual works, the public performance right applies to software. However, other than publicly available video games,[41] the performance right in software has not been developed.

Like the public performance right, the public display right is limited to certain works, namely, literary, musical, dramatic, choreographic, pictorial, graphical, and sculptural works, pantomimes, and still images from motion pictures and other audio visual works.[42] Whether a work is displayed "publicly" applies the same definition as the public performance right.[43]

---

36 17 United States Code, Section 101.
37 *Campbell* vs. *Acuff-Rose Music Inc.*, 510 U.S. 560 (1984) (repeated use of bass riff and theme was substantial and material, and not *de minimis*, but potential "fair use" as parody).
38 17 United States Code, Section 602(a), (b).
39 17 United States Code, Section 106(4).
40 17 United States Code, Section 101.
41 *Midway Mfg. Co.* vs. *Artic Intern., Inc.*, 704 F.2d 1009 (7th Cir.), *cert denied*, 464 U.S. 823 (1983).
42 17 United States Code, Section 106(5).
43 17 United States Code, Section 101.

Protections for Particular Classes of Works

Since December 1990, the Architectural Works Copyright Protection Act[44] has boosted copyright protection for architects, by treating constructed buildings, along with architectural plans, models, or drawings, as "architectural works" whose copyright is capable of infringement[45] — such as by constructing a building by copying another building or violating a licensing condition on the number of houses that can be built from proprietary home designs and plans.[46]

United States copyright law does not include an overall recognition or protection of "moral rights".[47] However, the Visual Artists Rights Act,[48] passed in 1990, amends United States copyright law to protect the moral rights of the creators of certain works of visual art, consistent with Article 6 *bis* of the Berne Convention.

The Visual Artists Rights Act provides additional and independent protections to authors of works of visual art. A work of visual art is defined to include "a painting, drawing, print, or sculpture, existing in a single copy" or in a limited edition. The definition specifically excludes a number of works that are otherwise copyrightable, including motion pictures and other audiovisual works, books, posters, periodicals, works made for hire, and merchandising, advertising, promotional, or packaging materials.[49]

The "rubric of moral rights encompasses many varieties of rights, but the two most widely recognized are attribution and integrity".[50] The Visual Artists Rights Act provides that, in addition to the exclusive rights

---

[44] Title VII of the Judicial Improvements Act of 1990, Pub. L. Number 101-650, 104 Stat. 5089, at p. 5133.

[45] United States Copyright Office, Circular Number 41, see https://www.copyright.gov/circs/circ41.pdf.

[46] *Kipp Flores Architects LLC* vs. *Mid-Continent Casualty Company*, 852 F.3d 405, at p. 407 (5th Cir., 2017).

[47] Moral rights generally refer to "rights of a spiritual, non-economic and personal nature" that exist "independently of an artist's copyright in his work" and "spring from a belief that an artist in the process of creation injects his spirit into the work and that the artist's personality, as well as the integrity of the work, should therefore be protected and preserved". *Carter* vs. *Helmsley-Spear, Inc.*, 71 F.3d 77, at p. 81 (2d Cir., 1995), *cert. denied*, 517 U.S. 1208 (1996).

[48] Pub. L. Number 101-650, 104 Stat. 5089, at p. 5128; 17 United States Code, Section 106A.

[49] 17 United States Code, Section 101.

[50] *Massachusetts Museum of Contemporary Art Foundation Inc.* vs. *Buchel*, 593 F.3d 38, at pp. 47 and 48 (1st Cir., 2010).

generally provided to works of visual art by copyright law, the author of a work of visual art has the right to:

(1) Claim authorship of that work (attribution); and
(2) Prevent the use of his name as the author of any work of visual art which he did not create (integrity), including the rights to prevent the use of his name as the author of the work of visual art in the event of a distortion, mutilation, or other modification of the work which would be prejudicial to his honor or reputation; prevent any intentional distortion, mutilation, or other modification of that work which would be prejudicial to his honor or reputation; and prevent intentional or grossly negligent destruction of a work of recognized stature.[51]

Electronic media receives specific protection under the Digital Millennium Copyright Act against "circumvent[ing] a technological measure that effectively controls access to a [copyrighted] work". Circumvention means "to decrypt an encrypted work . . . without the authority of the copyright owner".[52] The federal courts are in conflict over whether an "infringement nexus" is required, i.e., that the plaintiff must show that circumventing the technology infringes or facilitates infringement of the plaintiff's copyright.[53]

Works That Copyright Protects

Works Eligible for Copyright Protection

Under United States copyright law, the categories of works expressly eligible for protection include literary works; musical works, including any accompanying words; dramatic works, including any accompanying music; pantomimes and choreographic works; pictorial, graphic, and sculptural works; motion pictures and other audiovisual works; sound recordings; and architectural works.[54]

---

[51] 17 United States Code, Section 106A(a).
[52] 17 United States Code, Section 1201(a).
[53] Compare *MDY Industries, LLC* vs. *Blizzard Entertainment, Inc.*, 629 F.3d 92 (9th Cir., 2010) (no infringement nexus required) with *Chamberlain Group, Inc.* vs. *Skylink Techs., Inc.*, 381 F.3d 1178 (Fed. Cir., 2004) (infringement nexus required).
[54] 17 United States Code, Section 102(a).

These works are eligible for protection while unpublished, a provision of significance to biographers drawing from personal correspondence.[55] The topography of semiconductor chips and vessel hull and deck designs are eligible for protection under special provisions of the United States copyright law.[56] In general, computer programs, website and website content, and computer databases and compilations of data are eligible for protection as "literary works".[57]

Derivative works that add new original copyrightable authorship to a preexisting copyrightable work are themselves copyrightable. Compilations of data or compilations of preexisting works may also be copyrightable if the materials are selected, coordinated, or arranged in such a way that the resulting work as a whole constitutes a new work.[58]

Works that are specifically ineligible for copyright protection include ideas, methods, and systems; recipes; names, titles, and short phrases; typeface, fonts, and lettering (although computer code to create typeface designs is copyrightable); blank forms; familiar symbols and designs;[59] and works that have not been fixed in a tangible form.

An exception for unrecorded music performances prohibits "bootleg" recordings of live musical performances, even when there was no other fixation of the work.[60] The design of a useful article can be protected under copyright "only to the extent that [the] design incorporates pictorial, graphic, or sculptural features that can be identified separately from, and are capable of existing independently of, the utilitarian aspects of the article."[61]

The distinction between ideas (unprotected) and expression (protected) is particularly significant in assessing the protection of "non-literal" components of a computer program, including the program's sequence, structure, organization, and user interface. An "abstraction-filtration-comparison" test was initially formulated by the 2nd Circuit and has

---

55 17 United States Code, Section 104.
56 17 United States Code Chapter 9 and Section 1301; Copyright Office Circular Number 100, see https://www.copyright.gov/circs/circ100.pdf.
57 Copyright Office Circular Numbers 61, 65, and 66, see https://www.copyright.gov/circs/.
58 17 United States Code, Section 103; Copyright Office Circular Number 14, see https://www.copyright.gov/circs/circ14.pdf.
59 Copyright Office Circular Number 33, see https://www.copyright.gov/circs/circ33.pdf.
60 17 United States Code, Section 1101, added by the Uruguay Round Agreements Act (1994), Pub. L. Number 103-465, 108 Stat. 4809, at p. 4973.
61 17 United States Code, Section 101; *Star Athletica, LLC* vs. *Varsity Brands, Inc.*, 137 S.Ct. 1002 (2017) (surface decorations on cheerleading uniforms separable from utilitarian aspects of useful article, and therefore eligible for copyright protection).

been expressly adopted by several other circuits, for assessing whether the non-literal elements of a computer program constitute expression protectable by copyright. Under this test, the court first breaks down the allegedly infringed program into its constituent structural parts. In the filtration step, the court sifts out all non-protectable material, including expression that is necessarily incidental to unprotectable ideas. In the final step, the court compares the remaining creative expression for substantial similarity with the allegedly infringing program.[62]

Originality

The originality requirement in United States copyright law is a "low bar".[63] Copyrightable originality requires only "independent creation" by the author "plus a modicum of creativity". The degree of creativity required is "minimal"; the requirement is that the work possess "some creative spark, no matter how crude, humble or obvious".[64]

The United States has not adopted the "stamp of the author's personality" (*l'empreinte de la personnalite d'auteur*) standard prevalent in the European Union, or applied the German copyright law approach of applying a higher threshold of creativity to certain subject matter.[65]

National Origin

Published works that are first published in the United States or in a country with which the United States has a copyright treaty, or that are created by a citizen or domiciliary of a country with which the United States has a copyright treaty, are protected by United States copyright law. All works that are unpublished, regardless of the nationality of the author, also are protected in the United States.

Restored Works

The Uruguay Round Agreements Act (1994) restores United States copyright to certain foreign works that were in the public domain in the

---

62 *Oracle America, Inc.* vs. *Google Inc.*, 750 F.3d 1339, at pp. 1357 and 1358 (Fed. Cir., 2014), *cert. denied*, 135 S.Ct. 2887 (2015).
63 *Home Legend, LLC* vs. *Mannington Mills, Inc.*, 784 F.3d 1404, at p. 1409 (11th Cir.), *cert denied*, 136 S.Ct. 232 (2015).
64 *Feist Publ'ns* vs. *Rural Tel. Serv. Co., Inc.*, 499 U.S. 340, at p. 345 (1991).
65 Outfield and Suthersanen, *Global Intellectual Property Law*, at p. 82 (2008); Hick, *Artistic License: The Philosophical Problems of Copyright and Appropriation*, 61 (2017).

United States but protected by copyright in their countries of origin. The beneficiaries of restored copyright are mainly works that became public domain for failure to comply with formalities previously imposed by United States law.

Although copyright is restored automatically in eligible works, the Act requires the owner of a restored work to notify "reliance parties" (persons relying on the public domain status of the work), directly or through a filing with the Copyright Office, if the owner of the rights in a restored work plans to enforce those rights.[66]

Duration of Copyright

The United States Constitution restricts copyright protection to "limited [t]imes".[67] After the term ends, whether by expiration or otherwise, the work enters the "public domain" and is no longer protected by copyright.

The provisions of copyright law dealing with duration are complex. Different standards apply depending on whether federal statutory copyright protection was secured before or after 1 January 1978, the date the Copyright Act of 1976 took effect. In addition, several amendments enacted since 1 January 1978 affect duration.[68] The Copyright Information Center of the Cornell University Library publishes an annually updated copyright duration chart.[69] The most significant points, as of 1 January 2018 are:

For works published after 2002, the term of copyright in the United States is 70 years after the death of the author and 95 years from publication for works of corporate authorship (works made for hire). This term applies to United States works (registered or first published in the United States) and eligible foreign works (published in countries that are signatories to the Berne Convention or other copyright treaties, works first published outside the United States by foreign nationals, or United States citizens living abroad). For United States works, the maximum term is 120 years from creation.

---

66 17 United States Code, Sections 104A and 109, and Chapter 11; Copyright Office Circular Number 38B, see https://www.copyright.gov/circs/circ38b.pdf.

67 United States Constitution, Article I, Section 8. *Eldred* vs. *Ashcroft*, 537 U.S. 186 (2003) (upholding the 1998 Sonny Bono Copyright Term Extension Act as not exceeding the constitutional boundary).

68 Copyright Office Circular Number 15A, see https://www.copyright.gov/circs/circ15a.pdf.

69 Copyright Information Center of the Cornell University Library, Copyright Term and the Public Domain in the United States as of 1 January 2018, see https://copyright.cornell.edu/publicdomain.

Works that are in the public domain due to copyright expiration include works published before 1923, unpublished works of authors who died before 1948, anonymous and pseudonymous works, works made for hire (corporate authorship), and works created before 1898 when the death date of the author is not known. For works published between 1923 and 2002, calculating the term is more complex. The terms for works registered or first published in the United States are:

(1) Works published between 1923 and 1989 and following the formalities required at the time (copyright notice, registration, and/or renewal) have a copyright term of 70 years after the death of the author; for works of corporate authorship, the duration is 95 years from publication or 120 years from creation (whichever expires first).

(2) Works published from 1 March 1989 through 2002 have a copyright term of 70 years after the death of the author; for works of corporate authorship, 95 years from publication or 120 years from creation (whichever expires first); if created before 1978, the duration is the greater of the above term or 31 December 2047.

For works first published outside the United States by foreign nationals or United States citizens living abroad, the duration is calculated as follows:

(1) For works published in the United States less than 30 days after publication abroad, the United States publication chart should be used to determine duration;

(2) For works published between 1923 and 1977 and complying with United States formalities (notice and renewal) or solely published abroad and not in the public domain in their home country, a term of 95 years after publication date applies; and

(3) For works published between 1978 and 2002 in Berne signatory countries, there is a copyright term of 70 years after the death of the author, 95 years from publication for works of corporate authorship, or 31 December 2047, whichever is longest.

This is a simplified description. There are numerous additional rules and special cases, depending on the category of work, circumstances of publication (or non-publication), and country of origin.

Ownership of Copyright

When Copyright Exists

Copyright protection subsists in "original works of authorship" when created and "fixed in any tangible medium of expression . . . from which they can be perceived, reproduced, or otherwise communicated".[70]

An author "copyrights" a work by creating it. Notice and registration confirm the copyright owner's rights and maximize the owner's protections and remedies against potential copyright infringers, but neither is required to create or own a copyright.

Who Owns Copyright

Copyright ownership vests in the author or authors of the work. The authors of a joint work are co-owners of copyright in the work. However, in the case of a "work made for hire", the employer or other person for whom the work was prepared is considered the author and owner of the copyright, absent an express signed written instrument providing otherwise.[71]

A "work prepared by an employee within the scope of his or her employment" is automatically a work made for hire by operation of law.[72] The copyright law also lists specific categories of works that are "works made for hire" if the parties "expressly agree in a written instrument signed by them that the work shall be considered a work made for hire".[73] A "work for hire agreement" does not establish ownership in the hiring party except for these specific categories of work. However, ownership of a copyright "may be transferred in whole or in part by any means of conveyance or by operation of law".[74]

A transfer of ownership other than by operation of law is only valid if there is "an instrument of conveyance, or a note or memorandum of the transfer . . . in writing and signed by the owner of the rights

---

[70] 17 United States Code, Section 102(a).
[71] 17 United States Code, Section 201(a) and (b).
[72] 17 United States Code, Section 101; *Community for Creative Non-Violence* vs. *Reid*, 490 U.S. 730 (1989) (general common law agency principles decide whether individual is "employee" or independent contractor for copyright ownership purposes).
[73] 17 United States Code, Section 101.
[74] 17 United States Code, Section 201(d).

conveyed or such owner's duly authorized agent".[75] The document does not have to be notarized or otherwise officially authenticated, but doing so makes proving the transfer easier as *"prima facie* evidence of the execution of the transfer".[76] Transfers of copyright ownership or other documents pertaining to a copyright may be recorded in the Copyright Office.[77] Recording is not mandatory, but is valuable in proving ownership if contested in litigation.

Under certain circumstances, United States copyright law allows authors or their heirs to terminate after thirty-five years an agreement that transferred or licensed the author's copyright to a third party. To terminate a grant, the author or the author's heirs must serve an advance written "notice of termination" on the grantee or the grantee's successor-in-interest and must record a copy of that notice with the Copyright Office and pay the required filing fee.[78]

Copyright in separate contributions to collective works is owned by the contributing author, as distinct from ownership of the collective work itself. Copyright in the collective work is a limited right, granting "only the privilege of reproducing and distributing the contribution as part of that particular collective work, any revision of that collective work, and any later collective work in the same series".[79]

Copyright Notice

Copyright notice is a statement placed on copies of a work to inform the public that someone is claiming ownership of it. Use of a copyright notice is the responsibility of the copyright owner and publisher. Permission from, or registration with, the Copyright Office is not required.[80] A notice consists of three elements that generally appear as a single continuous statement:

(1) The copyright symbol © (or ℗ for sound recordings) or the word "copyright" or abbreviation "copr.";
(2) The year of first publication of the work; and
(3) The name of the copyright owner (© 2017 John Doe).[81]

---

75 17 United States Code, Section 204(a).
76 17 United States Code, Section 204(b).
77 17 United States Code, Section 205.
78 17 United States Code, Section 203; Copyright Office Circular Number 1, see https://www.copyright.gov/circs/circ01.pdf.
79 17 United States Code, Section 201(c).
80 Copyright Officer Circular Number 3, see https://www.copyright.gov/circs/circ03.pdf.
81 17 United States Code, Section 401(b); Copyright Office Circular Number 3.

Copyright notice is optional, except for United States works published before 1 March 1989.[82] However, using a copyright notice makes potential users aware that copyright is claimed in the work and, in the case of a published work, may prevent defendants in a copyright infringement action from attempting to limit their liability for damages or injunctive relief based on an innocent infringement defense.[83]

"All rights reserved", once used as a formality indicating that the copyright owner reserves all the rights provided by copyright law, no longer has any legal effect in any jurisdiction. Its frequent usage, however, has led to the use of "No rights reserved" or "Some rights reserved" ostensibly to disclaim or partially disclaim copyright protection.

Because nothing in United States copyright law specifies how to abandon copyright, these notices are ambiguous as a way for authors to dedicate their works to the public domain, and relying on them is risky. Organizations such as Creative Commons, Open Source Initiative, and Free Software Foundation have developed notices to guide authors who wish to share their work on open terms.[84] The resulting legal tools and standards are popular, widely used, and have strong communities. Open source licenses have been enforced by courts.[85]

Copyright Registration

Registering a claim to copyright with the Copyright Office is not mandatory. Besides establishing a public record of a copyright claim, however, registration offers several statutory advantages:

(1) Registration is necessary for works of United States origin before an infringement suit may be filed in court;[86]
(2) Registration establishes *prima facie* evidence of the validity of the copyright and facts stated in the certificate when registration is made before or within five years of publication;[87]

---

82 17 United States Code, Section 405(a); Copyright Office Circular Number 3.
83 17 United States Code, Section 405(b); Copyright Office Circular Number 3.
84 CC0 1.0 Universal Public Domain Dedication, see https://creativecommons.org/publicdomain/zero /1.0/legalcode; Open Source Initiative Licenses and Standards, see https://opensource.org/licenses; Free Software Licensing and Compliance, see http://www.fsf.org/licensing.
85 *Jacobsen* vs. *Katzer*, 535 F.3d 1373 (Fed. Cir., 2008); *Artifex Software Inc.* vs. *Hancom Inc.*, 2017 WL 1477373 (N.D. Calif., 25 April 2017), 2017 WL 4005508 (N.D. Calif., 12 September 2017).
86 17 United States Code, Section 411.
87 17 United States Code, Section 410.

(3) When registration is made prior to infringement or within three months after publication of a work, a copyright owner is eligible for statutory damages, attorney's fees, and costs;[88] and

(4) Registration permits a copyright owner to establish a record with the United States Customs and Border Protection for protection against the importation of infringing copies. The Customs and Border Protection records unregistered copyrights, valid for a limited period (mainly to cover the period while an application to register is pending with the Copyright Office) through its Intellectual Property Rights Electronic Recordation System.[89]

Registration can be made at any time within the life of the copyright. A copyright registered before publication does not need to be re-registered when the work is published, although the published edition may be registered, if desired.[90]

Affirmative Defenses to Infringement

Fair Use

Fair use is a legal doctrine that permits the unlicensed use of copyright-protected works in certain circumstances. Section 107 of the Copyright Act provides the statutory framework for determining whether something is a fair use and identifies certain types of limited and "transformative" uses, such as criticism, comment, news reporting, teaching, scholarship, and research, as examples of activities that may qualify as fair use.[91]

Because such uses can be done without permission from the copyright owner, fair use is considered a defense against a claim of copyright infringement. The fair use defense is highly subjective and fact-specific,

---

[88] 17 United States Code, Section 412.
[89] 19 Code of Federal Regulations, Part 133, Subpart D; CPB Intellectual Property Rights e-Recordation Application (see https://iprr.cbp.gov/).
[90] Copyright Office Circular Number 1, see https://www.copyright.gov/circs/circ01.pdf. Circular Number 2, see https://www.copyright.gov/circs/circ02.pdf.
[91] 17 United States Code, Section 107; United States Copyright Office Fair Use Index, More Information on Fair Use, see https://www.copyright.gov/fair-use/more-info.html. The Fair Use Index provides searchable summaries of major fair use decisions.

even at the Supreme Court level.[92] The history of copyright law abounds with battles between rights holders and new technologies for distributing content.[93]

Advances in digitization and Internet technologies have spurred public and private attempts to preserve a digital record of "the nation's memory"[94] and provide online access to digital copies of library, museum, and archive collections. Despite the absence of enabling legislation, there have been several independent attempts to make both orphan works and larger book collections available to the public under the "fair use" defense.

The most notable collections for online full-text searches and access to book content are the Google Books Library Project[95] — an effort to scan every book in the world — and its partnership with the Hathi Trust Digital Library at the University of Michigan.[96] Beginning with Michigan's collection in 2004, and making further arrangements with Harvard, Stanford, Oxford, the New York Public Library, and dozens of other library systems, Google had scanned approximately 25-million books at an estimated cost of US $400-million.

Google then delivered digital copies to participating libraries, created an electronic database of books, and made text available on the Google Books website for online searching through the use of "snippets", a few sentences of the search term in context.[97]

---

92 *Sony Corp. of America* vs. *Universal City Studios, Inc.*, 464 U.S. 417, at pp. 454–456 (1984) (finding use of video recorder for "time-shifting" of home television watching to be fair use, and therefore copying device manufacturers not liable for copyright infringement, because video recorder was capable of "substantial noninfringing uses"); *MGM Studios, Inc.* vs. *Grokster, Ltd.*, 545 U.S. 913 (2005) (peer-to-peer file sharing companies potentially liable for resulting acts of infringement by third parties).
93 Somers, "Torching the Modern-Day Library of Alexandria", *The Atlantic* (20 April 2017), see https://www.theatlantic.com/technology/archive/2017/04/the-tragedy-of-google-books/523320; Wu, "Copyright's Communications Policy", 103 *Mich. L. Rev.* 278 (2004), see http://repository.law.umich.edu/mlr/vol103/iss2/2.
94 Library of Congress, *American Memory, Mission and History*, see http://memory.loc.gov/ammem/about/index.html.
95 Google, Inc., *Google Books Library Project — An Enhanced Card Catalog of the World's Books*, see https://books.google.com/intl/en/googlebooks/library/. Google Books also collects content from publishers and authors cooperatively through its Google Books Partner Program, see https://books.google.com/intl/en/googlebooks/partners.
96 Howard, "What Happened to Google's Effort to Scan Millions of University Library Books?", *Edsurge* (10 August 2017), see https://www.edsurge.com/news/2017-08-10-what-happened-to-google-s-effort-to-scan-millions-of-university-library-books.
97 *Authors Guild, Inc.* vs. *Google, Inc.*, 804 F.3d 202, at p. 207 (2d Cir., 2015), *cert. denied*, 136 S.Ct. 1658 (2016); Somers, "Torching the Modern-Day Library of Alexandria",

Google did not obtain permission from the copyright holders for use of their copyrighted works. The ensuing legal saga, lasting more than ten years, was initiated in September 2005 as a class action by the Authors Guild and American Society of Media Photographers, along with representative authors and photographers, and joined in April 2010 by groups of photographers and graphic artists for use of their work in the Google Books Project.

A settlement agreement filed with the United States District Court in September 2009 was rejected in March 2011 on a number of grounds, including antitrust and international law concerns. In November 2013, the district judge granted summary judgment to Google on fair use grounds, which was affirmed by the United States Court of Appeals for the Second Circuit in October 2015. In April 2016, the United States Supreme Court declined to review the Court of Appeals' decision.

The Second Circuit held in favor of Google on each of the four fair use factors in Section 107 of the Copyright Act, noting at the outset that the ultimate goal of copyright is to benefit the public and expand knowledge and understanding. In particular, the court found Google's use of copyrighted works in a database "highly transformative" and that such use necessitated the complete copying of the works. The court noted that Google provides only discontinuous, tiny fragments at a time, amounting to no more than sixteen per cent of a book. Lastly, the court found that Google's use would not have a "meaningful or significant effect" on the copyrighted works' market, even if the snippet function might cause some loss in sales.[98]

First Sale

After the first sale or distribution of a copy, "the owner of a particular copy . . . lawfully made" under United States copyright law can sell or otherwise dispose of that copy without the authority of the copyright

---

(footnote 97 continued from previous page)
The Atlantic (20 April 2017), see https://www.theatlantic.com/technology/archive/2017/04/the-tragedy-of-google-books/523320; Wu, "Copyright's Communications Policy", 103 *Mich. L. Rev.* 278 (2004), see http://repository.law.umich.edu/mlr/vol103/iss2/2); Google, Inc., *Google Books Library Project — An Enhanced Card Catalog of the World's Books — Common Questions*, see https://www.google.com/googlebooks/common.html (explanation of snippets).

[98] *Authors Guild, Inc.* vs. *Google, Inc.*, 804 F.3d 202 (2d Cir., 2015), *cert. denied*, 136 S.Ct. 1658 (2016).

holder.[99] The first sale doctrine also limits the right to prevent importing or exporting copies "without the authority of the owner of copyright".[100]

Lawfully made copies purchased abroad can be imported to the United States and disposed of as freely as copies purchased in the United States. In 2013, the Supreme Court extended this rule beyond copies initially manufactured in the United States (and then sent abroad and sold) to copies manufactured abroad by or under the authority of the copyright holder.[101] This decision was commercially significant to publishers who sought to segment their market by producing cheaper editions for sale in other countries.

The first sale doctrine does not apply to a person who possesses a copy of the copyrighted work without owning it, however, such as a licensee. Whether the transferee of a copy is an owner or licensee has been problematic in cases involving software and digital media.

Possessing software as a licensee rather than as an owner of the copy also prevents the software user from invoking the "essential step doctrine" that allows the "owner of a copy of a computer program" to make "another copy or adaptation" of the program "as an essential step in the utilization" of the program "in conjunction with a machine" or "for archival purposes only".[102] The Ninth Circuit has established a well-accepted test under which "a software user is a licensee rather than an owner of a copy where the copyright owner (1) specifies that the user is granted a license; (2) significantly restricts the user's ability to transfer the software; and (3) imposes notable use restrictions".[103]

Public Domain, Abandonment, and Orphan Works

In addition to expiration of the copyright term, a copyright owner may deliberately place it in the public domain. Express dedication to the public domain is rare. Inadvertent public domain status — with potentially

---

99 17 United States Code, Section 109(a). Congress has enacted several limitations to the first sale doctrine, including a prohibition on the rental of software and musical recordings. 17 United States Code, Section 109(b).
100 17 United States Code, Section 602(a), (b).
101 *Kirtsaeng* vs. *John Wiley & Sons, Inc.*, 568 U.S. 519 (2013).
102 17 United States Code, Section 117(a). The "adaptation" right has become nearly vestigial with the standardization of computer platforms.
103 *Vernor* vs. *Autodesk, Inc.*, 621 F.3d 1102, at p. 1111 (9th Cir., 2010), *cert. denied* 565 U.S. 820 (2011); *UMG Recordings, Inc.* vs. *Augusto*, 628 F.3d 1175 (9th Cir., 2011) ("Promotional Use Only — Not for Sale" label did not create license where copyright owner dispatched promotional CDs without any prior arrangement as to the copies and without any attempt to track recipients' use or disposition).

momentous consequence — also can occur when the record of copyright ownership and transfer cannot be proved in court.[104]

Copyright investigations are frequently not conclusive, especially for registrations and records prior to 1 January 1978, which are not searchable in the Copyright Office's online catalog.[105] Sometimes, the creator of the work is not the copyright owner and does not have authority to control the copyright. Locating copyright owners is further complicated because the United States has an "opt-out" copyright system in which registration of copyright and recording of transfers are optional.[106] In addition, copyright law provides conditions under which authors can terminate previous transfers or licenses of their copyrights.[107]

Works published in 1923 or after (as well as unpublished works created in 1898 or after or by authors who died in 1948 or after) remain presumptively protected by copyright. However, significant numbers of these works are no longer commercially valuable to the copyright owner and have not been published or otherwise exploited for many years.

Generally termed "orphan works", often no owner can be located and, as such, there is no feasible way for persons who wish to use part or all of the work, including libraries and archives, to make the works available without the risk of a putative owner later appearing and suing.[108] Despite several Copyright Office studies and various legislative proposals, as of 2017, Congress has not passed any across-the-board legislation tackling the orphan works problem.[109]

---

104 *Maya* vs. *Warner/Chappell Music Inc*, 131 F.Supp.3d 975 (C.D. Calif. 2015) (longtime licensor lacked a valid copyright in the lyrics to "Happy Birthday" after court found that it could not establish who authored the lyrics and whether that author properly transferred any rights). Following this decision, Warner Music Group agreed to refund US $14 million in licensing fees it previously charged filmmakers and others for using the song. Sisario, "Details of 'Happy Birthday' Copyright Settlement Revealed", *New York Times* (9 February 2016), see https://www.nytimes.com/2016/02/10/business/media/details-of-happy-birthday-copyright-settlement-revealed.html.
105 Copyright Office Circular Number 22, see https://www.copyright.gov/circs/circ22.pdf; Copyright Office Circular Number 23, see https://www.copyright.gov/circs/circ23.pdf. The online catalog is at http:// www.copyright.gov/records.
106 17 United States Code, Sections 204 and 408. Registration of copyright and recording of transfer are, however, often necessary to enforce the copyright in court.
107 17 United States Code, Section 203.
108 Urban, "How Fair Use Can Help Solve the Orphan Works Problem", 27 *Berkeley Tech. L. J.* 1379, at p. 1382 (2012), see https://scholarship.law.berkeley.edu/facpubs/2199/.
109 United States Copyright Office, *Orphan Works and Mass Digitization* (2015), see https://www.copyright.gov/orphan/reports/orphan-works2015.pdf. Under a 2005 amendment, the copyright law grants libraries and archives limited privileges to make copies of certain orphan works. 17 United States Code, Section 108(h).

License

"Uses of the copyrighted work that stay within the scope of a ... license are immunized from infringement suits."[110] An exclusive license must be in writing.[111] This requirement does not apply, however, to non-exclusive licenses where ownership of the copyright is not transferred. "A copyright owner may grant such non-exclusive licenses orally, or they may be implied from conduct which indicates the owner's intent to allow a licensee to use the work."[112]

Digital Millennium Copyright Act Safe Harbor

The "safe harbor" provision of the Digital Millennium Copyright Act limits the liability of online service providers for copyright infringement that occurs "by reason of the storage at the direction of a user of material that resides on a system or network controlled or operated by or for the service provider".[113]

To qualify for protection, a party must meet a set of threshold criteria. The party must in fact be a "service provider", defined as "a provider of online services or network access, or the operator of facilities therefor". A service provider must satisfy certain "conditions of eligibility", including the adoption and reasonable implementation of a "repeat infringer" policy that "provides for the termination in appropriate circumstances of subscribers and account holders of the service provider's system or network". Finally, a qualifying service provider must accommodate "standard technical measures" that are "used by copyright owners to identify or protect copyrighted works".[114]

---

110 *John G. Danielson, Inc.* vs. *Winchester-Conant Props., Inc.*, 322 F.3d 26, at p. 40 (1st Cir., 2003) (internal citation omitted).
111 17 United States Code, Section 204(a).
112 *John G. Danielson, Inc.* vs. *Winchester-Conant Props., Inc.*, 322 F.3d 26, at p. 40 (1st Cir., 2003); *United States Auto Parts Network, Inc.* vs. *Parts Geek, LLC*, 692 F.3d 1009, at pp. 1019 and 1020 (9th Cir., 2012) (reversing grant of summary judgment because reasonable jury could find implied license).
113 17 United States Code, Section 512(c). Title II of the Digital Millennium Copyright Act established a series of four "safe harbors" that allow qualifying service providers to limit their liability for claims of copyright infringement based on (a) "transitory digital network communications", (b) "system caching", (c) "information residing on systems or networks at [the] direction of users", and (d) "information location tools". 17 United States Code, Section 512(a)–(d). Subsection (c) is by far the most pivotal to the explosive growth of social media since the Digital Millennium Copyright Act was enacted in 1998.
114 17 United States Code, Section 512(i)(1)(A), (i)(1)(B), (i)(2), and (k)(1)(B). *Viacom Intern Inc.* vs. *YouTube Inc.*, 676 F.3d 19, at p. 27 (2d Cir., 2012).

Once satisfying the threshold criteria, a service provider must satisfy the requirements of a particular safe harbor. The safe harbor for Section 512(c), which covers infringement claims that arise "by reason of the storage at the direction of a user of material that resides on a system or network controlled or operated by or for the service provider" will apply if the service provider:

(1) Does not have actual knowledge that the material or an activity using the material on the system or network is infringing;
(2) In the absence of such actual knowledge, is not aware of facts or circumstances from which infringing activity is apparent; or
(3) Upon obtaining such knowledge or awareness, acts expeditiously to remove or disable access to the material;
(4) Does not receive a financial benefit directly attributable to the infringing activity, in a case in which the service provider has the right and ability to control such activity; and
(5) Upon notification of claimed infringement responds expeditiously to remove or disable access to the material that is claimed to be infringing or to be the subject of infringing activity.[115]

This final item requires service providers to "designate [ ] an agent to receive notifications of claimed infringement", and specifies the components of a proper notification to that agent, commonly known as a "takedown notice".[116] Accordingly, actual knowledge of infringing material, awareness of facts or circumstances that make infringing activity apparent, or receipt of a proper takedown notice will each trigger an obligation to expeditiously remove the infringing material.[117]

A service provider that fulfills these requirements "shall not be liable for monetary relief, . . . injunctive or other equitable relief [except in limited circumstances, mainly designed to terminating the accounts of subscribers who commit repeated infringements] for infringement of copyright by reason of the storage at the direction of a user of material

---

[115] 17 United States Code, Section 512(c)(1)(A)–(C). *Viacom Intern Inc.* vs. *YouTube Inc.*, 676 F.3d 19, at p. 27 (2d Cir., 2012).

[116] 17 United States Code, Section 512(c)(3)(A). The target of a takedown notice may file a counter-notice. 17 United States Code, Section 512(g). Material misrepresentations by the copyright holder in the takedown notice may subject the copyright owner to liability, even nominal damages, for injury incurred as a result of the misrepresentation. *Lenz* vs. *Universal Music Corp.*, 815 F.3d 1145 (9th Cir., 2015) (requiring subjective good faith belief by copyright holder that content posted on Internet site was not fair use).

[117] 17 United States Code, Section 512(c)(2) and (3). *Viacom Intern Inc.* vs. *YouTube Inc.*, 676 F.3d 19, at pp. 27 and 28 (2d Cir., 2012).

that resides on a system or network controlled or operated by or for the service provider".[118]

The bounds of the Digital Millennium Copyright Act safe harbor were tested in the *Viacom* vs. *YouTube* litigation, in which Viacom, joined by copyright owner class plaintiffs, argued that YouTube lost its safe harbor by engaging in "brazen" and "massive" copyright infringement that knowingly and intentionally allowed and induced users to upload and view hundreds of thousands of infringing videos.

After several court rulings that largely upheld YouTube's reliance on the Digital Millennium Copyright Act safe harbor provisions, the case settled in March 2014, shortly before oral argument on a second appeal. No money changed hands. However, YouTube instituted more proactive technology to identify and disable suspected infringing context.[119]

Copyright Misuse

Copyright misuse forbids the use of a copyright to secure an exclusive right or limited monopoly not granted by copyright law.[120] The purpose of the defense is to prevent copyright holders "from leveraging their limited monopoly to allow them control of areas outside the monopoly".[121]

The contours of this defense are still being defined because courts do not need to address the issue when there is an unsuccessful claim for copyright infringement.[122]

Statute of Limitations

Copyright infringement has a statute of limitations of "three years after the claim accrued".[123] However, copyright follows a separate-accrual rule: "when a defendant commits successive violations, the statute of

---

[118] 17 United States Code, Section 512(c)(1).
[119] Stempel, "Google, Viacom Settle Landmark YouTube Lawsuit", *Reuters*, see https://www.reuters.com/article/us-google-viacom-lawsuit/google-viacom-settle-landmark-youtube-lawsuit-idUSBREA2H11220140318.
[120] *Practice Management Information Corp.* vs. *American Medical Ass'n*, 121 F.3d 516, at p. 520 (9th Cir., 1997).
[121] *Apple Inc.* vs. *Psystar Corp.*, 658 F.3d 1150, at p. 1157 (9th Cir., 2011).
[122] *MDY Indus., LLC* vs. *Blizzard Entm't, Inc.*, 629 F.3d 928, at p. 941 (9th Cir., 2010) (declining to address copyright misuse issue because there was no infringement).
[123] 17 United States Code, Section 507(b).

limitations runs separately from each violation . . . . [E]ach infringing act starts a new limitations period".[124]

In a 2014 decision, the United States Supreme Court ruled that the equitable defense of laches (unreasonable delay in bringing suit) did not displace the copyright statute of limitations, although the plaintiff's delay and defendant's reliance on that delay would be relevant "in determining appropriate injunctive relief and assessing profits".[125]

Extraterritoriality

United States copyright law reaches only "domestic conduct".[126] However, domestic conduct may have a long reach in applying United States law to activities commenced outside the United States which result in domestic conduct, such as copies manufactured abroad but imported, distributed, acquired, or further reproduced in the United States.[127]

Similarly, the "act of state doctrine", which bars United States courts from adjudicating the legality of a foreign sovereign's public acts, does not provide a "first sale" defense unless the copies made abroad were "lawfully made under this title", i.e., the United States copyright law.[128]

Sovereign Immunity

The Copyright Remedy Clarification Act, enacted in 1990,[129] attempts to abrogate the sovereign immunity of states for copyright infringement:

> "Any State, any instrumentality of a State, and any officer or employee of a State or instrumentality of a State acting in his official capacity, may not be immune, under the Eleventh Amendment of the Constitution of the United States or under any other doctrine of sovereign immunity, from suit in Federal Court by any person, including any governmental or non-governmental

---

124 *Petrella* vs. *Metro-Goldwyn-Mayer Inc.*, 134 S.Ct. 1962, at p. 1969 (2014).
125 *Petrella* vs. *Metro-Goldwyn-Mayer Inc.*, 134 S.Ct. 1962, at p. 1978 (2014).
126 *Geophysical Service Inc.* vs. *TGS-NOPEC Geophysical Co*, 850 F.3d 785, at pp. 790 and 791 (5th Cir., 2017).
127 *Geophysical Service Inc.* vs. *TGS-NOPEC Geophysical Co*, 850 F.3d 785, at pp. 797 and 798 (5th Cir., 2017); *Kirtsaeng* vs. *John Wiley & Sons, Inc.*, 568 U.S. 519 (2013).
128 *Geophysical Service Inc.* vs. *TGS-NOPEC Geophysical Co*, 850 F.3d 785, at pp. 795 and 796 (5th Cir., 2017).
129 Pub. L. Number 101-553, 104 Stat. 2749.

entity, for a violation of any of the exclusive rights of a copyright owner . . . under this title."[130]

The Copyright Remedy Clarification Act has been struck down as unconstitutional by district and appellate courts in the 1st, 2nd, 4th, 5th, 6th, 9th, and 11th Circuits. In these cases, the courts held that the 11th Amendment of the United States Constitution prohibits Congress from using its Article I powers to abrogate state sovereign immunity. To date, no court has enforced the Copyright Remedy Clarification Act against a state.[131]

Remedies for Infringement

Federal district courts have exclusive subject matter jurisdiction over copyright cases, along with jurisdiction of any civil action asserting a claim of unfair competition when joined with a substantial and related claim under the copyright law.[132] Potential remedies for copyright infringement available to the copyright owner or exclusive licensee include (a) "temporary and final injunctions . . . to prevent or restrain infringement",[133] (b) impounding and disposition of infringing articles,[134] (c) actual damages and any additional profits of the infringer,[135] (d) "statutory damages",[136] (e) "additional damages" in certain cases,[137]

---

[130] 17 United States Code 511(a).
[131] *Chaves* vs. *Arte Public Press*, 204 F.3d 601 (5th Cir., 2000), *Salerno* vs. *City Univ. of N.Y.*, 191 F.Supp.2d 352 (S.D.N.Y. 2001); *Hairston* vs. *N.C. Agricultural and Technical State University*, 2005 WL 2136923 (M.D.N.C. 5 August 2005); *Marketing Information Masters* vs. *The Trustees of the California State University*, 552 F.Supp.2d 1088 (S.D. Cal., 2008); *Romero* vs. *California Dept. of Transportation*, 2009 WL 650629 (C.D. Cal., 12 March 2009); *Jacobs* vs. *Memphis Convention and Visitors Bureau*, 710 F. Supp.2d 663 (W.D. Tenn., 2010); *Parker* vs. *Dufreshne*, 2010 WL 2671578 (W.D. La., 18 May 2010); *Whipple* vs. *Utah*, 2011 WL 4368568 (D. Utah, 25 August 2011); *National Association of Boards of Pharmacy* vs. *University of Georgia*, 633 F.3d 1297 (11th Cir., 2011); *Coyle* vs. *University of Kentucky*, 2 F.Supp.3d 1014 (E.D.Ky.), appeal dismissed (6th Circ. 14-5401, 15 July 2014).
[132] 28 United States Code, Section 1338(a).
[133] 17 United States Code, Section 502(a) and (b).
[134] 17 United States Code, Section 503.
[135] 17 United States Code, Section 504(a).
[136] 17 United States Code, Section 504(c).
[137] 17 United States Code, Section 504(d).

(f) court costs and attorney's fees,[138] and (g) seizure and forfeiture of infringing articles excluded from import into the United States.[139]

Following the United States Supreme Court's 2006 *eBay* decision,[140] federal courts have reversed the longstanding standard for preliminary injunctions that when a plaintiff was likely to prevail on the merits in a copyright case, a detailed showing of irreparable harm was not needed because such injury could normally be presumed when a copyright was infringed. Although *eBay* involved the propriety of a permanent injunction after a finding of patent infringement, Courts of Appeals have held that *eBay* applies with equal force to preliminary injunctions that are issued for alleged copyright infringement.

Accordingly, when a plaintiff seeks a preliminary injunction in a copyright case, a court may not presume that the plaintiff will suffer irreparable harm. For a preliminary injunction to be granted in a copyright case: (a) the plaintiff must demonstrate either likelihood of success on the merits or sufficiently serious questions regarding merits to make them fair ground for litigation and the balance of hardships tipping decidedly in plaintiff's favor; (b) the plaintiff must demonstrate a likelihood that it will suffer irreparable injury in absence of an injunction; (c) the balance of hardships between the plaintiff and the defendant must tip in plaintiff's favor; and (d) the court must ensure that public interest will not be disserved by issuance of a preliminary injunction.[141]

Section 504(b) of the Copyright Act provides that the copyright owner is entitled to recover the actual damages suffered as a result of the infringement, as well as any profits of the infringer that are attributable to the infringement and that are not taken into account in computing the actual damages.[142] The "actual damages must be suffered as a result of the infringement, and recoverable profits must be attributable to the infringement".[143] In establishing the infringer's profits, the copyright owner is required to present proof only of the infringer's gross revenue, and the infringer is required to prove the deductible expenses and the elements of profit attributable to factors other than the copyrighted work.[144]

---

[138] 17 United States Code, Section 505.
[139] 17 United States Code, Section 603; 19 Code of Federal Regulations, Section 133.43 (administrative procedure on suspicion of infringing copies).
[140] *eBay, Inc.* vs. *MercExchange, L.L.C.*, 547 U.S. 388 (2006).
[141] *Salinger* vs. *Colting*, 607 F.3d 68 (2d Cir., 2010).
[142] 17 United States Code, Section 504(b).
[143] *Polar Bear Prods., Inc.* vs. *Timex Corp.*, 384 F.3d 700, at p. 708 (9th Cir., 2004).
[144] 17 United States Code, Section 504(b).

"Statutory damages" may be a potent weapon where actual damages are small or it is difficult to prove by a preponderance of the evidence. The plaintiff may "elect, at any time before final judgment is rendered" whether to seek actual or statutory damages. If the copyright owner elects to recover statutory damages, the owner cannot also recover actual damages.[145]

In the absence of a finding of willful infringement, the amount that may be awarded as statutory damages is not less than US $750, nor more than US $30,000, for each work that was infringed. However, statutory damages may be reduced to as little as US $200 for each work infringed if the infringement is shown to have been innocent. In a case where the copyright owner obtains a finding that the infringement was willful, an amount as much as US $150,000 for each work willfully infringed may be awarded.[146]

Because the multiplier for statutory damages is the number of works infringed, threats of statutory damages have been potent weapons in illegal file sharing cases.[147] Statutory damages are only available if the copyright owner has registered copyright in the work prior to infringement or within three months after publication of the work.[148]

Awarding attorney's fees is discretionary. Among the "several non-exclusive factors" to guide the court are "frivolousness, motivation, objective unreasonableness and the need in particular circumstances to advance considerations of compensation and deterrence". These factors are exercised in an evenhanded manner with respect to prevailing plaintiffs and prevailing defendants.[149]

The Supreme Court has also endorsed an "objective-reasonableness approach" — putting substantial weight on the reasonableness of a losing party's position.[150] As with statutory damages, attorney's fees are

---

[145] 17 United States Code, Section 504(c).
[146] 17 United States Code, Section 504(c)(1); *Derek Andrew, Inc.* vs. *Poof Apparel Corp.*, 528 F.3d 696, at p. 699 (9th Cir., 2008); *L.A. News Serv.* vs. *Reuters Television Int'l*, 149 F.3d 987, at p. 995 (9th Cir., 1998).
[147] See *Capitol Records, Inc.* vs. *Thomas-Rasset*, 692 F.3d 899 (8th Cir., 2012) (statutory damages award of US $222,000 for willful infringement sustained against individual for making recordings available for distribution to public through online media distribution system). After winning this case and settling many others out of court, the Recording Industry Association of America adjusted its anti-piracy strategy largely to stop suing individual downloaders. Holpuch, "Minnesota Woman to Pay US $220,000 Fine for 24 Illegally Downloaded Songs, *The Guardian* (11 September 2012), see https://www.theguardian.com/technology/2012/sep/11/minnesota-woman-songs-illegally-downloaded.
[148] 17 United States Code, Section 412.
[149] *Fogerty* vs. *Fantasy, Inc.*, 510 U.S. 517 (1994).
[150] *Kirtsaeng* vs. *John Wiley & Sons, Inc.*, 136 S.Ct. 1979 (2016).

available to the prevailing party only if the copyright owner has registered copyright in the work prior to infringement or within three months after publication of the work.[151]

---

[151] 17 United States Code, Section 412. The courts have not addressed the paradox that a defendant's entitlement to attorney's fees may depend on whether the plaintiff registered its copyright within this period.

Index

A

Affirmative Defenses to Infringement
    act of state doctrine 250
    across-the-board legislation 246
    antitrust and international law 244
    claim of copyright infringement 242
    copyright infringement 249
    copyright investigations 246
    copyright law 246
    copyright misuse 249
    Copyright Office studies 246
    Copyright Office's online catalogue 246
    Digital Millennium Copyright Act Safe Harbor 247
    digital record 243
    Eleventh Amendment of the Constitution of the United States 250
    expiration of copyright terms 245
    extraterritoriality 250
    fair use 242
    Federal Court 250
    first sale 244–245
    Google Books Library Project 243–244
    Hathi Trust Digital Library 243
    legislation proposals 246
    license 247
    Ninth Circuit 245
    public domain, abandonment, and orphan works 245
    record of copyright ownership 246
    Second Circuit 244
    sovereign immunity 250
    statute of limitations 249–250
    successive violations 249
    The Copyright Remedy Clarification Act 250–251
    United States copyright law 244, 250
    United States Supreme Court 244, 250
Authorship and Ownership
    presumptions relevant to computer programs 200
    presumptions relevant to films 200
    presumptions relevant to literary, dramatic, musical,
        and artistic works 198
    presumptions relevant to sound recordings and films 199
Author's Rights
    Copyright and Related Rights Code 118

    copyright infringement 118
    economic assets 118
    economic rights 118
    legal monopoly 118
    moral rights 119
    Portuguese copyright law 119
    Portuguese law 118

C

Choice of Venue
    civil copyright infringement cases 127
    Constitutional Court 126
    court system 126
    criminal copyright infringement cases 127
    judicial courts 127
    Supreme Court of Justice 127
Civil Copyright Infringement Proceedings in Judicial Courts
    appeals 131
    civil court proceedings related to copyright infringement 128
    Civil Procedure Code 130, 132
    collective rights management 129
    confessions and other forms of evidence 134
    Copyright and Related Rights Code 129
    copyright infringement cases 129
    cross-examination 134
    documentary evidence 133
    evidence-gathering measures 135
    final hearing and judgment 131
    initial claims and counterarguments 130
    Intellectual Property Court 132
    length of civil copyright infringement proceeding 132
    Portuguese case law 129
    Portuguese civil procedural law 131
    summarization and improvement 130–131
    Supreme Court of Justice 131–132
    witness evidence 134
    written expert opinions 133
Civil Enforcement Proceedings
    Civil Procedure Code 45
    exemptions to infringement of copyright 46
    piracy in Brazil 45
    public domain 48

Index

Copyright
    Civil Code 146–150, 153–155, 157–161
    computer software 151
    items of design and architectural works 154
    lawful use of works without author's consent 159
    management of copyright on collective basis 156
    Russian Supreme Court 148
    theatrical shows and audiovisual works 153
    web pages 152

Copyright Enforcement in Brazil
    civil enforcement 43
    criminal enforcement 42
    criminal enforcement proceedings 43
    enforcement authorities 41

Copyright Infringement
    accessory sanctions 122
    cancellation of the right 122
    Civil Code 121, 123
    civil liability 120
    Civil procedural law 123
    civil proceedings 121
    Copyright and Related Rights Code 119–123
    copyright infringement as crime 119
    copyright privacy 119
    counterfeiting 120, 122
    criminal liability 120
    criminal proceedings 121
    criminal sanctions 121–122
    EU Enforcement Directive 123
    financial remedies 123
    indemnification 123
    misdemeanors 120
    monetary sanctions 122
    passing-off 120
    plagiarize 120
    Portuguese case law 124
    Portuguese law 119–120, 122
    sanctions and remedies 121
    temporary or permanent closing 122
    temporary prohibition 122
    third-party interests 121
    usurpation 119, 122

Copyright Infringement Criminal Proceedings
    Copyright and Related Rights Code 140
    copyright infringing goods 140
    criminal proceedings related to copyright infringement 140
    proceedings related to crime of infringement of moral rights 141
    public crimes 140
    Public Prosecutor's Office 140–141
Copyright Infringement Defense Strategies
    absence of protection 124
    Berne Convention 124
    Copyright and Related Rights Code 125
    copyright infringement cases 125
    copyright protection 124–125
    dissimilarities between original work and plagiarized work 126
    duration of copyrights 125
    EU Member States 125
    expiry of protection 125
    free uses 125
    lack of legitimacy of claimant 124
    limitations of copyright protection 125
    Portuguese law 125
    private use exception 125
Copyright Protection and Soundreef Judgment
    copyright assignment and license 75
    duration 76
    exhaustion principle 76
    protected works 73
    rights enjoyed by author 74
    rights of artists and performers 78
    rights of movie producer 77
    rights of phonogram producer 77
    rights of radio and television stations 78
    rights on databases 80
    rights on engineering works 80
    rights on photographs 79
    rights on titles of books or magazines 81
    territoriality 76
    website copyright 81
Criminal Liability
    claims of civil infringement 217
    Department of Economic Development in Northern Ireland 218
    HM Revenue and Customs 218

D

Defenses
    caricature, parody, or pastiche 215
    copies for text and data analysis for non-commercial research 214
    criticism, review, quotation, and news reporting 214
    dealings with computer programs and databases 215
    defenses on burden of proof 212
    designs 216
    incidental inclusion of copyright material 215
    intermediary safe harbors 217
    making temporary copies 213
    miscellaneous defenses 212
    personal copies for private use 213
    procedural defenses 211
    representation of certain artistic works on public display 216
    research and private study 214
    statutory defenses 212
Dispute Resolution Alternatives
    arbitral tribunal 128
    Law on Voluntary Arbitration 128
    Portuguese Bar Association 128
    Portuguese Intellectual Property Association 128

E

Elements of Copyright Infringement
    activity by the defendant 229
    cause of infringement 229
    copyright infringement 230
    direct infringement 229
    infringing activity 230
    limited liability entity 229
    ownership of a valid copyright 229
Enforcement
    audiovisual works 93
    cease and desist proceedings 85
    damages 90
    description 87
    destruction of removal of result of infringement 86
    evidence 90
    injunctions 90
    interim remedies, inventories, and expert appraisals 87
    legal costs 91

penal remedies and sanctions 91
  prevention of threatened infringement 85
  proceedings in respect of moral rights 86
  protection of public performances 85
  public enforcement 94
  publication of judicial decisions 91
  seizure 88
  software 92
  unauthorized rentals and records 93
Exemptions from Copyright Infringement
  Federal Copyright Law 110
  limitations on economic rights 110

I

Infringement
  criminal infringement 104
  dealings with infringing copy 207
  direct infringement 52
  economic rights infringement 103
  indirect infringement 53
  infringement by communication to public 204
  infringement by issues of copies to public 202
  infringement by making adaption or act done in relation
    to adaption 205
  infringement by performance, showing, or playing work
    in public 204
  infringement by rental or lending work to public 204
  infringement of copyrights by copying 201
  intermediaries and joint tortfeasorship 208
  moral rights infringement 101
  non-commercial file sharing 53
  permitting use of premises for infringing performance 207
  primary infringement 200
  providing means for making infringing copies 207
  provision of apparatus for infringing performance 208
  secondary infringement 206
  types of infringement 52
Infringement and Subject Matter of Resale Right
  Austrian implementation of Directive 29
  categories of works subject to resale right 24
  de minimis standard or fully harmonized legal concept 28
  originals 26
  subject matter — notion of originality 23

Index   261

Infringement Proceedings
    administrative proceedings for economic rights 105
    civil proceedings 6
    criminal proceedings 4
    customs enforcement 105
    damages 106
Interim Relief and Other Measures
    administrative injunctions 137
    border control measures 138
    cease-and-desist letters 135
    civil procedural law 138
    Copyright and Related Rights Code 138
    preliminary injunctions 136
    seizure of assets 138
    seizure of evidence 138

L

Legal Basis for Copyright Protection in the United States
    Agreement on Trade-Related Aspects of Intellectual
        Property Rights (TRIPS) 229
    Architectural Works Copyright Protection Act 227
    Artists' Rights and Theft Prevention Act 228
    Berne Convention for the Protection of Literary
        and Artistic Works 227, 228
    Berne Convention Implementation Act of 1988 227
    bilateral agreements 228
    Computer Software Copyright Act of 1980 226
    copyright infringement liability Internet 227
    criminal copyright infringement 227
    criminal penalties 228
    Digital Millennium Copyright Act 227
    Federal Copyright Legislation 226
    Fraudulent Online Identity Sanctions Act 228
    international copyright treaties and conventions 228
    Library of Congress 228
    No Electronic Theft (NET) Act 227
    protection of foreign works 228
    safe harbor guidelines 227
    Semiconductor Chip Protection Act 227
    Sonny Bono Copyright Term Extension Act 227
    statutory licensing provisions 228
    The Copyright Act of 1976 226
    The Register of Copyrights 228

United States Copyright Office 228
Universal Copyright Convention 228
Uruguay Round Agreement Act 227
Visual Artists Rights Act of 1990 227
World Trade Organization 229
Liability for Violation of Intellectual Rights to Copyrighted Material
    civil liability 164
    protection of copyright on Internet 166
    provisions on liability 162
Liability of Internet Service Providers
    Argentine law 10
    Court of Appeals 10
    Federal Court of Cassation 11
    Google 10, 13
    National Court of Appeals 10, 11
    Supreme Court 10, 12
    Yahoo 10

M

Movimento Cívico Anti Pirataria na Internet
    copyright infringement 139
    MAPiNET procedures 139
    multi-lateral cooperation effort 139

O

Online Intermediary Liability
    piracy 55
    Telemedia Act 54, 55
Ownership of Copyright
    claiming ownership 240
    copyright notice 240, 241
    Copyright Office 240–242
    copyright registration 241
    copyright symbol 240
    Creative Commons 241
    Free Software Foundation 241
    Intellectual Property Rights Electronic Recordation System 242
    Open Source Initiative 241
    United States copyright law 240, 241
    United States Customs and Border Protection 242
    when copyright exists 239
    who owns copyright 239

P

Procedural Law
- appeals 66
- arbitration and alternative dispute resolution 67
- criminal investigations 67
- duration 64
- evidence 62
- hearings 61
- judgment 63
- jurisdiction 61
- making temporary restraining orders permanent 66
- obtaining judgment 58
- provisional measures 64
- service of process 61
- temporary restraining orders 65
- warning letters 64

R

Remedies
- account of profits 219
- action by licensee 221
- action by non-exclusive licensee 221
- claim for information and an accounting 57
- criminal liability 58
- damages 57, 219
- injunction 56, 219
- inspection 57
- order for delivery up of infringing articles 220
- recall and destruction 58
- seizure of infringing articles 221

Remedies for Infringement
- attorney's fees 252
- Copyright Act 252
- court costs 252
- Court of Appeal 252
- *eBay* 252
- preliminary injunction 252
- preponderance of the evidence 253
- statutory damages 251, 253
- Supreme Court 252, 253

Resale Right Regime of Berne Convention
- mythical economic rationale for resale right 18

    no Austrian implementation of droit de suite 20
    resale right enters international stage 16
    subject matter of Berne Convention 17
Rights Covered by Copyright
    copyrights and protected works 98
    creativity requirement 70
    economic rights 100
    employers and projects 71
    form of expression 71
    moral rights 99
    neighboring rights 101
    presumption of authorship or ownership 71
Rights Protected by Copyright
    length of protection 41
    moral rights 34, 36
    neighboring rights 37
    property rights 34, 35
    registration of copyright 40
    types of copyrightable works 38
Rights Covered by Copyright in the United States
    Digital Millennium Copyright Act 234
    distribution right 232
    electronic media 234
    exclusive rights of owner of copyrighted work 231
    fair use 231
    first sale doctrine 232
    protection for particular classes of works 233
    protection of moral rights 233
    public display right 232
    public performance right 232
    right to reproduce 231
    The Architectural Works Copyright Protection Act 233
    The Berne Convention 233
    The Visual Artists Rights Act 233, 234
Russian Intellectual Property Law
    Agreement on Trade-Related Aspects of Intellectual
        Property Rights (TRIPS) 146
    Berne Convention for the Protection of Literary and Artistic
        Works 146
    Civil Code 145
    Madrid trade mark agreements 146
    Paris Convention for the Protection of Intellectual Property 146
    World Trade Organization (WTO) 146

S

Subsistence
- combined works 195
- duration 196
- original literary dramatic, musical, or artistic works 192
- requirement of originality 193
- requirement of recording 193
- sound recordings, films, and broadcasts 194
- typographical arrangement of published editions 195
- unclear status of design classics 193

T

Turkish Intellectual Property Law
- civil remedies 179
- compensation for damages and acting without authority 182
- copyright and authorship 171
- criminal remedies 183
- determination of owner of work 180
- direct infringement 178
- economic rights 172
- exemptions to infringement of copyright 185
- indirect infringement 179
- infringement of economic and moral rights 178
- infringement proceedings 179
- interests of individuals 186
- Law on Industrial Properties 170
- moral rights 175
- personal use 186
- prevention of infringement 182
- prohibition of infringement 180
- protected rights 171
- public interest 185
- public order 185
- related (derivative) rights 178
- remedies regarding prevention of piracy 184
- reproduction and exhibition 187
- right of adaption and translation 172
- right of attribution 176
- right of broadcasting of performance and making it
  available to public 174
- right of distribution 173
- right of public performance 174

right of reproduction 173
right to disclose work to public 175
right to integrity of work 177
right to payment of share on resale of specific copies 174
rights of author against persons who own or possess work 178
statute of limitations for civil remedies 182
use of works in public premises 187
works 170

W

Works Protected by Copyright Law
    Copyright and Related Rights Code 115–117
    exclusions from copyright protection 116
    industrial property rights 117
    Portuguese case law 117
    Portuguese copyright law 117
    Regulation for the Registration of Literary and Artistic Works 117
    The Berne Convention 117
Works that Copyright Protects
    anonymous and pseudonymous works 238
    Copyright Office 237
    corporate authorship 238
    duration of copyright 237
    national origin 236
    originality 236
    reliance parties 237
    restored works 237
    The Berne Convention 238
    The Copyright Act of 1976 237
    The Copyright Information Center of the Cornell University
        Library 237
    The United States Constitution 237
    The Uruguay Round Agreement Act 237
    United States copyright law 235, 236
    United States copyright protection 234, 235
    works eligible for copyright protection 234